D1555454

Indiraji

Indiraji

Through My Eyes

USHA BHAGAT

PENGUIN
VIKING

VIKING
Published by the Penguin Group
Penguin Books India Pvt Ltd, 11 Community Centre, Panchsheel Park, New Delhi
110 017, India
Penguin Group (USA) Inc., 375 Hudson Street, New York, New York 10014, USA
Penguin Group (Canada), 90 Eglinton Avenue East, Suite 700, Toronto, Ontario,
M4P 2Y3, Canada (a division of Pearson Penguin Canada Inc.)
Penguin Books Ltd, 80 Strand, London WC2R 0RL, England
Penguin Ireland, 25 St Stephen's Green, Dublin 2, Ireland (a division of Penguin
Books Ltd)
Penguin Group (Australia), 250 Camberwell Road, Camberwell, Victoria 3124,
Australia (a division of Pearson Australia Group Pty Ltd)
Penguin Group (NZ), cnr Airborne and Rosedale Roads, Albany, Auckland 1310,
New Zealand (a division of Pearson New Zealand Ltd)
Penguin Group (South Africa) (Pty) Ltd, 24 Sturdee Avenue, Rosebank,
Johannesburg 2196, South Africa

Penguin Books Ltd, Registered Offices: 80 Strand, London WC2R 0RL, England

First published in Viking by Penguin Books India 2005
Copyright © Usha Bhagat 2005

Copyright for material quoted from *Freedom's Daughters* and *Two Alone, Two
Together*, edited by Sonia Gandhi © Rahul Gandhi and Priyanka Gandhi Vadra

Copyright for letters written by Indira Gandhi to Usha Bhagat and the sketches made
by Indira Gandhi © Rahul Gandhi

Page 286 is an extension of the copyright page

All photographs in the book are courtesy the author, except those acknowledged
otherwise.

The views and opinions expressed in this book are the author's own and the facts
are as reported by her, and the publishers are not in any way liable for the same.

Typeset by Elevenarts, Keshav Puram, Delhi 110035
Printed at Chaman Offset Printers, New Delhi

Shadow is in itself unrestrained in its path while sunshine, as an incident of its very nature is pursued a hundredfold by nuance. Thus is sorrow from happiness a thing apart; the scope of happiness, however, is hampered by the aches and hurts of endless sorrow.

A favourite quotation of Indira Gandhi's
from *Rajatarangini*, a history of
Kashmir, by Kalhana, twelfth century
(translated by R.S. Pandit)

Contents

~

INTRODUCTION

Really speaking, I do not know myself why I have written this book. So much has already been written about Mrs Gandhi during her lifetime and also after her death, perhaps even more than has been written on her father.

After Mrs Gandhi's death, people would often accost me with the question, 'When are you writing a book?' I used to find the suggestion ridiculous and would dismiss it immediately. The reasons were many. I did not think that everyone has to write a book. After Mrs Gandhi's tragic and traumatic end, I could not even think clearly. I was not a writer and had never kept a diary, only some notes on very few occasions. Mrs Gandhi was a political person. Though I am not apolitical, I was not associated with her at a political level. Thus I could not contribute anything which would add to the assessments of her as a political figure. I am also a lazy person and was satisfied with these reasons for not pursuing the project.

I had thought that gradually the suggestions to write would peter out, but the refrain continued from friends and acquaintances. I never considered them seriously. Then another rationale for writing the book was mentioned: that I owe it to history and that even if what I write is not of political relevance, anything written about persons of historical significance has dimensions which throw new light on them, their decisions and actions and the working of their mind. Perhaps at the back of my mind this made some sense.

More than two years ago I began to sort out old papers. Along with other papers, I came across Mrs Gandhi's letters to me, mainly written in the 1950s and 1960s. Her letters were very personal. I was very diffident and hesitant about making them public, feeling that if they were published I might be crossing the line of privacy. Then I reasoned that with the passage of time even classified documents and papers get declassified. Over twenty years have elapsed since Mrs Gandhi left us. I felt her letters would convey her sensitivity and charm, her interests and concerns, besides other aspects of her personality which are not generally known. Some letters form part of the narrative but there are many more interesting letters which have been included in the Interlude. Except for a very few, all the letters are handwritten; only a few have been included in facsimile, as sometimes Mrs Gandhi's writing is not easy to read.

Gradually the idea of writing a book started to grow within me but I was confused regarding the form it should take. It would not be a biography. Many have already been written, and I was neither interested in writing another biography nor accomplished enough to do so. It had to be based on my memories of our long association of thirty-one years. Though there had been three breaks, the association had continued. I let the narrative flow but I could not focus only on Mrs Gandhi, and many other people and incidents are interwoven throughout it. The narrative began to meander in places, and I let it do so.

When I started writing, I was disturbed by 'I' figuring in it again and again. However, I could not escape this because I realized that memoirs cannot be written in the third person.

Another realization was that many of my views were at variance with those of others, but I could only write from my own perception. Besides the eternal truths, the other truths very often depend upon individual perceptions. This has been aptly mirrored in Akira Kurosawa's classic film *Rashomon*, depicting multiple perceptions of the same incident. The perceptions of people are based on their background, environment, and experiences. For this reason, I have included the Prologue which gives the background of the perceiver. As far as possible, I have tried to refrain from value judgements, otherwise one is likely to add one's own values, biases, and prejudices. My purpose has been to narrate, and I think it is for the readers to form their own opinions.

The book is not meant for scholars or political analysts who may find it lightweight. It is more for the general public who is interested in and intrigued by Mrs Gandhi's enigmatic persona. She was a very complex person and anyone who thought that she or he knew her well, I think, did not understand her. Even after so many years of close association, I cannot claim this.

This account is not comprehensive. There are many gaps chronology-wise. As the book is based on my personal memories, I have only written what I saw and experienced. Also, my description of the foreign visits may seem superficial. I was not part of the official delegation. While the Prime Minister and the delegation were busy with serious pursuits, I used to utilize the time to visit places of cultural interest and would later apprise Mrs Gandhi about what I had seen, and sometimes she would visit one of those places if time permitted.

Along with Mrs Gandhi's letters and other material, I also have a large collection of photographs. It has been possible to include only very few of them in the book. I did not possess a camera until 1981. The earlier photographs taken in Mashobra in 1954, on the visit abroad in 1956, and on a few other occasions were taken with borrowed cameras. After acquiring an auto-focus camera in 1981, I took a large number of photographs, mainly during the trips abroad. I wish I had had a camera all along for capturing many other occasions which are now part of history. All the photographs in the book, however, have not been taken by me. Some from other sources have also been included.

Mrs Gandhi had a habit of leaving little slips indicating things to do or her comments. I have a large collection of these slips and a few have been included in the book to convey her style of functioning, her sense of humour, and many other unknown facets of her personality. The images at the end of each chapter are sketches which Mrs Gandhi often used to make during meetings.

My entry into the Prime Minister's House in 1953 was a mere coincidence. I could never imagine then that one day Mrs Gandhi would become the prime minister. Power did not attract me all through the years I was with her. I used to remember Kabir's couplet:

Prabhuta ko sab koi bhajay
Prabhu ko bhajay na koy
Jo bhaje Prabhu ko sada
Prabhuta cheri hoy

(Everyone worships power, not the Lord.
If one worships Him, power becomes a slave.)

I liked the play of the words *Prabhu* (Lord) and *Prabhuta* (power).

This book has been possible only due to the persistence and perseverance of many friends and acquaintances, who pushed me into writing it in spite of my reluctance. I owe them my thanks. Whether it will be of value, I do not know. At least now I will not be confronted with the query as to when I am going to write a book. That is a matter of satisfaction!

My thanks to Chandrika for her secretarial assistance, the editorial staff at Penguin and Vinay Jain for the basic design of the cover.

~

PROLOGUE: PRE-1947

Before the partition of the country in 1947, our family used to live in Lahore. I could not have even dreamt then that one day I would be working for Mrs Indira Gandhi. National and personal destinies sometimes intertwine.

Our family was originally from Rawalpindi, now in Pakistan. Our great-great grandfather, Bhagat Jawaharmalji, although a householder, was a saintly person, almost like a sufi, and was known as Sain Sahib. He had a large following among people of all communities in and around Rawalpindi and the adjoining areas of the NWFP. When he passed away in 1866, he was cremated close to a small stream on the outskirts of the city. A simple samadhi was built there and the large plot of wooded land around it was acquired and called Tapovan. As children, when we went to Kashmir or Abbottabad for the summer vacation, we always stopped in Rawalpindi and visited Tapovan. In 1986, when I visited Pakistan for the first time after the Partition, I along with my sisters especially went looking for Tapovan and the samadhi there. When we found the large wooded plot of land, we were shocked to see that it had been turned into a *kabristan* (graveyard). We hoped that the samadhi had been left intact and trudged through the graveyard looking for it. We were saddened to find no trace of it.

The followers of Sain Sahib tried to persuade his eldest son, Bhagat Hiranand, to take on the mantle of his father but he did not accept this. He had perhaps a modern outlook and decided to educate his four sons. Except for the eldest who had poor eyesight, the other three sons did their MA and then law. The two older brothers had to appear for their MA examination in Calcutta as the facility did not then exist in Punjab University. Bhagat Ishwar Das was a leading lawyer in Lahore at the beginning of the twentieth century, and his house had a tennis court and a swimming pool. However, when his eldest son died in the plague epidemic in 1907, the shock affected him so deeply that he left his legal practice and became increasingly involved in the Arya Samaj movement. Bhagat Narain Das joined the judicial service and served in Kashmir State, besides other places.

My grandfather, Bhagat Govind Das, received his MSc. degree from Punjab University and then studied law. As children we were very impressed to learn that he had topped the university in the MSc. examinations and had received a gold medal. We learnt later that there were only two students who had graduated that year. My grandfather was to go to London to study law, but perhaps he got cold feet and returned from Bombay; thereafter he pursued his law degree in Lahore.

As the High Court was in Lahore, the family had moved to the city and our generation was born and brought up there. The only good school for girls in Lahore used to be the Sacred Heart Convent. It is said that at one stage when it was learnt that a girl wanted to become a nun, some eminent citizens led by Sir Ganga Ram became concerned and thus the Sir Ganga Ram High School was founded.

My sisters and I studied in this school. It was completely secular, with a nationalist atmosphere, and gave the teaching of Hindi more attention. Raksha Sondhi was the principal when I joined the school. After her marriage she became Raksha Saran, a well-known social worker in Delhi. Music was another subject taught at the school. When I was in the third standard, Rabindranath Tagore visited our school and I have memories of singing along with a few other girls before the gracious and distinguished guest. When I was in the fifth standard, Mrinalini Chattopadhyaya (sister of Sarojini Naidu) became the principal of our school. She was a remarkable person and infused a new spirit among the students. In those days, Sarojini Naidu, their brother Harindranath Chattopadhyaya, and other sisters used to visit the school and imparted a nationalist and cultural flavour to the institution.

Ours was a joint family. My grandfather, though mostly involved in his professional work, enjoyed the company of children. He used to pile us into the car and take us to the Baisakhi mela on the banks of the river Ravi, to the Basant mela at the Hakikat Rai Samadhi, and in summer for a drive on the canal bank. While driving towards it on the Mall, we sometimes saw Tommies (British soldiers) walking by. We would burst out singing loudly with nationalist fervour: 'Goray ghas ke boray, udenge tope ke agay!' (The white soldiers are like sacks of hay who will be blown up in front of the cannon!)

Our family was fond of music. Our grandfather had not only arranged a music teacher for us but also used to take us to concerts to listen to the classical musicians of the time. We owe our love of music to him.

During the summer holidays most residents of Lahore used to go to the hill stations. Our destination used to be mainly Abbottabad (in the NWFP) where an aunt was married and to Dunga Gali, between Abbottabad and Murree; or we went to Kashmir. Once we went to the Kulu valley, and across the river Beas we were attracted by a big red rooftop in Naggar. We decided to walk up—a very stiff climb— and on reaching our destination we learnt that a Russian, Nicholas Roerich, stayed there with his family. They lived a very secluded life. He had moved from Russia to India at the time of the Revolution. Our request to meet the family was returned with a basket of apples. We did not know then that Nicholas Roerich was a famous artist, nor did we recognize his son, the handsome young Svetoslav, who went riding past us.

In 1939, during the term of the Congress government in the NWFP, Dr Khan Sahib, the chief minister, and his illustrious brother, Khan Abdul Ghaffar Khan, invited Gandhiji to the province and made arrangements for a one-month stay in Abbottabad at the house of my aunt's brother-in-law, Rai Sahib Parmanand. We were there for our summer vacation at that time, and as young excited schoolgirls we used to be in and out of the house. An aunt and I sometimes used to sing bhajans during Gandhiji's prayer meetings. Once when Gandhiji got up to go for his afternoon walk, he saw us hovering around and said he could not find the khadi cord he used to wear around his waist to suspend his watch and enquired if we would look for it. We were very excited that Gandhiji had asked us to do something. We looked around everywhere, but were unable to trace the lost object. On his return he found us looking dejected, and on learning that we had been unsuccessful in our quest, Gandhiji, shrewd as he was, must have identified the one place we may have missed. He turned the wastepaper basket upside down and there, mixed in with the discarded papers, was the missing cord. I still remember Gandhiji telling us with a twinkle in his eye: '*Ankhon ka hona ek baat hai, istemaal karna doosri.*' (It is one thing to have eyes and another to use them.) We walked away sheepishly.

Once when Gandhiji was sitting and working, an elderly Sikh couple came and stood near him with folded hands, and began to shower praises on him. Gandhiji carried on with his work, but when the couple continued in the same vein endlessly, he looked up with a smile and said that such praises were generally bestowed after a person's death. I think his sharp remark, accompanied with a gentle smile, made an impact and the couple quietly left the room.

We would go into the kitchen to see Gandhiji's food being cooked. The steamed salt-less vegetables, all mixed together, would be served in a metal bowl on a thali along with a glass of goat's milk and a tablespoon of crushed garlic. We would squirm when we saw him mix everything together and eat this with relish. However, the fruit was served on a plate and he ate these with a fork and knife. When Gandhiji heard that my grandfather had fractured his wrist, he came to see him during his walk. Gandhiji was in Abbottabad when World War II broke out on 1 September 1939 and, as far as I can remember, he issued a statement about it from there.

We often used to see Badshah Khan (as Khan Abdul Ghaffar Khan is popularly known) there. We got another opportunity to see him from close quarters after a couple of years, when he along with his sons Ghani Khan and Wali Khan and daughter Mehar Taj came to stay in Dunga Gali. Our family was also staying in Dunga Gali, where my aunt's family had a hotel named Mokshpuri. It was named after the highest point of the hill called Mokshpuri (place of salvation) which, according to myth, the Pandavas are supposed to have visited during their *agyatvas*, the period during which they had to remain incognito. I remember our family going to Badshah Khan's house for tea. When my grandfather invited Badshah Khan for dinner and especially arranged for the serving of halal meat, he was very annoyed with my grandfather and said he was very happy with the vegetarian food. I have yet to come across anyone else like him— tall, well-built, but with such gentleness, simplicity, humility, and dedication. I was deeply impressed, and he has always been one of my heroes.

A year or two before Gandhiji's visit, the Working Committee of the All India Congress Committee was also held in Abbottabad, and Babu Rajendra Prasad, Pandit Nehru, Maulana Azad, and a few others came to attend it. We young girls were in charge of their rooms. Babu Rajendra Prasad came to our house for dinner at the invitation of my grandfather. At another time, a committee meeting of the All India Women's Conference was also held there, when I saw Aruna Asaf Ali for the first time.

My grandfather was a trustee of a women's college in Lahore and my aunt also used to teach mathematics there. Once my grandfather invited some professors for tea. I remember three of them quite vividly, because I met them again in Delhi after 1947. One was Frieda Bedi, the British wife of B.P.L. Bedi, a direct descendant of Guru Nanak. They were both involved in the leftist movement and later in life took to the spiritual path, Frieda becoming a Buddhist nun. After the partition her son Kabir Bedi was one of the students in the kindergarten school in Delhi where I taught and he later became a film actor. Another professor was Miss Muga Seth, a Parsi lady, who later married G. Parthasarathy, a journalist and diplomat, the son of Gopalaswamy Ayyangar, a member of the Constituent Assembly. The last but not the least was Teji Suri, who later married the well-known poet Harivansh Rai Bachchan and whose son is the well-known actor Amitabh.

After school, I joined Kinnaird College, a Scottish mission college, which had Christian, Hindu, Muslim, and Sikh students and thus had a cosmopolitan outlook. Although the atmosphere at the Sir Ganga

Ram High School and Kinnaird College were somewhat different, I think the composite effect of both the institutions was very wholesome and I owe a great deal to both of them.

In 1945 Madame Montessori (she had come to India at the invitation of the Theosophical Society, Madras, and could not return to Italy as World War II had broken out) conducted a short course in Srinagar, Kashmir. I attended it and it opened my eyes to the world of the child as the child views it.

I experienced another revelation. Having lived in Lahore and being exposed only to Punjabi Muslims, I thought they represented all Muslims in general. This impression was shaken while attending the Montessori course. Amongst those who attended the course were two Bengali girls, Himani from Calcutta and Lutfunnissa Begum from Dhaka. In our free time we had great fun interacting with each other. Himani would recite Tagore's poetry, Lutfunnissa would sing Bengali folk songs, and the rest of us pooled together whatever talent we had to relax and entertain each other. A Punjabi Muslim day student lived nearby with her family. On the festival of Id, this girl invited Lutfunnissa to her home for a meal. However, Lutfunnissa was very reluctant to go as she felt she had nothing in common with the Punjabi family. At our urging, she agreed to go provided we also accompanied her. We had to self-invite ourselves. Lutfunnissa sat quietly, replying in monosyllables, while the Punjabi family and I had a lot in common, besides our language; we chatted and enjoyed the meal. I felt a bigger jolt when Lutfunnissa took us for an Id dinner to a hotel where she had already made arrangements earlier. The hotel turned out to be the Khalsa (Sikh) Hotel which serves jhatka meat. In Lahore, the issue of halal and jhatka meats was such a sensitive matter between the two communities that it often led to controversies and violence. I was in a dilemma and felt uncomfortable during the dinner, but Lutfunnissa was in high spirits. All this made me realize that religion and culture are not necessarily synonymous.

From 1946 onwards, with the shrill cries and increasing activities of the Muslim League, the atmosphere of the cosmopolitan city of Lahore had started becoming charged and tension had begun to build up. It increased in 1947, and from March onwards violent incidents would frequently flare up in the old city.

We were then living in Model Town, a garden-like suburb, far from the city. Although no actual incident took place there, the fear psychosis was building up and the residents had taken to night patrolling.

PART I

~

1947–60

ONE

~

FLIGHT FROM KASHMIR

Towards the end of July 1947, a family friend, J.N. Khosla (a professor who after the Partition was inducted into the foreign service), tried to persuade my father to come to Kashmir where our families had had a wonderful time in Gulmarg the previous year. My father sent my sister Uma and me to Kashmir with Mr Khosla, to be followed later by the rest of the family. We went by train to Rawalpindi and by taxi from there onwards. I remember seeing some burnt villages between Rawalpindi and Murree where the residents had either been killed or had fled.

In Srinagar, we stayed with my aunt's family, who had come from Abbottabad in the NWFP and were staying in a houseboat on the Jhelum. When India became free on 15 August, we heard the famous 'Tryst with Destiny' speech of Panditji in the houseboat and we were on a jubilant high, not realizing that soon we would come down to earth, and that too with a thud.

The rest of the family, except for my father, came to Kashmir in early August and from Srinagar we moved to Gulmarg. Hardly any news reached us from the plains and our family was having a relaxed and enjoyable holiday. (Things were cheap then; apples were Rs 6 for 100.) Gradually, however, Gulmarg began to look deserted. All the Muslim families which had come to Kashmir for the summer vacation started to leave; perhaps they had received an inkling of what was to come in October. By the end of September when our family decided to come down to Srinagar, we learnt that buses had stopped plying. As both the existing roads to the Valley passed through the recently formed Pakistan (the Jammu-Kathua road was developed later), supplies of petrol had ceased. We did the forty-kilometre journey from Tangmarg to Srinagar in tongas.

Back in Srinagar, the news of the happenings in Punjab had begun to trickle in and our elders realized that now there could not be any going back to Lahore. It was not possible to leave the Valley by road. The only alternative route was by the twice weekly Dakota air service to Delhi. Bookings were hardly available, especially for a large group such as ours.

The weather had begun to turn crisp and the chinars were aglow with autumn colours. One began to hear faint rumors of the attack from Pakistan, though not many believed them and life went on as usual.

On 23 October, when I switched on the radio at 9.00 p.m., I heard, 'This is All India Radio. Here is the news', and suddenly the electricity failed. I said half jocularly, 'Mahura (the power station about 90 km away on the Baramula Road) has been taken over', and was reprimanded for making a silly statement. It turned out to be true.

On the night of 25 October, there was a loud thumping on the outer gate of the house in Ram Munshi Bagh where we were staying. It was my uncle and aunt who had come a few days earlier from Calcutta and were staying at the Nedous Hotel. They seemed in a panic and told us that they had learnt that the tribals from Pakistan had reached Pattan, 25 km from Srinagar and were expected to reach the city the next day. An important official had come from Delhi in a special plane and he contacted my uncle to take back the daughter of an ICS colleague who had accompanied my uncle. As she had already been sent back, the official agreed to take two or three persons in his plane. My uncle therefore came to our house and said in a high-pitched, shrill voice, 'Give me the young girls.' As news of the atrocities in Punjab had begun to reach the Valley, we were asked to pack up a few clothes, which we bundled up in bed sheets.

A car had to be found to take us at dawn to the airport. I accompanied my uncle to a neighbour's house. A lot of activity was on there and the head of the family was lying in bed, all dressed up. The telephone rang continuously and the word 'juice' came up again and again in the conversation. It was known that our neighbours owned a canning factory but the repeated mention of 'juice' at that time did seem rather strange to me. Our request for a car was refused with an excuse that they had no petrol. However, a frank relative confided that they were all ready to leave for Jammu in half-an-hour's time and that it was petrol that was being referred to as juice.

It was around 11.00 p.m. by now, so it was decided to go by tonga to the Nedous Hotel where my uncle and aunt were staying. A tonga arrived and five youngsters—I was the eldest among them—were piled in with our bundles. Such was the panic that rather than waiting for the other tonga in which my uncle and aunt were to accompany us, our tonga was sent off ahead. When it reached the nearby Sonwar Bagh, a group of ten to twelve men wrapped in blankets with lathis in their hands, suddenly emerged from behind some shops and asked us to stop. Reports of the gruesome happenings in Punjab were fresh in our minds, so I shuddered and almost said my last prayers. As they came near, the men assured us that they were National Conference workers and only wanted to check if there was any kerosene in the tonga. They had information that the Muslim Conference men were planning to burn the bridges (made of wood), and so they were keeping a watch. We heaved a big sigh of relief. After being checked at various points, we finally reached the Nedous Hotel at midnight. The two tongas were asked to stay for the night, as they were to transport us to the airport in the early morning.

The younger children went to sleep, but I could not sleep a wink. My mind was full of anxiety as my mother and some other members of the family were being left behind and I remembered the panic-stricken face of my mother. I had tried to argue with my uncle to persuade him to leave me behind, but he had snapped at me, saying that young girls couldn't be left behind. Had I been older, I would no doubt have refused to obey him. When leaving, I had told my mother that the family should all move to the Nedous Hotel in the morning, as it might be somewhat safer than the house.

It was a fearful night. All those who could get out of the city were fleeing. Petrol was being sold at Rs 80 a gallon (equal to 4.5 litres), when the normal price as far as I remember used to be Rs 2 to Rs 4

5

per gallon. The clip-clop of the tongas and the whizzing sound of cars and buses speeding by continued throughout the night and would resound in my ears for years afterwards. At 4.00 a.m. when it was pitch dark and pretty cold, we left in the tongas for the airport. Lal Chowk near the Amira Kadal bridge was full of National Conference workers who had gathered around a bonfire to keep warm and the place was buzzing with activity. As our tongas were being checked at various points, a procedure which would have delayed our arrival at the airport, my uncle met Bakshi Ghulam Mohammad (he became chief minister after Sheikh Abdullah) in the chowk, and he assigned a volunteer to facilitate our movement. Just as we reached the airport, we saw a jeep with the crew arriving.

The special plane was an IAF Dakota, a freighter without any seats. We were seven in our group and there were seven or eight other people. Our *potli*s (bundles) came in handy for passengers to sit on. I did not know then the significance of the special flight or the special status of a person on the plane. I came to know later that he was Mr V.P. Menon, Secretary, Ministry of Home, who under Sardar Vallabhbhai Patel had played an important role in the integration of the States into the Union. When the Maharaja's militia was unable to control the onslaught of the tribals, he was finally compelled to abandon his vacillation and decided to accede to India. He then appealed to the Government of India for help. Mr Menon was sent to Kashmir to study the situation on the spot and report to the Defence Committee headed by the Governor General, Lord Mountbatten. We were travelling on the same flight carrying Mr Menon. Mr Mehar Chand Mahajan, the then chief minister of Kashmir, was also on this flight. After meeting Mr Menon in Srinagar, the Maharaja had fled to Jammu.

As soon as the plane took off around 6.00 a.m. on the morning of 26 October, the impact of the separation from my family left behind hit me and the pain turned into tears. To hide them from the others, I wept quietly while looking out of the window. I saw then perhaps the most glorious sunrise I have ever seen, the golden orb bathing the snowy ranges with pinky-orange and mauve hues, but my eyes were full of tears and my heart too heavy to appreciate it. Mr Menon who was sitting opposite me must have noticed my sobbing. On learning the reason, he spoke to me and said that he would see to it that my mother and other members of my family were brought to Delhi, and to reassure me further he asked me to write a note for my mother. I had neither pencil nor paper and my aunt took out from her purse a cash memo and her eyebrow pencil and I scribbled a note. Of course, the note never reached my mother, but Mr Menon's reassurance came from the knowledge that the State was going to accede to India and that our troops would be flying out immediately. (After Mr Menon reported the Maharaja's acquiescence to the Defence Committee in Delhi, he was sent to Jammu on the afternoon of 26 October where the Maharaja signed the Instrument of Accession.) I will never forget Mr Menon's kindness and concern for a young girl when his mind must have been preoccupied with the anxiety and tension of the historical mission he was on.

When we arrived at the Delhi airport, I saw my father; his face beamed when he saw us, but it fell when he did not see the rest of the family. I felt terribly guilty and could hardly meet his eyes. He was again at the airport in the early hours of 27 September, when the planes were leaving with the troops, hoping to find someone who would agree to carry some money for the rest of our family stranded in Srinagar. He gave it to Sheikh Abdullah who was also present at the airport seeing the troops off. Sheikh Abdullah did not have time to undertake such personal errands, but realizing that the gesture would satisfy my father, he took the money.

In Srinagar, the rest of our family moved to the Nedous Hotel on the morning of 26 October and the next morning, on 27 October, along with some others they were taken to the airport by the army. Troops were disembarking from the planes and civilians waiting to be rescued were being taken on board. Our family reached Delhi on the evening of 27 October. The tension and emotion of the family's reunion were released by the remark of my ten-year-old brother who was also on the flight, that while we had come in a freighter, he had come in a plane with corduroy-covered seats. In that moment of release our tears and laughter mingled.

My father had stayed back in Lahore to look after his business; most people at the time were not thinking of leaving their hearths and homes. On 15 August, he even went to salute the Pakistan flag at a function. When the massacres started, a Muslim friend told my father that he had better leave.

He thus left Lahore in September for Delhi via Ferozepur in an old Ford with friends, a couple and a young Sikh boy who worked for him. To hide him he was doubled up in between the seats. When the car reached the border, at the bridge over the Satluj river, near Ferozepur, they found a few children who were crying. My father learnt that a couple of families from the same colony as ours had left for Ferozepur in tongas. On the way, in the small town of Kasur the tongas were ransacked, the women abducted, the men killed, and the children spared, who were now crying. This incident had occurred about an hour before my father's car passed through Kasur. Since the situation in East Punjab was also grim, the Sikh boy from then onwards was hoisted up to mark the identity of the passengers. After a day, when they reached Delhi, the tyre of the car punctured just when the vehicle reached the house of a relative. It seems that God's protective hand was on them.

My father was penniless and had to start both his life and his business anew. My mother had a small savings account in a bank, which had failed a couple of months before Partition. Only my royal account of Rs 3,000 was transferred to the Delhi Bank.

We became refugees twice. We had left Lahore with a few belongings necessary for the summer holidays and then departed Kashmir with the bare necessities tied in a bundle. Leaving Lahore was not traumatic because we had planned to return home after our vacation. However, the fateful events of the exodus from Kashmir will forever remain etched in my mind.

~

REFUGEES TWICE OVER

Coming from Lahore, I found New Delhi as it was then a very dull place. No doubt it was a well-planned city with broad tree-lined avenues, but it lacked spirit and soul. It was a purely bureaucratic city with very few other families (mainly those of contractors and local business people) living in it. In contrast, Lahore was an important educational, commercial, cultural, and legal centre, and interaction between different people created a lively atmosphere. The people were more spirited and avant-garde in their outlook. Thus to people who had grown up and lived in Lahore, Delhi seemed a sleepy village in comparison. In the evenings, one could hear the jackals wailing even at Curzon Road, where we lived for many years.

In Delhi, our family stayed in the homes of various relations for a few days. My father was busy running from pillar to post to start his business afresh. Then there was the family to look after. A cousin offered two rooms to my father in a ramshackle old bungalow in Meerut, 60 km from Delhi. My father decided to take the family there and come back to Delhi to start work from scratch. He was in Meerut for two days to make the necessary arrangements for the family. However, I began to feel suffocated and felt I could not swallow even 'dal-roti' while doing nothing. I persuaded my father and returned with him to Delhi to look for a job. I went to AIR and to a couple of other places, but refugees who had arrived in August and September had occupied the vacant posts.

I remembered Mohini Gauba, who had done her Montessori course with me in Srinagar in 1946. I went to meet her and was introduced to her mother, Mrs Elisabeth Gauba, who ran a small kindergarten school. Learning of the plight of our family, she straightaway asked me not only to work in her school but also said

I could stay with her and share Mohini's room till my family made some arrangements. She had been working in a refugee camp and was sensitive to the hardships suffered by the refugees. Mrs Gauba was a German married to a Punjabi. I stayed in her house for nearly six months. I was young and had led a sheltered life. Working with Aunty Gauba (as she was called) and especially staying with her was quite an experience.

My family moved from Meerut to Delhi after a month. A young cousin of ours found two vacant bungalows in Lodi Estate, a government colony. He broke open their locks and his family moved into one and our family moved into the other. The families enjoyed living in the spacious bungalows for at least three months and did not feel particularly bad occupying the houses illegally as we rationalized that the government was responsible for our being refugees. When the concerned government department finally woke up, they sent a truck with policemen and women to get the houses vacated and take the families to the Purana Qila refugee camp. My father was not at home and my mother seeing the police began to cry. Luckily an aunt was present at the scene and she was able to persuade them to leave for the time being. We were a large family of ten, consisting of my parents, four sisters, two brothers, my grandfather, and an aunt.

Fortunately for us, my uncle's wife had come to Delhi from Calcutta. My uncle (father's elder brother) was a friend of Lala Shri Ram, the leading industrialist from Delhi; he also had business connections with Lalaji. My aunt came to meet us accompanied by Lalaji's daughter-in-law, Sheila Bharat Ram. They found our family in a state of turmoil and reported the situation to Lalaji, who very kindly offered us accommodation for a few months. In the summer of 1948, the family moved into two rooms and a kitchen in Lalaji's brother Shankar Lal's large house, adjoining Lalaji's own house on Curzon Road. My father was struggling not only to set up his business but also to look after our large family. The strain was so tremendous that he suffered a heart attack in early 1949 and instead of a few months, we had to stay in that house for two years.

Lala Shri Ram's house was a hub of activity, not only concerning business affairs but also social and cultural activities. There were hardly any cultural organizations or programmes held in Delhi in the late 1940s and early 1950s, and Lalaji's house used to be a venue for music recitals and similar activities.

In the summer of 1948, the ballet *Discovery of India* (based on Nehru's book) came to Delhi, and the troupe stayed in the same big house in which we were living. Ravi Shankar had composed the music for the ballet and Lalaji's family organized a small concert by him. It was the first time that I heard Ravi Shankar play. He was young and hardly known then. In early 1949, Ravi Shankar was invited by AIR to start the Vadya-Vrinda (orchestra). He came with a few musicians who had earlier been with his elder brother Uday Shankar. They all were accommodated in the same big house. The ambience was wonderful, and besides attending the small concerts one could listen to the *riyaz* (practice sessions) as well.

At the time of the first Republic Day, in 1950, Rukmini Devi and her Kalakshetra Troupe based in Madras were especially invited by the government for a performance. All of them also stayed in the house we were living in. Kalidas's *Kumarasambhavam* was performed, in which Rukmini Devi herself danced.

On the eve of Independence Day in 1950, Lalaji's family organized an all-night concert in the big house, at which Ustad Allaudin Khan, Kanthe Maharaj, Ravi Shankar, Ali Akbar Khan, and others performed. When I reached home early in the morning, my father was reading the newspaper!

The big house on Curzon Road (now Kasturba Gandhi Marg), where the *Hindustan Times* building now stands, was not only a physical abode for our family, but for me it also provided an impetus for furthering my interest in art and culture.

11

~

THREE

AUNTY GAUBA AND INDIRAJI

I continued to work for Aunty Gauba at her school on Hailey Road, off Curzon Road. She was a phenomenon. All those who came in contact with her felt her impact—the more intimate the relationship, the more intense the impact. One either liked or disliked her. Aunty had a special ability to draw out of children and others their latent talents and to help develop their intellectual and creative skills. She was against any formal or rigid method of teaching. Instead she stressed the importance of encouraging and fostering each individual child's creativity and imagination. She had some brilliant streaks but also quite a few eccentricities. Her teaching methods and approaches were very personalized, but her ideas often came in erratic spurts and could cause tensions and problems. During the time I stayed with her, we often used to talk late into the night. Although it was tiring, I used to find our conversations very stimulating as her views and ideas were original and unconventional.

In the early years, her home was a Mecca for many young people from different spheres and backgrounds. They used to assemble in the evenings for intellectual interaction and stimulating conversation. She ignited the creative spark in many but her intensity burnt some too. While she held court, her family remained on the sidelines and often one sensed resentment among them.

Relationships with Aunty could never be on an even keel as she was a volatile person. My own relationship with her also had its ups and downs, but I tried to keep it fairly steady by refusing to get provoked by her intensity. This was not always an easy task. Nevertheless, I owe a great deal to her for opening the doors of my perception.

Rajiv and Sanjay Gandhi joined Elisabeth Gauba's school in late 1951. It was Mr Krishna Menon who had suggested the school to Mrs Indira Gandhi. Aunty Gauba had met Mr Menon in England when she had gone there to fight the case of her father-in-law, Harkishanlal Gauba, in the Privy Council. Her father-in-law was a self-made man and perhaps the richest man in Lahore in the early 1930s. Due to various reasons, he became insolvent and he and his son Jeewan Lal (Aunty Gauba's husband) were jailed. The case went before the Privy Council, and Aunty Gauba travelled to London to attend to the matter. There she met Mr Menon who was very helpful and he retained Sir Stafford Cripps for her as her counsel. When Sir Stafford Cripps came to India on the Cripps Mission in 1942, he went to meet Aunty Gauba at her flat, and she owed her telephone connection to his visit! Through Mr Menon, Aunty Gauba first met Indira Nehru (as she was then) in the UK when she was studying there.

Aunty Gauba's was a very small kindergarten school run in her own flat on Hailey Road, and had only thirty-five to forty children when I joined at the end of 1947. Every child received individual attention. She did not believe in formal education. There were no regular classes, nor textbooks. However, there were a large number of books for reading and reference purposes. The stress was on learning through creativity.

The two Gandhi boys were quite different from each other. Rajiv with his beautiful face and eyes was shy and introverted. Sanjay was an extrovert and had a naughty and impish streak. They did not show much interest in the usual studies. Rajiv used to counter any reprimand with a bewitching smile, which was enough to dissolve any firmness. He enjoyed drawing and often drew aeroplanes. Sanjay had no qualms in announcing what he wanted or did not want to do. To keep him interested, work had to be made into a game involving writing, colouring, cutting, and pasting. When the boys were studying at Aunty Gauba's school, Mrs Gandhi came there a few times. I saw her from a distance and thought that she seemed somewhat haughty and aloof. I did not push myself forward to cultivate acquaintance with the First

Family, but it seems our paths were destined to cross again and again in the years to come.

I worked in the school for four or five years and was getting a little tired of teaching and wanted a change. However, attempts to leave Aunty's school, either by the children or by staff, without her consent used to be a traumatic experience, and I had seen many unpleasant scenes. Knowing of Aunty Gauba's reactions, I carried on working and may have continued even longer. But in August 1953 she told me that she wished to work more on the academic side of education and wanted me to take on the entire responsibility of running the school, of course under her supervision. This was a big jolt to me, especially since I wanted to leave the job. When I told her of my desire, she was taken aback and said I was making a big mistake. Suddenly I got the good sense to reply, 'Perhaps I am making a mistake, but let me realize it for myself and if I do, I will come back.' She had no answer to this and had to let me go.

After a month or so, when I visited her, she told me that she had been to see Mrs Gandhi who was looking for someone to help her and that she had suggested my name. She added that Mrs Gandhi wished to meet me and that I should go to see her. Knowing Aunty's sometimes strange and quirky ideas, I didn't take her seriously and dismissed the suggestion from my mind. I also did not think I was qualified for the work, especially when Mrs Gandhi could have had the best candidates. I did not wish to make a fool of myself before her.

After a few days, Aunty Gauba came to my house and asked me if I had been to see Mrs Gandhi. I said, 'Certainly not.' When Aunty Gauba insisted, I told her I would go with her but not alone. She agreed to take me but said she would leave shortly afterwards. After making an appointment, she took me with her. As she was a regular visitor, she walked straight into the Prime Minister's House and then upstairs into Mrs Gandhi's large bedroom, which also served as her study. I had gone in a simple but neatly ironed white silk saree. I found Mrs Gandhi sitting cross-legged on a sofa in a crumpled khadi saree. Both the ladies talked while I sat there, quite tense, wondering what replies I would give to her questions as I did not know any secretarial work. Mrs Gandhi must have sensed my discomfiture, so when Aunty Gauba was leaving, she told her, 'It seems that you are leaving poor Usha for an inquisition.' I burst out laughing and the tension broke. Without asking me any questions, she told me the nature of her work and then asked me when I could start coming. This is how I started to work for Mrs Gandhi in September 1953.

I had thought the Prime Minister's House would be very grand and that I would be overawed. No doubt the building was very impressive, but the décor was like that of a better class circuit house as it was looked after by the CPWD (Central Public Works Department) of the government. It was only later that some improvements were made.

Mrs Gandhi gave me her sitting room for my office, which opened onto the ballroom, and the window overlooked the beautiful garden at the back. A couple of days after I had started working, N.K. Seshan, PA to the PM, to whom I had been introduced earlier, entered my room with another person. This second person looked arrogant and crude to me. I wondered what a man like him was doing in that house. I learnt later that he was M.O. Mathai. They entered without saying hello and discussed the need for a filing cabinet and walked out. Coming from a different background, I thought them to be lacking in manners. Seshan told me later that the staff were so afraid of Mathai that they maintained their distance and did not show any familiarity as Mathai often misinterpreted such behaviour.

When I started to work for Mrs Gandhi, I felt that though she talked very freely, she also kept her distance as if assessing the other person. I realized that for any meaningful relationship to develop between us, she must feel the need to relate and reach out herself. This suited me fine as I myself was reticent and shy. It took her nearly six months to gauge and form an opinion about me and then she began to reach out. However, one always had to be careful not to trespass or encroach on her privacy. In 1953, her main area of work was helping her father in every way—personally, as official hostess, and in the political field acting as her father's ears and eyes. At the same time, she took her duty of motherhood seriously. In addition to these responsibilities, she also served on a couple of committees, mainly that of the Indian Council for Child Welfare.

Mrs Gandhi had accompanied her father to the coronation of Queen Elizabeth II in June 1953 and had later visited the USSR and Sweden to study child welfare programmes in these countries. She was impressed by the Children's Palaces in the USSR and the idea of establishing Bal Bhavan emerged out of this experience. Later, moved by the plight of some vagrant beggar children, she started Bal Sahyog, an institution for vocational training to equip them for employment.

It is interesting, however, to see her letter to Panditji dated 13 August 1953 written from London before she returned to India.

> On my return to Delhi, I do want to reorganise my life and get out of all the silly committees. I am so sick of people doing social work as a step up [the] political & social-set ladder, and equally sick of the vague goodness of the so-called Gandhians.[1]

I think the above views reflect Mrs Gandhi's mood and thinking at that time when she was looking at things from the outside, resisting getting involved in happenings around her. Gradually, she allowed circumstances to pull her into the vortex of the public and political arena.

[1]Sonia Gandhi, *Two Alone, Two Together*, p. 598.

~

FOUR

THE AMAZING INCIDENT

In 1954 Mrs C.J. Vakil, in whose Pupils' Own School in Poona Mrs Gandhi had studied in the early 1930s, came to stay with her former student. Aunty Vakil expressed a desire to see Aunty Gauba's school as Rajiv and Sanjay were studying there. Aunty Vakil was a very different person from Aunty Gauba. She was very methodical and practical while Aunty Gauba was very unconventional. I think Aunty Vakil did not form too good an opinion of Aunty Gauba's school. As the school catered to children only till the ages of eight or nine years, Mrs Gandhi was already thinking of admitting the boys in a regular school. Soon they were sent to Welham Boys' School in Dehra Dun.

Once Rajiv and Sanjay were taken out of Aunty Gauba's school, the relationship between Mrs Gauba and Mrs Gandhi began to diminish. Earlier Mrs Gauba had free access to the Prime Minister's House. Security in those days was minimal anyhow, and as she was a constant visitor her Volkswagen Beetle was not stopped at the gate; even if it was, she would drive her little car under the outstretched arms of the security persons. Nor did she stop at the reception office—she used to walk almost straight into Mrs Gandhi's room. In addition to discussing Rajiv and Sanjay, their personalities and progress, with their mother, perhaps Mrs Gauba also used to talk about other things—personal matters, philosophical problems, and political issues. Mrs Gandhi was lonely, she was not so busy then, and perhaps found Mrs Gauba's insights interesting. Aunty loved to 'see' into people. In a letter to someone in 1955, she observed:

> Indira is an introvert, but for my sixth sense for the human potential— a seed that can flower and bear fruit 'if given the right climate'.

After the boys had moved to Dehra Dun, the raison d'être of Aunty's visits to the Prime Minister's House no longer existed. At the same time, Mrs Gandhi was gradually becoming more involved in public and political activities. In addition to taking an interest in the Bal Bhavan Board and in Bal Sahyog, she also became an active member of the Central Social Welfare Board when it was set up under the chairmanship of Durgabai Deshmukh; this organization planned and conducted welfare activities through various State Boards.

In 1956 the scope of Mrs Gandhi's involvement in politics expanded when she was elected to the Congress Working Committee, and in that connection she was frequently on tours in various states. Due to Mrs Gandhi's busy schedule as well as a lack of interest on her part now in Aunty Gauba's school, the meetings between the two women became less and less frequent. As a result Aunty Gauba started becoming restless and unhappy. She did not have free access to Mrs Gandhi as before. She then took to writing long letters to Mrs Gandhi and would leave them at my house to deliver. I used to faithfully leave these envelopes on Mrs Gandhi's table. The first few times Mrs Gandhi opened the letters but later the unopened long and rambling letters used to be put into my tray.

Aunty Gauba was a member of the Bal Bhavan Board and when she realized that her ideas were often not taken note of when compared to those of other members such as Tara Ali Baig, her frustration started to increase. I had shared a close rapport with Aunty earlier, but now our meetings also started to become painful. Rather than being interesting and stimulating, I had to listen to critical remarks about Mrs Gandhi. In anger she quit the Bal Bhavan Board and now she had no opportunity to meet Mrs Gandhi. She was obsessed by Mrs Gandhi and her pent-up feelings added to her frustrations. Many of the problems, I think, lay within her, as her earlier relationship with Mrs Gandhi had given her a sense of fulfilment as well as perhaps a feeling of power. To some extent, Mrs Gandhi also perhaps did not realize that after giving Aunty Gauba free access and having opened up and shared her feelings and problems, this withdrawal could possibly cause hurt and unhappiness, especially to a person like Aunty Gauba.

An echo of such a situation occurred many years later vis-à-vis Mrs Gandhi and Maneka. Perhaps one of the reasons for the souring of their relationship was similar to the one which created a rift between Mrs Gandhi and Aunty Gauba. During the Emergency, along with Sanjay, Maneka had also tasted power. After Sanjay's death in 1980, she may have thought that power was not reflected but belonged to her and she would be able to exercise it as before. Had Mrs Gandhi restrained here earlier, the situation may not have developed into what it did.

In early 1958 Aunty Gauba rang me up at home early one morning to say that she wished to come to the Prime Minister's House to see Mrs Gandhi on some important matter. (I learnt later that she wanted Mrs Gandhi and Panditji to resolve the Kashmir problem according to her suggestions.) As Sir Harold Macmillan, the British Prime Minister, and his wife were staying at the Prime Minister's House and Mrs Gandhi was giving a coffee party for Lady Macmillan, I told Aunty Gauba that this would not be possible. When I reached the Prime Minister's House around 9.00 a.m., I heard the sound of a piano being played loudly in the ballroom upstairs. I guessed who it was. As I approached her, Aunty Gauba started thumping the piano even more loudly and stared at me with a look that was a mixture of guilt and defiance. I learnt later that the piece she was playing was the Death March. I was annoyed and managed to send her away. But the incident was not over yet.

After lunch she again walked into my room with a strange look on her face. She told me that from the Prime Minister's House she had gone to the Ashoka Hotel, where the Prime Minister was hosting a lunch for Sir Macmillan. She sat there for hours and when Panditji came out she tried to accost him, but he brushed her aside. Then she went to Mr Krishna Menon and when he also did not give her a satisfactory hearing, perhaps she was overtaken by frustration and a kind of desperation. She then once again made her way to the Prime Minister's House and into my room. When I realized that she had had no breakfast and lunch, I thought I would calm her down with some food and send her away. In the meantime Mrs Gandhi sent for me and I had to go downstairs to attend to her work, which took time. As I was coming up, I saw Aunty Gauba coming down with her eyes glazed and with an almost deranged look. A servant was agitatedly running after her and told me that she had hit Mrs Gandhi. I could not understand and rushed upstairs into Mrs Gandhi's room. She was sitting in her bed sobbing and I could see the imprint of the heavy German hand on her delicate skin. I was horrified. It seems that in my absence, Aunty Gauba's mad streak must have taken over and she walked into Mrs Gandhi's room, argued with her, and when Mrs Gandhi replied angrily, Aunty Gauba hit her. I could not believe and understand such behaviour. After this, naturally, Aunty Gauba's entry into the Prime Minister's House was stopped.

Mrs Gandhi eventually got over the incident but the effect on Aunty Gauba was terrible. She gradually started going under. I realized the depression she was going through. Although I was extremely upset by her inexcusable behaviour, I also felt sorry for her. As I had feelings for both Mrs Gandhi and Aunty Gauba, the situation depressed me. In June, when Panditji, Mrs Gandhi, and children went to Manali, I wrote a letter to Mrs Gandhi trying to explain the causes of Aunty Gauba's frustration and the likely reasons for her unfortunate action. I wrote the letter more to express my own feelings at the unhappy incident. There was no response to my letter and neither did I expect one. However, after more than a month had passed, Mrs Gandhi wrote the following letter to me while she was on tour:

Raj Bhavan
Hyderabad
7.7.58
11 p.m.

My dear Usha

I cannot remember whether I made it clear that all the middle part of the Manali article is to be deleted for the Statesman *but kept for the 'Women on the March'.*[1] *The paragraph about the Rishis and the Pandavas.*

---

[1]Mrs Gandhi had written an article, 'Manali: A Place for Contemplation', for *The Sunday Statesman*, Delhi, which was published on 13 July 1958.

As usual the programme gets fuller & fuller—with interviews, inaugurations of the Upper House by the President, President's party and so on. However, having once acknowledged the philosophy of 'gracious acceptance' one cannot grumble.

I meant to talk to you about your letter re Aunty Gauba. It is true she has many fine qualities but I find she is the very opposite of what she imagines herself to be hence all the conflict and tension. I do not find her stimulating. On the contrary she drains me of ideas & energy, so that I am left utterly exhausted. I was attracted to her when I first met her but on deeper acquaintance I found many traits with which I could not reconcile myself & being a very bad actress, I cannot help showing this. That is what has really led to the tension between us. The things she wants me to do & the way she would often like me to behave I consider quite ridiculous & wrong. We really do not have much in common. Her latest letter proves this once again. It is, of course, a very nice & friendly letter. Life is a travelling. You meet people and sometimes you can travel together for a while, or for a long time but most often one moves forward & one gets left behind or takes another path.

Indira

URGENT
P.S.
8.7.58 at 5 a.m.

How about starting the Statesman article like this? This would then be the first paragraph.

[Stephen Spender says:
'Different living is not living in different places.
It is creating in the mind a map an image
And willing on it a desert
A pinnacled mountain or a saving resort.'
'Or an air-conditioner' adds my father. But then comes a time when the best of maps get worn. Then is it that one looks towards the Himalayas.]

Delete the few lines about the paddy & buckwheat field—it makes the description too long.

Show the whole thing plus photographs to Padmajaji if she has the time.

I am in a mood to write realms [sic], especially on the subject of 'travelling' mentioned yesterday, but physically I am feeling half dead . . .

Indira

The maturity of her reply regarding Aunty Gauba impressed me.

Aunty Gauba, on the other hand, was gradually going down. A year had passed and she was losing weight and looking more and more unhappy. I felt sorry for her, although she herself was responsible. When I went to see her once, she seemed very depressed, and suddenly asked me, 'Tell me, what is wrong with me.' I was taken aback as it was she who used to diagnose people and their personalities. I did not believe in doing so, but I found her looking very anxiously into my eyes for an answer. Suddenly I heard myself say, 'Aunty, I think you lack intellectual humility.' I myself was surprised at my reply but later thought that perhaps it was not wrong, because she used to feel that she knew other people better than they did themselves.

A few friends of Aunty Gauba were also concerned about her state although they did not know the reason behind it. On Aunty Gauba's birthday, we decided to bring some eats and gather at her house to surprise and cheer her up. However, I knew that only some gesture from Mrs Gandhi would be a real solace. I was not working for Mrs Gandhi at the time and thus with hesitation wrote a letter to her telling her of our plan and mentioning that though I was aware of Aunty Gauba's unforgivable behaviour, Mrs Gandhi's presence at the surprise party could perhaps lift her depression and gloom. I added that this was merely a suggestion and it was perfectly understandable if she chose not to come. Mrs Gandhi was then the Congress President and I sent the letter to her AICC office. We, the friends, arrived at Aunty Gauba's home. Soon after, Mrs Gandhi entered with a gift, a saree. Aunty Gauba's expression was to be seen to be believed. I looked at Mrs Gandhi gratefully, and felt that by overcoming her feelings she had been gracious. The rift, of course, could never be healed. Mrs Gandhi moved ahead, while Aunty Gauba continued to hold on to the past relationship and remained unhappy.

Another surprise birthday party was attempted much later in 1967, which turned out to be a fiasco. More about that later.

While in Manali in 1958, Mrs Gandhi wrote a short piece on that hill station. I liked it and persuaded her to get it published, which it was in the *Sunday Statesman* of 13 July 1958. Reproduced below are excerpts from the article:

Awe-inspiring snow-covered mountains, forests of deodars, aged and dignified, dozens of springs and rivulets, bubbling and laughing down the hillsides . . .

The River Beas itself, at this stage of its journey, is a rushing, roaring torrent, drowning all other sounds and inviting to its waters some of the loveliest of our hill birds. Here are the terraced fields of paddy and buckwheat, their varied shades of green set off by the rich brown of the plots still to be planted. And permeating it all an undercurrent of the utmost peace. That is Manali.

A year ago I took a two-day holiday in Manali in the midst of a most tiring, hot and dusty tour of our welfare projects in Himachal and the Kulu and Kangra Valleys. It struck me then as an ideal spot for those who love solitude and who do not mind, indeed would welcome, a rough and simple life far from the so-called amenities of civilization. It is not a place to escape from life but rather to become more poignantly aware of its many facets . . .

A deputation came to me requesting a visit from my father. I knew my father would love the place. I knew that his visit would draw attention to the difficulties of the people and be of help to them. It gladdened my heart when he agreed to choose it for his vacation. And yet at the back of my mind there was a lurking fear too. How would this opening-up affect the valley and its attractive people? Would contact and competition with the 'clever' people of the plains not destroy their charming naiveté? Cannot greater comfort and material grain [sic] be achieved without lessening the people's spiritual quality? Is there no way of improving the economy and bringing in better education, health and transport services without also introducing the restlessness of the plains, which might cause a weakening in their vital touch with nature?

. . . For those who want urban comforts, tarred roads and organized entertainment there are many hill-stations to go to—Simla, Mussoorie, Darjeeling, Ootacamund and Mahableshwar, to give only a few examples. Let the Kulu Valley attract a different type—those who are young at heart and eager for adventure: those who yearn to conquer the peaks and those who seek quiet contemplation; those who can appreciate the beauty of nature and draw from it spiritual, mental and physical vigour. The aim is not a cessation of effort but, in the words of Charles Morgan, 'the stilling of the soul within the activities of the mind and body so that it might be still as the axis of a revolving wheel is still.'

Humanity is losing itself in the unnatural and is showing signs of suffering a severe deficiency because 'it no longer takes its strength direct from nature, which alone is eternally young and eternally true.'

Her description is imbued with her love for the unspoilt natural beauty of the Kulu valley as well as concern for the way of life of its people and their culture. It speaks of Manali as it was then and was not ruined by crass tourism as at present. Unfortunately, what she had feared has now happened. It is good that she is not there to see the violation of nature.

~

FIVE

HOLIDAYS WITH THE FAMILY

In June 1954, Panditji, Mrs Gandhi, and the family went to Mashobra, eight miles beyond Shimla, for a short holiday and stayed at 'The Retreat', a bungalow where the Viceroys used to retreat for peace and quiet from the hustle and bustle of the Viceregal Lodge in Shimla, then the summer capital.

One day I received a message from Mr Mathai stating that Mrs Gandhi had enquired if I could come up to Mashobra, as both Panditji and she had to come down to Delhi for the visit of Mr Chou En-lai, Prime Minister of China, to New Delhi. Mrs Gandhi wanted me to be with Rajiv and Sanjay during her absence. The meeting with Chou En-lai was the famous meeting where the Panchshila principle was enunciated. On his return to China, Mr Chou en Lai sent a large basket of litchis for Panditji which was brought to Mashobra. The litchis were small in size but most luscious with a wonderful flavour. When Panditji and Mrs Gandhi returned to Mashobra, she asked me to stay on. This gave me an opportunity to see Panditji from close quarters, especially at meal times. Panditji was not much of a talker and used to be engrossed in his thoughts, but Sanjay would provoke him with questions and riddles. Panditji was very patient in his replies. At lunch one day Sanjay was not eating properly, so Panditji told him that the food items on his plate were his friends and one must not waste anything. Sanjay at once retorted that one does not eat one's friends. Once at dinner time, Sanjay asked if Nanu's (Panditji's) *achkan* was made on the charkha, and Panditji then patiently explained the entire process of the production of the woollen cloth.

Another time Sanjay wanted to know why Chandragupta was called Maurya, and Panditji replied that the word came from 'mayur' (peacock). Being young and eager to contribute to the conversation, I said that in our history lessons we had been told of another interpretation, that the word came from Mura, the name of Chandragupta's mother. Panditji responded rather brusquely, 'Maybe'. I realized then that he did not like intervention or interruption and was more careful about making interjections after that.

One day Mrs Gandhi said that she saw everything in colours. Panditji was intrigued and asked what colour she saw him in. I observed, 'Surely everything cannot be represented by colours.' Panditji, with a twinkle in his eye, replied, 'Things are sometimes exaggerated.'

I used to marvel at Panditji's energy. He was impatient and restless, too. His hands were very alive. He hardly ever relaxed and used to work very hard. The only difference in the routine at Mashobra was that Panditji used to go for long walks both in the morning and evening and would rest after lunch. Once I met his PA coming out of Panditji's room at 11.00 p.m. and Panditji was to leave early in the morning. I remarked to the PA that the members of the staff did not let Panditji rest or sleep. He replied, 'It is the contrary', which was true.

In the summer of 1955, Panditji and Mrs Gandhi were to visit the USSR where Nikolai Bulganin and Nikita Khrushchev had arranged a tumultuous welcome for them. This tour coincided with Rajiv and Sanjay's summer vacations. Mrs Gandhi was in a dilemma. Mrs Raksha Saran, a social worker and well known to Mrs Gandhi, had already made arrangements for the boys to go to the hill station of Dalhousie. While going on a tour, Mrs Gandhi left the following letter for me:

Prime Minister's House,
New Delhi
7.5.55

Usha,

Had especially wanted to have a talk with you this afternoon but in the hubbub about blouse pieces I forgot.

Perhaps you know that I am in a bit of a spot with regard to the children's summer holidays. I seem to be getting more and more involved in the Russian trip. And so far no satisfactory arrangements have been made for Rajiv & Sanjay.

I had hoped they would be able to go to Kashmir and, on that basis, had asked Miss Naidu (Padmajaji) to stay with them. But it has not been possible to make any satisfactory arrangement for their stay there.

In Dalhousie, Raizada Hansraj has offered me his guest cottage, which is 700 yds from his own house. He and his family will be staying there.

The cottage has 2 bedrooms with bathrooms, sitting, dining rooms, kitchen, etc. Tulsi & Prabhu will go from here.

Now to come to the point. If Feroze's willing to go there & stay the whole time, there is no great problem. He has not yet given his reply.

If he does not go, will it be possible for you to take the children up? I can arrange for a police officer or Srinivasan to escort the party up to Dalhousie.

If you would not like to be quite alone, perhaps Vimla could go too.

Think this over and let me know when I return. I should like to tell the children exactly what has been decided when I go to see them on the 14th.

I should like the boys to stay there for a month—the whole of June, which is the hottest time here.

ING

Thus Rajiv, Sanjay, Mrs Clark, a teacher from Welham School, and I went to Dalhousie.

In her instructions, Mrs Gandhi had told me that the boys could also go for riding. A few days later, at about 8.00 a.m., when I was in my room, which overlooked the approach road, I heard some sounds. When I looked down through the window, to my horror I saw a man carrying Rajiv in his arms. I rushed down and learnt that Rajiv had fallen from his horse just near the entrance. He did not seem to be hurt, but complained of pain in his elbow. I felt terrible as Mrs Gandhi had left the boys in my care. I informed Raksha Saran, who had arranged the trip to Dalhousie and was also staying there with her father Raizada Hans Raj. She quickly organized a jeep and we took Rajiv down to the military hospital for an x-ray. We were told that there was no fracture but nevertheless his arm was put in a sling. I wrote about this to Mrs Gandhi who was away on her tour.

Persuading the boys to write to their mother was an uphill task.

The following two letters were received from Mrs Gandhi from the trip.

7.6.55

Usha—

I hope all is going well! We are travelling in three planes—just the eight of us. PM, Pillai, Azim Husain & I are in this one with two Russians.[1]

Yesterday in Prague I saw a most impressive hospital for women & children. There was a premature baby which was born at 5 months weighing 400 grammes. It was now $1^{1/2}$ months & twice its original weight but still miserable to look at.

There was an attractive American woman doctor who said she was a 'political refugee' from her country.

Give my greetings to Miss Clark and the family next door.

> *Best wishes*
> *Indira*

P.S. Have arrived in Moscow. Staying night out of the city in a beautiful house with a heavenly garden.

ING

The second letter was from Salzburg, Austria.

> *Hotel Schloss Fuschl*
> *Land Salzburg*
> *29.6.55*

My dear Usha,

Your letters and the children's all came by bag and reached me in Vienna on the evening of the 27th. I was very happy to get them, and to have, at long last, news of you and the children. I am glad you gave me detailed news of Rajiv's arm.—This way one is less worried as one is sure that nothing will be kept hidden! I hope he is quite all right now.

Since Feroze is there, you need not have stayed, but naturally it is

---

[1]Sir Raghavan Pillai, Secretary General and Mr Azim Husain, joint secretary were from the Ministry of External Affairs.

reassuring to have you there. About the future programme—you must help the children to decide.

My own arrival in Delhi has been delayed by a few days. As you know we are now going to England too. We arrive there on Friday evening, motor to Chequers (the Prime Minister's country house). On Saturday we go to Windsor Castle (the Queen's country place) & from there to Broadlands (the Mountbattens' country house). The result of all this is that we get only a few hours on Sunday in London. This seemed silly to me since no one knows when I shall get a chance of coming this way again. So I have decided to stay on in London until the next Air India service which is on Thursday. Papu & our ambassador in Cairo insist that I must stay a day in Cairo as it will be rude to cancel the programme fixed for me. So I shall reach Delhi on the 16th July.

<u>Question to be decided</u>: Would the children want to stay on in Dalhousie for so long & would they like me to come up there?

Otherwise they can come down to Delhi whenever they please after PM's arrival which will be on the 14th, most probably. I suppose Delhi will not be so hot then.

Mathai wrote to say that there was some confusion about money. I had thought that he would give you as much as was needed and I would pay him back on my return.

We are here for the Conference of Heads of Missions. So far as I am concerned it is a holiday. Yesterday I slept for 2 hours in the day. After the excitement of the USSR I have a let-down feeling!

I hope the children have not been giving trouble & that Miss Clark is content. How are the lessons going?

Best wishes,
Indira

Feroze Gandhi came up to Dalhousie twice to be with Rajiv and Sanjay for a week (and on both occasions he gave me some money to cover the expenditure). We returned to Delhi a couple of days before Panditji was due to return. Mrs Gandhi came a few days after Panditji. Once in Delhi, Feroze Gandhi took Rajiv to Safdarjang Hospital for an X-ray and it was discovered that there was a hairline fracture in his elbow; his arm had to be put in a plaster cast. When

Mrs Gandhi returned, I felt very embarrassed as I had been writing to her that there was nothing to worry about.

After their visit to the USSR, Mrs Gandhi started receiving letters from some parents in that country who had named their newborn daughters 'Indira' as a mark of respect and love for Mrs Gandhi and India. I opened a file labeled 'Little Indiras of the USSR' and it soon started swelling. Mrs Gandhi was particular about replying to these letters and from time to time she also sent them souvenirs. I wrote a short piece about a few of the little Indiras in the USSR in 1958 which was published in the *Illustrated Weekly* with photographs. Some excerpts:

LITTLE INDIRAS OF THE USSR

Indira Ivanova, Indira Muratbekovna Tanikeeva, Indira Alekssevna Doroshenko, Indira Abdul Kadirovna Yunisova and Indira Haluhaeva. These names sound interesting and intriguing. There are about fifty such names in the USSR.

Ever since the Prime Minister and Shrimati Indira Gandhi visited the Soviet Union in the summer of 1955, Mrs. Gandhi has been receiving requests from parents for naming their daughters after her and for becoming their god-mother.

The parents of little Indiras come from all walks of life. Among them are a colonel, a doctor, a school teacher, an agronomist and an air-gymnast.

Mrs. Jamaldinova writes, 'I would remember throughout my life the day when I saw you and Mr. Nehru in Tashkent. When I saw you, my heart began to beat and tears came out of my eyes—these were the tears of happiness and pleasure at the thought that we are living at such a good time when the peoples of different countries know each other closely and establish friendly contacts. Let the life of all children in this world be shining and full of happiness as a May Day, and beautiful as a rose. Let them never see the horrors of war.'

Doctor Dairbekovich writes, 'In the Middle Asia as in Kirghiz particularly, the names are quite similar to those found in India. The name of my wife is Nadira and that is why we like the name Indira all the more. We will bring up our daughter with the real love and respect for the talented Indian people.'

Mrs. Vilma Ozola from Latvia, giving reasons for naming her daughter Indira, writes, 'We did it out of the deep esteem and sympathy we feel for the great people of India, whose ancient and bright culture, famous history, love of freedom and endeavours for the strengthening of peace and understanding between the nations always evoke our admiration and enthusiasm.'

Mrs. Haluhaeva from Alma Ata asked for permission to name her fourteenth child Indira. Mrs. Gandhi, while agreeing to her request, wrote, 'Your family must be a joy to you. Being an only child myself I can appreciate the fun and companionship of a large family.' Mrs. Haluhaeva replied, 'We, as parents of fourteen children, would like to consider you our fifteenth daughter and your parents as our relations.' Mrs. Haluhaeva is a Mother Heroine of the USSR.

Besides Indiras in USSR, there are little Indiras in Yugoslavia, Bulgaria and Rumania also.

Shrimati Indira Gandhi sent dolls to some Indiras and has been receiving appreciative letters, press cuttings and photographs since then. Her 'Indira file' is swelling day by day.

One of her god-daughters Lilya Predit from the Ukraine wrote: 'Dear God Mother, Thank you for the doll. I have named her Venera. I love her very much. I wish to see you. Grandmother hold my hand. Please allow me to kiss you many many times. Your god-daughter—Lilya.'

~

SIX

FIRST TIME ABROAD

The next summer, in 1956, Panditji was to attend the Commonwealth Prime Ministers' Conference in London. From there, he was to fly to the USA to meet President Eisenhower and later he was to visit other countries in Europe. Mrs Gandhi was to accompany him along with Rajiv and Sanjay.

One day I received the following brief note from Mrs Gandhi:

PRIME MINISTER'S HOUSE.

——

Message—
~~To the Reception Officer~~.

Ush–

Papu has agreed to your accompanying me to England. So I think about it & let me know.

Indu.

9/5/17

P.T.O.

Don't tell
broadcast it yet!

I was thrilled, as I had never gone abroad till then.

In June, the Prime Minister and his party left in an IAF Viscount. Not being a jet, it had to go hopping and stopped for refuelling at Jamnagar and Bahrain, and reached Damascus in the afternoon. Next morning we left and stopped for refuelling at Athens, where the Greek President came to the airport for talks with Panditji. From there we went to Rome and reached London late in the evening. While flying over the islands of the Aegean Sea, Panditji asked the IAF crew for a map, he spread it out, and started explaining the geography of the region to Rajiv and Sanjay. Suddenly, lo and behold, he began reciting Lord Byron's poem on the struggle in Greece (I think from 'Childe Harold'). In London, we were received by Mrs Vijaya Lakshmi Pandit who was then the Indian High Commissioner there.

After the Commonwealth Prime Ministers' Conference in London, Panditji and Mrs Gandhi were to go on a state visit to the US when the news came that President Eisenhower had suffered a heart attack, so the trip to that country was cancelled. Instead Panditji went to Ireland with Mrs Pandit, and Mrs Gandhi stayed on in London. After the visit to the United States, Panditji was to visit Germany, France, Yugoslavia and Egypt. It had been arranged therefore that when Panditji and Mrs Gandhi went to the US, the boys and I would go to Cologne, Germany.

Two German boys, Walter and Reinhard Frey, had studied in Aunty Gauba's school for a short while when Rajiv and Sanjay were there, and they had invited the Gandhi boys to stay with them in their home on the banks of the Rhine. The Freys had a modest home and had to work hard to look after us. The food was simple, the boiled kind. Sanjay being Sanjay, said on the second day—in Hindi—that he wanted a poached egg. The Freys looked at me and I, somewhat

33

embarrassed, told them of his wish. They did not know what a poached egg was. Thus I produced a misshapen poached egg. There was no running hot water, so we had not had a bath for a day. Sanjay announced that he wanted to have a bath. Again there was confusion and Father Frey and his sons went to the backyard to chop wood to heat the boiler. One day both Rajiv and Sanjay were having a pillow fight and making noise. When I scolded them, Sanjay gave me his 'Dennis the Menace' book and said with a smile, 'See page 73.' I thought he was trying to distract me, so I scolded him even more. When he persisted, I opened the page and found Dennis telling his mother, 'Don't scold me. I am not your husband.' We all burst out laughing. Sanjay was quite a prankster, and he enjoyed the discomfiture of others.

Mathai had also come with us from London and was staying with Ambassador Nambiar. When they both came to visit us, I quietly told them that we had better move to the Ambassador's residence as we were proving to be quite a strain on the Freys.

After a few days, Panditji and Mrs Gandhi came for the state visit to Germany and we moved to the beautiful Hotel Petersburg overlooking the Rhine. The next day with Chancellor Konrad Adenauer we went for a boat ride on the Rhine up to Koblenz and back. Panditji and Adenauer had talks over lunch and the rest of us relaxed. Later Rajiv, Sanjay, and I went to visit Beethoven's house in Bonn where the genius had lived and worked and where some of his finished and unfinished manuscripts of music were displayed. The next night we left for Hamburg by a special train. After a day's stay, we flew to Paris for a day and then went on to Yugoslavia.

President Tito had invited Panditji and President Nasser to Brioni, his favourite vacation island in the Adriatic Sea. All three held long and intense talks, which led to the genesis of the non-aligned movement. On the second day the talks were held on another very small island, Vanga, off Brioni Island. The lunch and talks continued in a kind of fisherman's shack. After lunch Rajiv, Sanjay, and I went around the island and also examined the President's cellar! We were to leave for Cairo in the evening. However, the talks between the three stalwarts of the non-aligned movement were continuing, and Panditji sent a message that we could go to Cairo in our plane and that he would come later with President Nasser.

In Cairo, Ambassador Ali Yavar Jung and his charming wife Zehra took us to their house on the Nile. It was late, and as the boys were half-asleep I took them to their room. When I came out, Mrs Gandhi and the Begum were coming out of the adjoining bedroom, and Mrs Gandhi said with a mischievous look (knowing that I would be embarrassed) that she and I were going to share the room. We did not share a room again, but had to share a bathroom in Warsaw and Thimphu, Bhutan.

~

SEVEN

THE MOODINESS OF MRS GANDHI

When I joined Mrs Gandhi in 1953, I was the only person helping her. In 1955, Amie Crishna came to meet Mrs Gandhi. She was the sister of General Thimayya and had married into the Crishna family of Allahabad; the Crishnas were known to the Nehrus. A major tragedy befell the Crishnas when Amie's husband, who was an officer in the Himachal Government, was washed away in a flash flood in a stream in the state. Amie was left alone to bring up four young children. Mrs Gandhi was moved by her plight and gave her a job that came with a cottage in the grounds of the Prime Minister's House. Thus Amie also came to work for Mrs Gandhi and shared the room with me.

In 1956 Yashpal Kapoor, a clerk from the Prime Minister's Office, was brought to the Prime Minister's House and he also started helping Mrs Gandhi. He sat with the other PAs on the ground floor. He was a plump and bouncy person, always ready to oblige. He obviously understood the intricacies of handling those in power; thus he gradually managed to enter the corridors of power and besides being useful to Mrs Gandhi in her political work, became an MP as well.

Work began to increase, but the style of functioning somewhat disturbed me. There wasn't any proper division of work. Sometimes I found that Kapoor had been given the same task which I had been assigned. When this began to happen more often, I started feeling that perhaps Mrs Gandhi had less confidence in me now. This coincided with a certain coolness in her behaviour towards me. Later I realized that such phases of aloofness and distance were part of her personality. Perhaps her earlier life had something to do with it.

It seems that she was moody and had phases when she withdrew from the people around her, even when she was very young. This is evident from Panditji's letter to his sister, Mrs Pandit, written from the Dehra Dun Jail on 6 March 1933, when Mrs Gandhi was about sixteen years old. He wrote:

> During the last fourteen months or more I have written to Indu regularly. It has been a very one-sided correspondence as letters have evoked practically no response . . . I gather that Kamala is treated in the same way. It is not casual. It is persistent . . . I know that Indu is fond of me and Kamala. Yet she ignores us and others completely.[1]

I came from a different background and had not faced the kind of situations that she had, except the trauma of Partition, which was also faced by millions and had toughened them to face the challenges that came into their lives. I therefore could not comprehend such an attitude.

After some time I came to the conclusion that perhaps I had outlived my usefulness and should quit. I wrote a letter thanking Mrs Gandhi and saying that I had enjoyed working for her and being a perceptive person she must surely have known this. However, I continued, I had lately sensed a lack of confidence in me on her part and hence I found it difficult to work in such a situation. I left the letter on her table before leaving for home. The next morning the following five-page handwritten letter came from the Prime Minister's House:

Prime Minister's House,
New Delhi
15 September 1956

Usha—

I have just seen your letter.

I must say I have been singularly 'unperceptive' to let you feel this way.

Believe me you are <u>not</u> at all superfluous. If there wasn't enough work, why should I want to engage another person?

Amie Crishna came for her sake than for mine—she was in such distress that I felt that we had to get her a job. Kapoor came without any planning on my part. The day I couldn't get to Auntie Gauba's, I had an interview

[1]Nayantara Sehgal, *Before Freedom*, p. 114.

with Dhebarbhai which really scared me. He expected so much of me. In front of him I protested mildly but really it seemed so unfair that when I got home I exploded! Mathai decided then and there to get Kapoor over for the increasing election and other Hindi work, much of which is really my father's.

Actually neither Amie nor Kapoor are encroaching on your domain. They are doing PA's work and it is more than enough to (keep) them occupied. Although I had not planned it that way, I was afterwards rather glad because I thought this would give you more time for other work. I wanted you more and more to 'take charge' of things. You know my taste and my reactions, so I felt I could trust you to do the right thing and to deal with almost everything on your own, even if I were away. I had hoped that gradually you could also deal with the mail—with the exception of personal letters.

I realize now that I should have said all this to you more explicityly [sic]. There is no question of distrust. I could certainly trust you more than the others since you are obviously more discreet.

I have been under such a strain and so preoccupied with a number of problems that I hardly realized I was not speaking.

I don't know if all this will make sense to you. If you really feel you should have a break, take a holiday by all means. But don't feel that you have been slighted or distrusted because that won't be true. I do need you and shall miss you.

Think it over and come and have a talk when you feel like it.

Love
Indira

I was moved by her letter and naturally continued working for her. Soon after this Rajiv had a hernia operation and Mrs Gandhi planned to take him to Srinagar to convalesce. Perhaps to assuage my feelings, she asked me to accompany them. We stayed with Dr Karan Singh, who was then the Sadr-e-Riyasat of Kashmir.

When I began working in 1953, and received my first salary cheque, I was dumbstruck when I saw that it was signed 'Jawaharlal Nehru'. People used to be very anxious to get his autograph and here was a cheque for me signed by him! For three months I could not bring myself to send the salary cheques to the bank!

In 1956, I was sent for by Mr Mathai in his Parliament House

Office. He told me that it was being planned to put me in government service (ex-cadre). I still remember reacting rather unhappily to this suggestion. Mathai seemed a little surprised at my response and asked for the reason. In our family, no one had ever been in government service and I associated it with various kinds of restrictions and red tapism. Mathai was amused and must have thought me to be quite foolish as people used to clamber around him for jobs and favours. I was given the designation of PA to SA (special assistant, who was Mathai) to the PM. I did not particularly relish the designation, but luckily I had nothing to do with him.

~

EIGHT

LIFE AT THE PRIME MINISTER'S HOUSE

There was hardly any security system in the Prime Minister's House. A security man once told me that when the public used to come to meet Panditji and even if someone looked angry or agitated, on encountering Panditji their anger would melt away. One could see that while mixing with or talking to ordinary people, Panditji used to be happy and relaxed, and in his element. However, this was not so when he met others such as politicians and officials, with whom he could become withdrawn, serious, and even irritatable. Nevertheless, politicians in those days were of another calibre. Many stalwarts of the freedom struggle such as Babu Rajendra Prasad, Maulana Azad, Govind Ballabh Pant, and others, were still active in politics, holding various positions. But power then had a presence and dignity and was not reduced to a scramble for position, fuelled by ambition and corruption, as it was later.

The atmosphere in the Prime Minister's House in the 1950s used to be delightful. November used to be a festive month in the Prime Minister's House. There were three birthdays in close succession, Panditji's on 14 November, Padmaja Naidu's (who was always there during that time) on 17 November, and Indiraji's on 19 November. Once on Panditji's birthday, there was a dinner party where some of the staff members were also invited. Everyone was supposed to come in fancy dress. Mrs Gandhi looked elegant in a Sikkimese dress, Mrs Pandit came smartly dressed in a Chinese suit, and Padmaja Naidu was grand in a saffron-coloured robe. Panditji entered last, in an old 'jamewar choga' (a Kashmiri embroidered long coat), looking handsome and dignified as usual.

On Indiraji's birthday in 1959, there was another fancy dress dinner party. She looked beautiful in a 'garara' (a Muslim dress from Lucknow) and Panditji appeared handsome as usual in a Central Asian robe and cap.

On Panditji's birthday, the breakfast was special and even the staff were invited. As the day was also celebrated as Children's Day, a rally of hundreds of children was held at the Prime Minister's House. Once the rally was held in the National Stadium. On this occasion, on my return from the rally, I witnessed an interesting and embarrassing scene. Panditji and Indiraji, who had returned earlier from the National Stadium, were in the small entrance hall, which could not be avoided if one had to go anywhere into the House. Indiraji was very angry and was shouting at Panditji. Perhaps something had gone wrong at the National Stadium and Panditji was bearing the brunt of her ire. He stood quietly with his head bent and a little smile on his lips. It seemed a scene from a school—Indiraji the teacher scolding Panditji the student. On entering the hall, I felt terribly embarrassed and tried to slink through unobtrusively. I learnt later that after this incident Panditji went to Padmaja Naidu's room and happily told her about the scolding he had received. Who could have scolded him but Indiraji, and I am sure he must have cherished the experience.

Being young, I would try out various ideas to celebrate the birthdays and other occasions in the Prime Minister's House. We used to plan a cake for Panditji's birthday, keeping some topical theme in mind. For instance, to commemorate Panditji's visit to China in 1954 we got a cake made displaying a map and the route with the Qutab Minar (India) and a pagoda (China). After Panditji's visit to Japan in 1957, we ordered a cake in the shape of Mount Fujiyama. Another cake commemorated Panchshila in the form of five crazy stones with the five principles inscribed on them. Vimla Sindhi, the receptionist in the Prime Minister's House, and I would go to the bakery of Standard Restaurant (above Regal Cinema in Connaught Place) where I would give the finishing touches to the cake. I do not know if Panditji and the family were impressed or not by our efforts, but we used to find the enterprise exciting and enjoyable.

The birthdays of Rajiv and Sanjay were also special occasions, especially Sanjay's, as it was in December. Rajiv's was in August when schools were closed for summer vacations. Mrs Gandhi used to take a lot of interest in planning the food, games, and other entertainment for the occasion.

I also tried to be innovative regarding some menus. When the well-known African American singer, Marion Anderson, was invited by Panditji for dinner, I persuaded Indiraji to name the items on the menu after Indian ragas. When Yuri Gagarin, the first human to go into space, was invited by Panditji for a reception, once again interesting names were given to the items on the menu.

DINNER
MONDAY, THE 18TH
NOVEMBER, 1957.

Soup Pilu

Fish Desi

Chicken Darbari
Potato Mridang
Peas Chayanut

Gateau Spiritual
Kafi

TEA
FRIDAY, THE 13TH
DECEMBER, 1957.

Sputnik
Laddoo Lunar
Flying Saucer Samosa
Rocket & Shooting Star
Sandwiches
Meteorite Sweets
Milky Way

Lunches and dinners, even though formal, had a personal touch and warmth. If there were many guests, such as MPs, Panditji would move from table to table to personally interact with all of them. When the meal was finished, he would walk down the stairs to the porch to personally see off the guests.

In the winter months when the garden at the back used to be in bloom, some important lunches would be held on the side lawn, such as those for Queen Elizabeth and the lunch to celebrate the 2,500[th] anniversary of the Buddha in 1957. This lunch was attended by both the Dalai Lama and the Panchen Lama, who had come from Tibet with other important monks. For some time the Panchen Lama disappeared, causing concern. He was later found coming out of the small tent that Rajiv and Sanjay had erected on the main lawn, causing much amusement.

An important resident of the side lawn was a red panda to whom Panditji used to feed bamboo shoots in the morning before going to the office. The main central garden was planned in a British style with hedges and flowerbeds. I think Panditji and Mrs Gandhi were more interested in trees. The boys had planted a tree each in the side lawns.

Before being actively involved in politics herself, Mrs Gandhi was not only Panditji's eyes and ears, but she was also his official hostess. Along with looking after the family, she took a keen interest in official hospitality and related matters such as menus, table plans, flowers, linen, service, etc. Both father and daughter were good hosts and there was always a quiet grace about such occasions.

They were also interested in projecting the national heritage of the country to state guests. Thus a short dance recital used to be organized after state banquets at the Rashtrapati Bhavan. Over a period of time, almost all good dancers performed in these programmes. As the programme used to be for half an hour only, Mrs Gandhi felt that there should be a variety of short items rather than long ones depicting mythological themes which were quite unintelligible to the state guests. The proposed programme was put up to her for her approval; it came back with remarks such as, 'The visitors do not appreciate the finer points of classical dances. They much prefer younger and faster dances.' Once when I suggested two names from which she could choose, she asked, 'Who is a better dancer and also is prettier?' The slip below conveys her sensitivity towards authenticity as well as tribal culture.

The dance recital last evening was very bad. We should not have Naga dance (which anyhow was not at all authentic)

After Mrs Gandhi became the Prime Minister, she maintained her interest in such matters in spite of her heavy involvement in official and political work. The programmes continued till some Presidents, especially Giani Zail Singh, became bored with them and they were discontinued.

Teen Murti House was no doubt an imposing building, but the style of living of Panditji and his family had a simplicity. Panditji's bedroom did not have an air-conditioner. On very hot days when he returned home for lunch, he would rest for a short while on a sofa in the drawing room which had an air-conditioner for guests. In his large bedroom, besides the ceiling fan, there was a rickety old table-fan near his bed. When I saw it one day, I reprimanded the person in charge and asked him to provide a new one immediately. The next day he came and smilingly told me that Panditji was annoyed at the change and had asked for the old dilapidated fan back.

I would often see the Nehru family's old tailor-master Mohammad Hasan, who had come with them from Allahabad, mending and darning Panditji's khadi clothes. He told me that Panditji did not like to discard his old clothes and new ones were made only when necessary. Who would have realized this streak of austerity behind his gracious and charming personality? Although born in luxury, I think Gandhiji, the national movement, and the time spent in various jails had profoundly touched Panditji's personality.

NINE

~

INTERESTING VISITORS

In the Prime Minister's House one came across a wide cross-section
of people from all spheres. Panditji liked people with courage. One
such person who came into his life was Krishna Mehta.

In October 1947 Krishnaji's husband Mr Duni Chand Mehta was
the wazir-e-wazarat (district officer) in Muzaffarabad on the border
of Jammu and Kashmir state, near Domel, where the Krishanganga
meets the Jhelum. When the tribals attacked Kashmir, Muzaffarabad
was the first town that was sacked and Mr Mehta was brutally killed
in his own house. Krishnaji with her five young children, the eldest
being fourteen years old, tried to escape alongside the Jhelum, but
did not succeed. The Mehta family along with some others (mainly
women and children as the men had been killed) were kept in a camp
near the river.

I came to know of Krishnaji's experiences from her. She also
described these in her book *This Happened in Kashmir*.

> The raiders led us out . . . along the river bank to Domel bridge. What
> I saw there, I shall never forget . . . I saw the tragic spectacle . . . They
> (the women) threw their children first into the rushing river and
> seemed impervious to the shrieks and yells of their own children . . .
> Then they jumped in themselves and it was all over in the twinkling
> of an eye . . . I cannot say . . . how many women and children that day
> gave up their lives in the river. Only myself and three other women
> did not kill ourselves . . . many of the raiders had broken down and
> were weeping. The scene they had just seen moved them . . . I dared
> to tell them . . . 'and now why are you weeping? It is too late for regret
> and remorse.'[1]

[1]Krishna Mehta, *This Happened in Kashmir*, pp. 47–49.

Krishnaji was not only courageous but also tactful, and perhaps she had luck on her side. In the terrible ordeal she went through, some senior tribal leaders, impressed by her courage, became protective towards her. One of them told her, 'You are a mother whom everyone will envy. I have not seen anyone who faced us without fear.' Another Khan when leaving brought a notice in red ink and pasted it on the door of the old burnt house into which the Mehta family had moved. It read: 'No person, either Hindu or Muslim, is to enter the house without permission. The offender will run the risk of the whole Kabuli area turning against him. Aga Khan, Kabuli Leader.'

A few months later, they were moved and after more stops in other camps and in a jail in Rawalpindi, when the transfer of refugees took place, they finally reached India after nearly six months. They were taken to the Kurukshetra camp, where nearly two lakh refugees were staying. Krishnaji was keen to meet Panditji and wrote a letter to him. As he was coming to visit the camp, he asked to meet her. Krishnaji writes:

> I stood speechless before him . . . It happens very often in the presence of an acknowledgedly superior person. You do not have to make an effort, because so much is taken for granted. You can always hope to be judged as much as by what you do not say.[2]

Panditji was very moved by the account of her experiences and impressed by her courage, he asked her to accompany him in his car to Delhi to continue with her story. She was put up in the guest room at the Prime Minister's House and Panditji told her: 'Krishna, you should now look upon yourself as one of our own family. I shall arrange to have the children sent to school.' She writes: 'We (the family) stayed there (the Prime Minister's House) for over two months and Mrs Indira Gandhi was extremely kind and solicitous.' Panditji educated and rehabilitated her children, and two daughters became doctors. Panditji treated Krishnaji as a sister. Later she became a member of the Rajya Sabha.

---

[2]Krishna Mehta, *This Happened in Kashmir*, p. 169.

Krishnaji told me that once she was worried and went to Panditji with her problems. He told her not to worry and said that when he was faced with problems, he first tried to resolve them. If they did not get resolved, he put them on a shelf. After some time, when the situation changed either the problem would get resolved by itself or another way was discovered. I have found this advice very useful.

In 1955 Satish Gujral, the artist, returned from Mexico where he had gone on a scholarship and had been exposed to the works of the three great Mexican Social Realist muralists, Rivera, Orozco, and Siqueiros. He held an exhibition of his recent works, whose scale and boldness was influenced by his Mexican visit and the paintings expressed the anguish and tragedy of the Partition that he had personally experienced.

Mrs Gandhi and I visited the exhibition and later Satish was invited to the Prime Minister's House to meet Panditji and show his work. He took to the artist as despite his impaired hearing Satish had shown courage. Panditji always liked such people. Because of Satish's handicap, his older brother Inder Gujral used to accompany him to act as his interpreter. Inder Gujral was always politically inclined; in Lahore he had been an active member of the Students Federation movement and his parents had also taken part in the freedom movement. Coming close to Panditji and Indiraji eventually led to his political ascendancy.

Satish later painted the portraits of Panditji and Mrs Gandhi. We were surprised to see Mrs Gandhi's portrait, where she looked stern, much older, and weary, although she was still young and attractive and not yet forty. When queried about this, Satish's response was that this was the way he saw Mrs Gandhi. Strangely enough, later on as she plunged deeper into the hurly-burly of politics, she would sometimes look like the portrait painted some years earlier.

Another person who used to come frequently to Teen Murti House was Teji Bachchan, wife of the well-known Hindi poet Harivansh Rai Bachchan, whom I had first seen as a young girl in Lahore. Bachchanji, a professor of English literature at Allahabad University, had burst on the Hindi literary scene with his poetic work *Madhushala*, which was considered path-breaking at the time. He and his wife were introduced to the Nehru household in Allahabad by Sarojini Naidu. Bachchanji came to Delhi to join the Ministry of External Affairs as Hindi Officer. He was an introvert and a serious personality, while his wife was a lively and social person who was also fashion conscious. She often used to drop in to meet Mrs Gandhi. The two Bachchan sons, Amit (Amitabh) and Bunty (Ajitabh), who were in school in Nainital, would also visit Rajiv and Sanjay when in town for their vacation.

I think Teji had big dreams for Bachchanji and later for her son Amit. She was interested in theatre, especially acting, and produced Shakespeare's *Othello*, translated into Hindi in blank verse by Bachchanji. She herself enacted the role of Desdemona. Panditji and Mrs Gandhi attended the performance. She also took a keen interest in Amit's endeavours to become a film actor. The film actress Nargis, who was then an MP and knew Mrs Gandhi, also helped in this direction. Teji Bachchan must be a proud mother with the great success that Amitabh has achieved in the Hindi film industry.

Another interesting person whose life intertwined with that of Mrs Gandhi, and also with mine, was Marie Seton. She came to India towards the end of 1955 at the invitation of the Ministry of Education as a British Film Institute lecturer to help in their audio-visual programmes, especially films. I met her at a dinner party within the first couple of days of her arrival. She expressed a desire to meet Mrs Gandhi. An appointment was fixed and when she came to the Prime Minister's House, I left them together on a sofa in the sitting room. After an hour or more, Srinivasan, Panditji's private secretary rang up, and said Panditji had been waiting to speak to Mrs Gandhi but there was no response from her room. I went looking for her and found Mrs Gandhi and Marie sitting on the same sofa where I had left them, engrossed in deep conversation. Marie writes that when they were interrupted, 'We were still discussing the most varied subjects from art to family relations. It seemed as if we had known each other a long time.'[3] About Mrs Gandhi, Marie observes:

[3]Marie Seton, *Panditji*, p. 189.

Complex facets of her personality emerged: one intimate, leisurely and provocatively intelligent with the strongest inclination for the company of creative people; the other side, businesslike cool in appearance and with a swift withdrawal to irritability . . .[4]

This meeting led to Marie's long association with Mrs Gandhi as well as with Panditji. Before writing about Marie's involvement with India from 1955 onwards, some snippets about her past make interesting reading and give some glimpses into her personality. Marie was quite an unusual person and was a rebel from her childhood. She writes:

> I was taught to honour my Scottish heritage of resistance to English conquest and from it to learn the courage to stand up for my own opinions, right or wrong . . . The accident of this heritage was to play a very considerable role in the formation of an expanding consciousness of India's struggle to attain freedom from alien rule.[5]

One learns that Marie's mother liked to move in high society and was a social climber. She had cultivated an acquaintance with Queen Mary at Buckingham Palace and used to compose lyrics for songs sung to the royal family. Marie reacted to her mother and to high society by leaving home while still in her teens to go on to the stage, and later she became a theatre and film critic. Circumstances led her to Moscow. There 'through accident rather than design' she met and came to know Sergei Eisenstein, the well-known Russian film director. She later wrote a biography of Eisenstein who, according to Marie, was 'the genius of Soviet cinema, who had his work condemned and impeded under both Communist and capitalist dogmatists.'[6] After his death, she salvaged the footage of his unfinished Mexican film ¡Que Viva Mexico! (1930). From this footage she produced and edited the film Time in the Sun (1940).

Marie met D.G. Tendulkar, a mathematics student, who later

---

[4]Marie Seton, Panditji, p. 189.
[5]Ibid., p. 34.
[6]Ibid., p. 156.

authored some notable works on Gandhiji, in Berlin around 1932.[7]
He was keen to study film making under Eisenstein and Marie's letter
of introduction provided him the opportunity.[8] Marie was already
interested in the freedom movement in India, but Tendulkar also stirred
her interest and was in a way responsible for her coming to India
many years later.

Another person whom Marie came in contact with in 1932 and
who furthered her interest in India was V.K. Krishna Menon, who
was then building up the India League in London. When Marie met
him for the first time, she writes:

It was hard to decide if he was a very handsome man in a hacked out
sculptural manner, or if he was distinctly devilish to look at.[9]

She further observes:

As a personality, he might have walked out of a primeval forest, . . . But in
contradiction to this primal quality . . . his intellect was tempered to the
most scintillating impersonal steel . . . It crossed my mind that this man
might be possessed of a streak of what is called genius.[10]

Krishna Menon was Marie's lifelong obsession. Unfortunately, her
desire to write his biography remained unfulfilled.

Marie was in America in the 1940s where she became close friends
with Paul Robeson, the well-known African American singer and
activist, and his wife Eslanda. When the Robesons were persecuted
during the McCarthy period, Marie campaigned for them. She later
wrote Paul Robeson's biography. Marie's obsessions very often helped
her in her creative endeavours. Her biographies of Sergei Eisenstein,
of Paul Robeson, and last but not the least of Satyajit Ray, *The Portrait
of a Director*, are fine examples of her talent. She also wrote a book

[7]See *Gandhiji: His Life and Work* (1944), edited by D.G. Tendulkar and others,
Mahatma: Life of Mohandas Karamchand Gandhi (1951) and *Gandhi in Champaran* (1957).
[8]Marie Seton, *Panditji*, pp. 68–69.
[9]Ibid., p. 64.
[10]Ibid., p. 65.

on Panditji, not exactly a biography, but having been in and out of the Prime Minister's House and also having been present at some important occasions, it reveals her views on the events of that period. She wrote to me in 1966: 'I have always from childhood been attracted to people who will dare and undertake the impossible.'

Soon after her arrival in India in 1955, Marie saw a private screening of Satyajit Ray's first film, *Pather Panchali*, and she was struck by his genius. The film had been entered for the Cannes Film Festival but was having problems with the government in New Delhi. She campaigned for it and spoke to Mrs Gandhi and Panditji. The film was sent to Cannes and the rest is history. The film received the special jury prize for 'the Best Human Document' at the 1956 Cannes Film Festival. Despite this international honour, there was official hesitation in granting it recognition and there was a rumour about shelving the film as it portrayed poverty in India. Marie wrote a letter to Panditji protesting against this attitude; he responded by instructing the Ministry of External Affairs to acquire copies of the film for circulation in Indian embassies abroad.

After Marie's death in 1985, a few friends organized a memorial meeting in Delhi and requested Satyajit Ray and Rajiv Gandhi, then Prime Minister, for messages. Some excerpts from Satyajit Ray's message:

> . . . Her boundless energy was mostly spent on causes that she believed in . . . (When) I met Marie for the first time in the mid-fifties, I wanted to talk about the Soviet Master [Eisenstein], but Marie had just seen *Pather Panchali* in Delhi, and wished to talk of nothing else. I casually mentioned that the film was supposed to go to the Cannes Festival, but some officials in New Delhi didn't welcome the idea of an Indian film showing poverty being sent abroad. Marie at once produced note paper and dashed off a letter to the then Minister of Information & Broadcasting, urging him to intervene and make sure that the film was sent to Cannes.
>
> A few months before her own death, Marie suffered one of the greatest shocks of her life in the way Mrs Gandhi's life ended. Marie had long been a friend of the Nehru family, and 'Indu' had been especially close to her.

Some excerpts from Rajiv Gandhi's message:

> Marie Seton was an unusual person—warm, unconventional, generous, capable of intense enthusiasm, unfailingly sensitive. Her initial interests were in the arts . . . However, she did not dwell exclusively in the world of art. She was a political activist. India was among her special loves. My mother and I . . . were close to her.

In a span of twenty-nine years, Marie visited India often and stayed in the country a total of ten years. With her infectious energy and great enthusiasm, she contributed to many areas. She played an important role in building the film society movement. She also contributed to developing a course on film appreciation at the Film and Television Institute in Poona, where she also lectured on the subject. She had the quality of inspiring an interest in the cause of good cinema, an enthusiasm that touched many people, including me.

Along with pursuing her own work, Marie used to be in and out of the Prime Minister's House. She stayed there a few times and also travelled with Panditji and Mrs Gandhi. She therefore saw things from the inside and closely observed both the inmates of the House and various happenings too, some of which are recorded in her book *Panditji*.

Marie was a friend of Mrs Gandhi, knew both her strong and weak points, and remained her loyal friend till the end. She was a good friend of mine, too. When I had problems vis-à-vis Mrs Gandhi or otherwise, there were not many people to whom I could talk openly, being in the position I was. But I could safely confide in Marie because, knowing both Mrs Gandhi and me, and being fond of us both, she was sensitive to the situation and was objective in her comments. Some excerpts from her letters to me illustrate this. Before rejoining Mrs Gandhi in 1966, when I was in a dilemma, I wrote to Marie expressing my feelings. She responded as follows:

> You should consider very carefully indeed before you become involved again in work. If you do think of accepting, you must, I think, accept the hurting which cannot help but be part of it. There is an absence of

appreciation of people and crabbiness towards those too closely involved. It is an almost mechanical reaction and I think unconscious. (Letter dated 26 March 1966.)

Again, in 1983, when I was unhappy and wondering if I should continue, Marie counselled me:

Allowing the quirks of friend's [Mrs Gandhi] character, distrust, withdrawal, etc. I honestly doubt if she intentionally has ever intended to hurt, snub or be disloyal to you who has honestly been the best friend she ever managed to find. (Letter dated 19 December 1983.)

Earlier the same year she had written:

Very early on, I realized that to preserve a relationship with our friend [Mrs Gandhi] it was essential to preserve, or build up a certain detachment, otherwise one would inevitably become vulnerable to being hurt, not intentionally, but because friend is moody. (Letter dated 28 August 1983.)

Fredda Brilliant, a British sculptor (I think she was a Polish émigré), used to often come to India with her husband Herbert Marshall, a theatre person. In the 1950s, Fredda expressed a desire to sculpt Mrs Gandhi's head. However, after a few sittings Fredda gave up. She felt that while Mrs Gandhi's eyes were beautiful and visionary, her mouth conveyed a certain smallness. Fredda could not reconcile the two and eventually only did a sculpture called the 'Eyes of Indira'.

Once a British artist, Edward Halliday, came to India to do a portrait of Panditji. Panditji would give him a sitting after breakfast. One day Mr Halliday told me that it was very difficult to do his portrait, as Panditji was constantly thinking, and the contours of his mobile face would keep changing. He, the painter, had to start afresh almost every morning.

~

TEN

FAMILY RELATIONSHIPS

When I started to work in 1953, Feroze Gandhi was living in Lucknow working for the *National Herald*, but he came to Delhi quite often. He would stay in the Prime Minister's House until he became an MP and thereafter he moved to an MP bungalow allotted to him. When he was in the Prime Minister's House, I used to find him quite morose and not very communicative. Even at the dining table he would hardly speak. However, his mood changed when he was with his sons. Rajiv and Sanjay's room would be turned into a Meccano room. The floor would be littered with various parts and father and sons would become fully engrossed for hours in building various objects. I think Rajiv and Sanjay inherited their interest in mechanical things and their ability to use their hands from their father. Feroze Gandhi came less and less frequently to the Prime Minister's House after he became an MP. One could see that he did not feel particularly comfortable in the House. The only time I heard him pass a snide remark about Panditji was in Dalhousie, in 1955; however, I do not remember it now. There may be some merit in the following remarks made by a biographer of Indira Gandhi concerning Feroze Gandhi:

> Although he genuinely admired his father-in-law, he thought there was something counterfeit in the cult developing around Nehru. He intensely disliked being introduced as 'the Prime Minister's son-in-law,' . . . This only encouraged him all the more to establish his own identity. As Indira found a substitute satisfaction in attending to her father's needs, Feroze sublimated his energies in attending to the needs of his constituents and to parliamentary affairs.[1]

[1] Anand Mohan, *Indira Gandhi: A Personal and Political Biography*, p. 202.

Shanta Gandhi and Mrs Gandhi studied together in Aunty Vakil's school in Poona in the early 1930s. Later, when Mrs Gandhi and Feroze were in England for studies, Shanta also happened to be there. All three used to be together quite often.

Shanta came to Delhi in the 1950s to join the National School of Drama and became a good friend of mine. She would often talk about Mrs Gandhi in Poona and in England. About the latter, she used to say that though Mrs Gandhi and Feroze were very much in love, Feroze used to be quite apprehensive about marrying Jawaharlal Nehru's daughter.

Tariq Ali commented about Feroze Gandhi:

> He hated protocol, state banquets, formality in any shape or form . . . The children, under his care, would not have been so bedazzled by their proximity to power. . . Indira had grown up at a time when India was engaged in [the freedom] struggle . . . Rajiv and Sanjay by contrast were brought up in the shadow of power politics.[2]

Mrs Gandhi relationship with her mother was very close and intense.

She was charged with a fierce sense of responsibility. Mrs Gandhi said, 'I was looking after myself from the time I was three or four, and whether I was or not, I thought I was looking after my parents.' It was this feeling that made her fiercely protective when she saw her mother slighted or neglected or pushed into the background.[3]

Mrs Gandhi's relationship with Mrs Vijaya Lakshmi Pandit, as is known, was never comfortable or cordial. A lot has been written about Mrs Gandhi's early years and the causes of her insecurities and resentments. 'For Indira, old wounds never healed; nor could she forget or relinquish a grudge', observes Katherine Frank in regard to Mrs Gandhi's relations with her aunt.[4] When Mrs Gandhi became the prime minister, I thought she would be able to transcend her

[2] Tariq Ali, *The Nehrus and the Gandhis: An Indian Dynasty*, p. 265–66.
[3] Pupul Jayakar, *Indira Gandhi*, p. 11.
[4] Katherine Frank, *Indira*, p. 173.

earlier feelings, but that did not happen. Once or twice when Mrs
Pandit came to see Mrs Gandhi, she asked me to intervene after ten
minutes or so, perhaps because she did not feel comfortable during
these encounters.

Unlike the aunt and niece relationship, the relationship between
brother and sister, Panditji and Mrs Pandit, was very warm and close.
Mrs Pandit's was a strong extroverted personality while Panditji was
an introvert, gentle and vulnerable. I have a feeling, though I may be
wrong, that unconsciously perhaps this may have also been a factor,
besides others, which influenced Mrs Gandhi's decision to move to
Delhi to stay with her father to look after him and to protect him
from certain influences. Of course, the most important motive that
prompted her to move to Delhi is stated in her own words:

> When I went to live with my father at Teen Murti House, the residence
> of the Prime Minister, it wasn't really a choice. My father asked me to
> come and to set up the house for him. There was nobody else to do it.
> So I set up the house, but I resisted every inch of the way about becoming
> a hostess. I was simply terrified of the so-called social duties . . . I used
> to stay for a period of time and then go . . . It was a real problem because,
> naturally, Feroze didn't always appreciate my going away. I was living
> about half the month in Lucknow and half in Delhi, until Feroze became
> a member of the Parliament.[5]

In spite of her earlier reservations and initial reluctance, Mrs Gandhi
eventually became immersed in her duties at the Prime Minister's
House. I am not sure if she was fully reconciled to the situation, but
as usual her sense of duty prevailed.

It is interesting to observe the difference when she referred to
her grandfather Motilalji and her father Panditji. During Motilalji's
time, she was a child and then a young girl. Life in Anand Bhavan
then was not so difficult and insecure, physically and emotionally, as
it became later.

Mrs Gandhi remembered her grandfather with love and fondness,

[5]Indira Gandhi, *My Truth*, pp. 69–70.

a person who thoroughly spoilt her. According to her, 'when he laughed the whole house shook and laughed with him'. When she talked of him, her eyes used to gleam with happiness and affection.

However, when Mrs Gandhi used to talk about her father, it was always in the context of an incident or an anecdote. I do not recollect her mentioning him with the same emotion as she did her grandfather. Motilalji was an extrovert, while both Panditji and Mrs Gandhi were introverted and sensitive. Panditji was an intellectual influence on his daughter and gave her a sense of history and a wider vision. I think, however, that her earlier hurts and insecurities got mixed up with this. While both father and daughter were deeply attached to each other, I do not think she could communicate with him easily. Often she would convey her thoughts through letters, such as the one below and another reproduced in Chapter 12.

In April 1958, when Panditji expressed a desire to be relieved of the prime ministership, there was much furore and he had to agree to continue in office. There were discussions amongst the staff at the Prime Minister's House and I remember that I was the only one who felt that Panditji should follow his instinct and that it might be better for him to continue as an elder statesman.

It was only recently that I came across a letter dated 1 May 1958 that Mrs Gandhi had written to Panditji and found that we were on the same wavelength.

> *Prime Minister's House*
> *New Delhi*
> *1st May, 1958.*

Darling Papu,

I should not presume to advise you but I have been thinking over our little talk of an hour ago.

Having once suggested giving up the Prime Ministership and started a train of thought and discussion, is it wise to go back to the status quo? Will it not have an adverse effect? So much is rotten in our politics that everybody sees things through his own avaricious myopic eyes and is quite unable to understand nobility or greatness. There will therefore be a feeling that you had no intention of giving up the Prime Ministership and were only bluffing.

Let them try to manage by themselves, otherwise they will only drag you down with their own rottenness. If you are outside, it may at least reassure the general public that you are not responsible for all the wrongdoing.

I have so much to say but there is no time.

All my love to you,

Indu[6]

The above letter conveys Mrs Gandhi's anguish and her efforts to protect her father. Panditji's early life had been one of comfort, secure and loving, unlike that of Mrs Gandhi. Panditji's idealism and trusting quality made him what he was. Mrs Gandhi became tough and harsh partly due to the situation she had to face from her childhood and later, when Panditji was in power politics, seeing other people take advantage of his nobility. Mary Carras writes:

She [Mrs Gandhi] told a friend that her father was too gentle with those who were corrupt or who had crossed him in some way or who were simply dead wood. If it was within her power she would summarily dismiss such people. And indeed when she later came to occupy the 'gaddi', she exercised that option frequently.[7]

People do get conditioned by the situation and happenings they go through, especially if they are sensitive, as Mrs Gandhi was.

[6]Sonia Gandhi, *Two Alone, Two Together*, p. 623.

[7]Mary C. Carras, *Women in World Politics*, from the chapter 'Indira Gandhi: Gender and Foreign Policy'.

~

ELEVEN

ARROGANCE OF POWER

The staff at the Prime Minister's House was quite small. At the top was M.O. Mathai and there were about three PAs, including N.K. Seshan who had joined Panditji along with Mathai during the term of the Interim Government. Mathai was the kingpin who controlled and coordinated everything—work, staff, interviews, etc. Thus he wielded a lot of power and the staff were in awe of him. I do not think he was happy at my entering the House directly through Mrs Gandhi and not through his channel. Thus he had no hold on me and tried to ignore me. I had no use for him anyway.

Mathai, with his uncanny feel for power, had arrived and offered his services to Panditji in Allahabad (I believe gratis) in 1946, even before the formation of the Interim Government. Panditji was new to governance and Mathai (by worming his way in) would have not only made himself useful but also won Panditji's trust. By controlling different channels of access and communication, he increased his power. He also tried to play a similar game with Mrs Gandhi by working on her weaknesses and vulnerability. Taking advantage of Mrs Gandhi's diffidence in talking about mundane things directly with Panditji, he would get certain things done. With time Mrs Gandhi gained confidence in herself and perhaps she saw through Mathai's game.

In late 1958, there was an uproar in Parliament regarding the funding of the Chechamma Mathai Trust, which Mathai had set up in memory of his mother. It was alleged that he had raised large donations for the Trust from industrialists by exploiting his position. In January 1959, the AICC session was held in Nagpur and both Panditji and Mrs Gandhi had gone there to attend it. On the day they were to return, I got a telephone call from Mathai asking me to

Mrs Gauba (centre) in her school, c.1952. Habib Tanvir, theatre personality, is behind and the author is in front of her

Panditji explaining the sundial to Rajiv and Sanjay in Mashobra, Shimla, 1954

Mrs Gandhi at a picnic at
Okhla, Delhi, 1954

Mrs Gandhi, Rajiv, Sanjay and Aunty Vakil in Mashobra,
Shimla, 1954

At Sanjay's birthday party in 1954
(Photo courtesy Homai Vyarawala)

Mrs Gandhi in the
Lidder river in Pahalgam,
Jammu and Kashmir, 1956

Mrs Gandhi with her portrait by Satish Gujral, along with the artist
and his mother

'Eyes of Indira': a sculpture by Fredda Brilliant

Panditji, President Tito of Yugoslavia, Rajiv and Sanjay at
Brioni, Yugoslavia, 1956

Panditji and Mrs Gandhi with the Dalai Lama at
Teen Murti House, Delhi, c. 1957

At the fancy dress party held on Mrs Gandhi's
birthday in 1959

Mrs Gandhi and Jacqueline Kennedy at Teen Murti House,
Delhi, 1962 (Photo courtesy Photo Division)

Padmaja Naidu and the author, c.1970

Benazir Bhutto with Shri Y.S. Parmar, chief minister of Himachal
Pradesh, and the author in Shimla, 1972
(Photo courtesy Photo Division)

Mrs Gandhi and the author in Thimpu, Bhutan,
1968 (Photo courtesy Photo Division)

Mrs Gandhi at the Borobudur Temple in Jogjakarta,
Indonesia, 1969 (Photo courtesy Photo Division)

come down to his office. This was unusual, as there was no interaction between us and I wondered what had happened. When I went in, he asked me to sit down and pushed some papers towards me. These were copies of letters that he and Rajkumari Amrit Kaur (who was also a trustee) had written to Panditji regarding the controversy. I quietly read the letters and pushed them back. He asked me what I thought of them. I remember replying that this would unnecessarily drag the old man (Panditji) into the controversy. Mathai thumped the table and said he did not care and that he would sue the people who had tarnished his reputation. I quietly got up and left, wondering why he had decided to show those papers to me.

In the hall I found Vimla Sindhi pacing up and down, as usual with her antenna crackling. She knew of my antipathy towards Mathai and was curious to know why he had sent for me. When I told her, I still remember her remark that at this juncture Mathai wanted to hear truthful comments and reactions. Others were too afraid of him to give him their true opinion. A few days later Mathai resigned and Panditji accepted it. Marie Seton's remark indicates that Mrs Gandhi may have had a hand in the decision that led to Mathai's departure:

> To what extent the accusations made were true was never publicly established. Possibly, he might have convinced Jawaharlal Nehru, so loyal to his friends, that he was being wickedly maligned. But there was Indira Gandhi to be reckoned with. No matter how retiring or malleable she might appear at moments, when it came to protecting her father's interests, she could become as impenetrable as obsidian.[1]

Naturally, my job as PA to S.A. was also wound up. Soon after, when I learnt of Mathai's birthday from Vimla Sindhi, I felt sorry at the fall of such an arrogant person, and sent him a copy of Kahlil Gibran's *The Prophet* which had deeply impressed me. I am sure such a book must have been beyond him, but nevertheless he wrote the following letter to me:

[1]Marie Seton, *Panditji*, p. 273.

61

> *Prime Minister's House,*
> *New Delhi*
> *27ᵗʰ Jan 1959*

Dear Usha,

Thank you for the good words and the book. My 50ᵗʰ birthday has been rather a curious one for me. I shall take your book with me to Almora as a companion. I am mentally and physically tired.

I should like you to continue your work until I come back regardless of the termination of your Govt. job. I will be back here end of March or early April. I know you have the capacity to say 'hell with the Govt job'. I also know you never wanted it. When I come back I should like to have a talk with you. Until then please don't do anything irrevocable unless, of course, you find something after your heart.

Again thank you Usha

> *Yours*
> *M.O. Mathai*

Thank god, Mathai never came back. Mrs Gandhi became Congress President in February 1959, and knowing that her work would now become much more political, I thought the termination of my job had come at just the right moment.

~

TWELVE

INDIRAJI BECOMES CONGRESS PRESIDENT

Mrs Gandhi was elected Congress President at the Nagpur Session in January 1959. When I heard about it, I was quite taken aback. Although her work and activities had been increasing and she had also become a member of the Congress Working Committee, I used to think that her involvement in political and public affairs was more to help her father and the national cause. I did not think that she would come into politics on her own. I was a little disturbed at the news but then began to rationalize the situation and to assure myself that perhaps it was all for the best. One day when she was resting, I mustered some courage and told her that it was a good thing that she had become Congress President and that now she could bring younger people into the party. I was a little disappointed when she mumbled, 'There are so many old people', which seemed to me to convey a kind of helplessness on her part.

The day she was to be sworn in, I went for the occasion to the AICC office on Jantar Mantar Road. A 'shamiana' had been erected in the front grounds. After a while Mrs Gandhi, wearing a plain white khadi saree and a white knitted blouse, entered with U.N. Dhebar from whom she was taking over. She looked very delicate, almost like a lamb. When I looked around at the leaders assembled there, many of them looked somewhat coarse and loud, and sitting in the middle was Tarkeshwari Sinha, the glamorous MP, attracting a lot of attention from the men around her. I could not imagine then that some years later the same 'lamb' would put many of these leaders in their places!

It was difficult for me to believe the suggestion being made by some people that Panditji had groomed his daughter for this position. Mary C. Carras also observes:

Indira Gandhi herself has speculated that her principal foray into the political arena while he was alive may not have been wholly welcomed by her father. She said that he greeted her decision to accept the Congress party's nomination for the presidency in 1959 with a look of disapproval; and rather than encouraging her to accept the nomination, he told her the decision was hers to make . . .[1]

I tend to agree with this assessment and also feel that Panditji being democratic by temperament would not have liked to impose his views on his daughter.

There was much speculation about Mrs Gandhi's political ambition then and this assessment has since continued. I was struck and moved by the following letter I recently came across. Mrs Gandhi wrote to Panditji in October 1959, at a time when she was being pressured to continue with the Congress Presidentship, the term of which was to end soon.

30th October, 1959

Darling Papu,

It is now three forty-five a.m. It must be twenty years since I have felt compelled to get up at an odd hour of night to write letters! This will show how agitated I am. I just had to write to Pantji and I am sending you a copy of the letter to enlist your support in withstanding the 'affectionate pressure' which is being put upon me.

Many reasons, all equally valid and cogent, can be given for my wishing to discontinue. But deep down there is always 'the real reason' which one does not tell about because no one would understand.

Each person probably feels that he is different from the rest of humanity, but in my case there may be some justification for this thought. We are moulded by our experiences and our reactions to those experiences.

Few people could have had the fortune of such truly wonderful parents, and also rather remarkable grandparents—Dadu was known and admired, but not many discerned the deep compassion & understanding of my Nani. Since earliest childhood I have been surrounded by exceptional people and have participated in exceptional events. This has given me a somewhat

---

[1]Mary C. Carras, *Indira Gandhi: In the Crucible of Leadership*, pp. 26–27.

unusual attitude. I am not terribly concerned with public acclamation or the reverse, nor do I feel any honour in holding a high position. Some people are attaching importance to my presiding over a Congress session & delivering the address. To me it has no special meaning or attraction.

The circumstances in which I passed my girlhood—both the domestic and public spheres—were not easy. The world is a cruel place for the best of us and specially so for the sensitive. We are apt to guard ourselves with whatever armour we can lay our minds on . . . So it was at a comparatively late age that I began discovering the world and people and, above all, myself.

This brought a realisation of the richness of life but also of my debt to the world. I felt a burden on me and these last eight years or so, I have worked harder and longer as the years went by, always feeling that I could never do enough. Last year there suddenly came a moment of lightness, as if the last of the debt had been paid off. By the time I became President, I just was not in the mood for this sort of work and I have felt like a bird in a very small cage, my wings hitting against the bars whichever way I move.

The time has come for me to live my own life. What will it be? I don't know at all. For the moment, I just want to be free as a piece of flotsam waiting for the waves to wash me up on some shore, from where I shall arise and find my own direction.

The experience of being President of the Congress has been exhilarating at times, depressing at times, but certainly worthwhile. But I have already begun thinking of it in the past tense—my mind is racing ahead and I can only be warped & unhappy if I have to continue.

Sorry to inflict so many pages of illegible handwriting on you first thing in the morning.

> *All my love,*
> *Indu*[2]

What comes across from this letter are the two strong currents that shaped both Mrs Gandhi's personality and her life. The first was the urge to follow her own instincts of self-fulfilment through avenues which gave her happiness and joy, such as art, culture, literature, and nature, and the other was her strong sense of duty and commitment to her family, her country, and her people.

One can see that the second current was a much more dominant

---

[2]Sonia Gandhi, *Two Alone, Two Together*, p. 627.

streak in her personality and overrode the first time and again. Should she not have followed her instincts? The question does not arise, as destiny was always beckoning her from her personal self to that of the nation.

Gradually, with the changing times, especially after Mrs Gandhi became the Prime Minister, her personal desires and urges perhaps began to be submerged. Power has its own dynamic, and continued power can begin to somewhat erode one's sensitivities. This is evident from the remark Mrs Gandhi made to Siddharth Shankar Ray, then chief minister of West Bengal, on 12 June 1975 just before the Emergency, 'I must resign.'[3] She however did not follow her instinct. It is interesting that in 1958, when Panditji had wished to resign, she was unhappy at his not following his instincts.

When the due date of the end of my job came, I felt awkward about saying goodbye, so I left a short note on her table. Some excerpts:

. . . This is to thank you for all your kindness and consideration . . . What I have learnt from you and the House forms an important part of me and I treasure it.

My leaving at this moment seems to me as the end of a phase rather than the termination of a relationship . . . I feel that perhaps there is some meaning to it . . .

I know what you are going through. Sometimes I wish that we could carry another person's burden, but it cannot be and perhaps rightly so.

The next day I received the following letter from her and was greatly touched.

> Prime Minister's House,
> New Delhi
> 22nd Feb '59

My dear Usha,

Thank you for your letter. I had no idea you were leaving so soon or so suddenly. There is so much I have been wanting to say to you but I am rather

[3]Katherine Frank, *Indira*, p. 372.

an inarticulate person (although I talk such a lot!) and find it really difficult to find the right words to express my feelings.

You say you have learnt a lot here but can you not imagine how much it has meant to me to have a person like you around? It is not only that you have been taking an enormous burden off my shoulders by doing all kinds of odd jobs, pleasant as well as unpleasant—but just the fact of having some one like you around has been a great comfort. Believe me you have given as much as you have received.

Whenever you have been ill or on leave we have all missed you very much but I have hesitated to say anything because I did not wish to influence your decisions.

You have been through a trying time. I should have liked to help in some way but as Louis Golding has written 'in the last resort we are neither father nor mother, neither husband nor wife nor child; we are each a private and lonely universe, we must each live in the truth of our own law, our own quality.'

I hope you will regard me as your friend and remember that when you are feeling better there is always a place for you here. If you want work there is no dearth of it. But you will be equally welcome to come just to relax.

We have had very little time to talk but if you are free any evening, I should be glad if you would drop in.

With every good wish,
Indira

I did not realize then that this was indeed the end of a phase, as I said above in my letter, and that our paths would cross again. In her letter to me dated 7 July 1958, she had aptly observed, 'Life is a travelling. You meet people and sometimes you can travel together for a while or for a long time . . .'

~

THIRTEEN

DISCOVERING OTHER WORLDS

Now that I was free, I was not particularly keen to do anything specific straightaway. Nevertheless, I met some interesting people during this time. One such person was Rehana Tyabji, quite an amazing person. She was the daughter of Abbas Tyabji, a nationalist leader and a colleague of Gandhiji. When I came to know Rehana Behn, she was a mystic and a Krishna Bhakt (devotee). She used to share a house with Kaka Sahib Kalelkar, a Gandhian. Rehana Behn also used to read hands, not the palm but the back of the hand. She once told me that in my last life I had been a Norwegian, married to a French count, and that we both were drowned in a fjord. I found all this amusing and insisted that I felt that I have always been an Indian!

At Rehana Behn's place I used to meet different kinds of people, among whom was Shantibhai, a Gandhian. When I learnt from him that he was going to the Sarvodaya Sammelan being held in Ajmer in April 1959, and which was to be attended by Vinoba Bhave, J.P. Narayan, and other leaders, I expressed a desire to attend the meeting and he agreed to take me along. At the railway station, he introduced me to Jainendraji in the compartment. I had heard of this Hindi writer who was considered to be in the tradition of Munshi Prem Chand, the well-known luminary of the Hindi literary world. We talked late into the night and not once did Jainendraji make me feel the difference in our ages nor in our intellectual status. In Ajmer, he insisted that I stay in his enclosure in the camp reserved for the leaders. This provided me a wonderful opportunity to listen to the intellectual discussions he and other leaders used to have. However, I found the general atmosphere and ambience of the Sammelan lacklustre.

Early one morning, the leaders were to meet Vinobaji. Jainendraji took me with him, but I sat outside the door of the camp. Jainendraji came out of the meeting very dissatisfied. He said that Vinobaji had talked all the time and did not give an opportunity to the others to ask many questions or raise the problems they had regarding the Bhoodan movement. After a few hours, the principal of a local college met Jainendraji and requested him to come to his institution. After the principal introduced Jainendraji, praising him lavishly, he requested him to address the students. Because of his experience at Vinobaji's meeting, Jainendraji refused to address the students and instead said that he would only answer questions. This led to a long and embarrassed silence as young people in India are generally expected to obey their elders and are not encouraged to ask questions. Eventually the students who had earlier felt diffident about standing up and asking their questions slowly began to bring Jainendraji slips of paper with their questions. Many of these questions were pertinent to their generation and quite bold, and this led to a lively discussion.

My encounter with Jainendraji led to a long friendship and abiding relationship with him and his family. Every year in May, after Panditji's death anniversary was observed at Shantivana, his memorial on the banks of the Yamuna, I would go to Jainendraji's small house nearby in a congested lane in Daryaganj, climbing up a rickety wooden staircase, for breakfast.

During the Emergency, Jainendraji met Mrs Gandhi before he went to attend a meeting of intellectuals called by Vinoba Bhave in Paunnar, near Nagpur. At his meeting with Mrs Gandhi, he says, he tried to look for a 'dictator', as she was being termed those days, but instead found her very open, frank, and sincere in her explanations of the problems she faced in the governance of the country. However, at the meeting in Paunnar, Jainendraji expressed his opposition to the Emergency, the decision which proved right.[1]

A few months afterwards, Kamaladevi Chattopadhyay, who

[1]Mrinal Pande, *Indira Gandhi: Smriti-Sandarbh*, pp. 33–34.

was then the president of the Bharatiya Natya Sangh, a theatre NGO, sent for me and asked me to work for the organization as its honorary general secretary. I was not very clear about the nature of the work but I told her I would give it a try. I found the work haphazard and the organization beset with financial problems. Kamaladevi was also connected with organizations disbursing grants to the Sangh. So she persuaded Bharati Sarabhai, from the well-known industrial family of Ahmedabad, to become the president of the Sangh. However, differences between them soon emerged, and Bharati Sarabhai wanted to shift the office to Ahmedabad. I was surprised to see the power tussle between the two women. At one meeting there was such an angry exchange of words that Kamaladevi got up and walked out. I ran after her, trying to pacify her. Until then I had been unaware of the level of such power tussles. I had worked at the Prime Minister's House, which was the apex of power, yet one could hardly sense the play of power there, perhaps it being so subtle.

I could not comprehend this kind of functioning and thought of ways and means to make the organization somewhat more self-sufficient. We began to charge a fee for some cultural programmes that we arranged. We also organized a festival of Satyajit Ray's *Apu Trilogy*. These prestigious films were rarely screened in Delhi and on the few occasions when they were shown they were scheduled at early morning shows in far-away cinema halls for Bengali-speaking audiences. The *Apu Trilogy* had never been seen together in Delhi. We decided to organize the screening of the three films on three consecutive days so that they could be seen in continuity. It was a difficult task as the negotiations with the three different distributors took six months. The festival was finally held in April 1960 and was very successful. It also raised funds for the Bharatiya Natya Sangh. When we sent an album containing the press clippings, the brochure, and other material to Satyajit Ray, he was happy and wrote back:

Satyajit Ray

5 Lake Terrace Road, Calcutt. 29   June 17, 1960

Sm Usha Bhagat
34 New Central Market
New Delhi.

Dear Usha:

The Album of clippings has just arrived. I must say it
is most beautifully got up. Thank you ever so much.
Yes, Bombay has just had a very successful showing of
all six of my films. I was there for the opening. But
they were actually only following in your footsteps, and
the 'good leaders with a lot of persistence' that you
talk about are obviously you and the like of you.

If you want to show the three other films, there is no
other way but the usual one of getting in touch with the
respective distributors and hoping and praying for their
cooperation. Aurora fleeced the Bombay chaps well and
good and charged an enormous amount for the four films
that they own. J.IS and IS MS are owned by Aurora. About
DEVI – owned by Janata pictures – I should strongly
recommend a subtitled print, which ought to be ready in
about two months time. ∧

Yours sincerely

Satyajit Ray

I was not particularly happy with the work at the Bharatiya Natya Sangh and realized that my style of functioning did not fit in with that of the Sangh. In August 1960 my father suffered a stroke. As there was a lot of work in the house, I stopped working at the Sangh.

~

FOURTEEN

FEROZE GANDHI'S DEATH

In early September 1960, Mrs Gandhi on learning about my father's illness came to enquire about his health. As former refugees, we were still living in three tiny rooms measuring ten feet by ten feet above the garages at the back of an evacuee's bungalow on Curzon Road. When Mrs Gandhi came to visit, I could not take her upstairs and had a couple of chairs brought down into the open yard.

A week or so after that Feroze Gandhi suffered a heart attack. Ironically, he suffered it in the hospital where he had gone for a check up in the afternoon. Mrs Gandhi as Congress president was away in Kerala on a tour. Air connections in those days were not good, so she could reach Delhi only late at night and rushed straight to the hospital. She was there the whole night and in the morning Feroze Gandhi passed away. I was not working for her at the time, and on hearing the news I went to the Prime Minister's House. I found her in a stunned state—she had not cried till then. She told me that she wanted prayers and devotional music from different religions; these were arranged for five or six days.

On the second day I was also asked to sing a bhajan. I did not know then that while I was singing Panditji had also entered and was sitting at the back amongst other people. Vimla Sindhi told me that Panditji had asked her the next day if I was going to sing again. I was touched to hear this. On the last day of the prayers, after everyone had left except the family, Padmasi (as Padmaja Naidu was called by those younger than her) asked me to sing. As usual Vimla with her antenna up was hovering at the door. She rushed to tell Panditji who was, as far as I remember, meeting Air Marshal S. Mukherjee. I believe Panditji excused himself for a short while and came to hear me sing. I felt very privileged.

I can take pride in having sung before the three greats of modern India—Tagore, Gandhiji, and Nehru—not because I possessed any particular singing capabilities but because circumstances provided me the opportunity.

After Feroze's death, Mrs Gandhi went to meet Swami Ranganathananda, who was then the head of the Ramakrishna Mission in Delhi. Swamiji told me later that on seeing her deep anguish and sorrow, he arranged for her to stay at the Ramakrishna Mission Ashram in Dehra Dun for a few days.

Earlier in the summer of the same year, Mrs Gandhi, Feroze, and the boys had gone to Srinagar and stayed in a houseboat. They were all together as a family after a long time and came back happy. Perhaps there was hope for a better future. When sorrow comes after having lived a fulfilled life, perhaps it is somewhat easier to bear than when sorrow is compounded with regrets. Whatever may have been the differences and unhappiness between Indiraji and Feroze, Mrs Gandhi often used to say that she could have only married Feroze and no one else.

Marie Seton writes:

For many months following Feroze's death, Indira retreated into herself. When Indira was at last able to speak about his death, she said to me that it would have been a far greater tragedy for her had she and Feroze not discovered a revived understanding of each other during their month alone in Kashmir. This was her salvation. She confessed that on the day he died and people crowded about her, their sympathy only made her feel more alone in her stunned condition.[1]

She had expressed her desire for a perfect relationship in a letter to Dorothy Norman as early as on 31 May 1955:

I am sorry to have missed the most wonderful thing in life, having a complete and perfect relationship with another human being ... for only thus, I feel, can one's personality fully develop and blossom.[2]

[1]Marie Seton, *Panditji*, p. 288.
[2]Dorothy Norman, *Indira Gandhi*, p. 29.

I saw Mrs Gandhi during the deaths of three people to whom she was very close—Feroze, Panditji, and Sanjay. My impression is that she was most devastated by Feroze's death. Because with him there was a long relationship, intimate as well as unresolved and unfulfilled and yet maybe with hope for a better future. Panditji died after living a full and rich life. When Sanjay died, besides being a mother she was also the Prime Minister. She thus did not wish her personal emotions to be exposed to the public, retaining her deep sorrow and anguish within herself. I was not in Delhi then but learnt that in between meetings she would go to her room and cry.

PART II

~

1961–69

~

FIFTEEN

LETTERS FROM PARIS AND MOSCOW

The death of Feroze left Mrs Gandhi very depressed. In a letter to Dorothy Norman dated 21 September1960, she wrote:

> I am still quite weak with shock and although the burden of sorrow seems heavy enough even now, I feel it can only increase as the numbness wears off and one is faced with reality—I feel as if I were all alone in the midst of an unending sandy waste. And still life has to go on.[1]

To help her get out of her depression, Dr Radhakrishnan, the Vice President, who was fond of Mrs Gandhi, persuaded her to become a member of the Executive Board of UNESCO. She accepted the assignment with reluctance. However, she did not find the general atmosphere at UNESCO or even Paris particularly uplifting as is evident from her undated letter to me, written in November 1961, after her birthday.

Delegation of India to the
11th Session of the General
Conference of UNESCO
Paris

Dear Usha-

Do forgive this typed and circular letter but I feel that if I do not get this off to you I may not be able to write at all.

I was so happy to get your letters and to have news of the household. It was sweet of you to remember my birthday and to send your greetings. We enjoyed Onkar Nath's 'gota' and shared it with the Ambassador and Mrs Raghavan. This birthday was so different from the previous ones in Delhi when I am surrounded by your affection and cheer. Also

---

[1]Dorothy Norman, *Indira Gandhi*, p. 77.

November is such a lovely month in Delhi. Here in Paris it is grey and drab.

Amie did her best to hold the fort—she has given me a most elegant slim umbrella in a beige shade and some lovely soap in my favourite scent. Mrs Pandit had written to somebody to send me flowers and bright and early came a pot of gay cyclamen but after that it became more and more depressing—both outside from the weather point of view, in the discussions in the UNESCO, and inside us. Amie and I both feel that perhaps we are too old for gay Paris and I keep thinking of a song that used to be popular many years ago and said something like this: 'it is raining outside and it is raining in my heart!' However, it is a great help to have Amie around because being together we manage to grin through it all. The Raghavans of course are very sweet to us. He is still far from well and has to take things easy so we do not see much of him except at meals.

The UNESCO day is such a long one—sometimes starting at 9 a.m. and ending at 7 or later—after which there are always 2 or 3 receptions which have to be attended. In-between lunch is also out with the same group, and which is much worse, sometimes after-dinner receptions so that perhaps it is not fair to blame Paris, as we have hardly any chance of meeting anybody out of UNESCO groups or seeing anything of the city.

The day of our arrival here there was a wedding in the house; the elder daughter of Mr Baldoon Dhingra. Amie and I were told not to come down till the last moment but when we arrived we found the mother harassed and rushing around in circles and everyone else just standing around so we both got rather involved ourselves. The people concerned did not seem to know much about it themselves and everything seemed rather confused to us (it was a sort of Hindu ceremony), but since the bride and bridegroom and the Dhingras were all happy I suppose that is all that matters. The bridegroom is from Venezuela and they will be going there soon.

As soon as we arrived in Paris I was informed that I would have to attend the new UNESCO Executive Board meeting which takes place about the 13th of December and which might go on until the end of December. My heart sank so low that I felt it go down to the very sharp points of my fashionable new shoes (which Fory Nehru forced me to buy in New York). The Vice President then tried to cheer me by saying that I could go back on the 27th with him and return to Paris on the 13th Dec. for the meeting but then, according to UNESCO rules, they would not pay my fare for this first meeting, and of course you know the govt. of India's attitude in such things, so the going back was ruled out.

However, a minor mercy is that the meeting is only held for one day and this means that I have to stay only till the 14th December, which is long enough!

I am worried about Papu being alone for so long but there is nothing I can do now about this. How I wish I had not got involved in this business. I can now understand the loneliness and difficulties faced by our students and others who come to Europe for the first time. I do not know if Amie and I have just struck the wrong part of Paris but after the friendliness of the people in America, the French people seem not only uninterested but almost surly and hard. Ofoucrse [sic] their annoyance is not with us but with life in general including their own govt. and its measures, one of the most recent of which is a change-over in their money, they now have old francs and new francs which are most confusing to us and it seems equally confusing to the French themselves.

In America the maids at the hotel, the people at the post-offices, and shop people were so friendly and interested in India. Practically everybody seemed to know of Gandhiji & PM & knew of Shri Ramakrishna. One girl at the hairdresser's had even read the Gita, and they were all full of questions. Here one has a feeling that the French just resent all foreigners and could not care less whether they were here or not. Also to our surprise Paris has turned out to be more expensive than any other city in Europe or America—even New York.

We miss you all and Delhi!

Indira

P.S. One day, the meeting went on until 11.15 p.m. If there is a show it rarely ends before 1 a.m.

Earlier Mrs Gandhi had gone to Moscow with Rajiv, and her letter to me conveys some interesting aspects of the visit.

Hotel Windsor-Etoile
14 Rue Beaujon
Paris
2nd June 1961.

My dear Usha,

Thank you for your letter . . .

Rajiv and I had a wonderful time in Moscow, partly because the K.P.Ss. [Menon] are such sweet people and so very popular with everyone there and partly because as usual a great fuss was made over us by the Government. Though we stayed with K.P.S. we were the guests of the Minister for Culture. She has been to India, Furtseva. She told me that Khrushchev himself had told her to do this for us. We met Khrushchev during and after a Ballet and had a long and interesting talk. Everyone urged Rajiv to join Moscow University which he had visited earlier in the day.

The show which we saw together consisted of 3 one-act ballets, Les Sylphides, Pagnini and the Lights of the City. The last two are new ones and the Lights of the City is utterly different from the usual Russian ballet. It seemed very much akin to some scenes from West Side Story which is an American musical. The day-before [sic] Rajiv had gone to see Giselle with K.P.S. while I was attending a ladies' party in honour of Mrs. Khrushchev. By the way, I met three top ballerinas at various functions—Ulanova, Maya Plisetskaya (who had come to India) and Ludinskaya—they are all in the retiring list now.

One evening we went to the Puppet show. Obraskov (sic) [The name was Obvatsov] the Director made a short but brief speech about me and his trip to India.

There is a faint possibility that Rajiv may not return to India with me. I find that if he remains in London and joins tutorial classes to prepare for the qualifying exam, which is demanded of all students wanting to do Mechanical Sciences Tripos he would be able to sit for this exam in June 1962. If he fails he has another chance to sit in September 1962. He could then join college in October 1962. Whereas, if he returns to India there is no chance of his joining Cambridge until October 1963. It seems a pity to waste a whole year. However, everything depends on the Reserve Bank whose rules change from month to month.

I shall be going to London once again at the end of the UNESCO meetings before proceeding to Geneva and home. I hope everyone is well.

With all good wishes,

ING

[4th] We went to dinner with a nice young couple—a Bengali girl married to a Frenchman, Krishna and Jean Riboud. Amina was there (I just cannot remember who she is married to) [Chitamani Dar?] She seemed her usual bubbling self. She is very satisfied with her work here but is longing to return to India at the end of the month. She asked after you.

In the above letter Mrs Gandhi refers to Krishna and Jean Riboud and Amina.[2] Krishna's mother was from the Tagore family. While studying at Wellesley College in the USA, where Mrs Pandit's daughters Lekha and Tara were also studying, Krishna met Jean Riboud in New York. They later married and then lived in Paris. Jean and Mr Francois Mitterand, later the President of France, had known each other since their days in the French resistance; Jean was for sometime in a concentration camp too. The Ribouds were a couple very much interested in the arts and had a wide circle of artist friends. They became good friends of Mrs Gandhi, and mine as well.

[2]Amina was Amina Ahmad, a Bengali artist who was married to the sculptor Chintamani Kar.

~

SIXTEEN

THE PA CIRCUIT

I had ceased working for Mrs Gandhi in 1959, but this did not mean that I had lost touch with her in the intervening years. Besides reading about her activities, I also went to the Prime Minister's House from time to time to meet her and be of help if required. So the bond between us continued.

In September 1961 Mrs Gandhi sent for me and asked me to rejoin her staff. There was no job, but I was glad to help. A World Fair was going to be held in New York City in 1964–65. India decided to participate and a New York World Fair Advisory Committee was set up in 1962 under the Ministry of Commerce, and the Minister Mr T.T. Krishnamachari asked Mrs Gandhi to be the chairperson.

The Indian participation in the New York World Fair in 1964–65 was perhaps the first event aimed at projecting the cultural image of India officially on the international stage. The Advisory Committee went into all aspects, including the pavilion, its architecture and design, thematic content, items to be displayed, interior décor, and other related features. Mrs Gandhi took a keen interest in all aspects of the planning and travelled to New York for the inauguration.

In her capacity as the chairperson Mrs Gandhi was entitled to have a personal secretary, and as I had already been working gratis for her for some months, she offered the job to me. I later learnt that Yashpal Kapoor had gone up to Mrs Gandhi to ask for the same job, and had suggested that I could be given his present job. Mrs Gandhi did not agree to his request. However, people like him do not get disheartened easily, but make other moves. After a few days Kapoor told me that I was entitled to a PA and asked if I had anyone in mind. Not belonging to the PA cadre, I replied in the negative. Kapoor said he had a good person in mind. After a couple of days he brought R.K.

Dhawan to meet me and recommended him. I came to know only afterwards that they were first cousins.

Till then I had been quite ignorant of the importance of the PA circuits and the ways in which they operate. I realized later that they move spirally upwards and that the first step is to install one's own people in positions with different people in power. This allows access to information from different sources, which increases and widens the circle of information and power, leading to one's enhanced usefulness to one's boss. Gradually, the PAs make themselves quite indispensable to their superiors. All this makes them power centres and in some cases even power brokers. This of course does not apply to PAs in general.

Of course, the style and functioning of such people differed—it depended on their personalities and circumstances. Mathai, I think, showed the way. He became the first power centre when the governance of the independent country began. However, there were political heavyweights on the scene at the time who had direct access to Panditji and who neither needed the help of intermediaries like Mathai nor would they have been amenable to the power games indulged in by persons at the lower levels. Mathai's hold was mainly on members of the bureaucracy who often sought his favours for promotions or special appointments; he could make or mar things for them. It was rumoured that some wives used to intercede with him actively on behalf of their husbands. Mathai kept himself aloof to convey his arrogance of power.

The scene started changing later on with the entry of lightweights into politics. Not having their own power base and lacking credibility, these leaders sought ways and means to gain access to power and this is where the PA circuit was useful. The power of the PA circuit thus began to increase, and the scene started getting muddier. The working style of this circuit was also different. They were ever smiling, always ready to oblige so as to gain power in the process. There is no doubt that all such people were efficient and impressed their bosses, who however did not try to enquire into the modes sometimes employed to get the job done. Perhaps such ways are all a part of the power game or statecraft, which after all is a craft, often crafty, approved even by Chanakya!

85

~

SEVENTEEN

JACKIE KENNEDY'S VISIT

In November 1961 Panditji and Mrs Gandhi went to the USA on a state visit and Panditji invited the Kennedys to visit India. President Kennedy could not come but Jackie Kennedy decided to visit India in March 1962. She was to be the guest of the Ambassador John Kenneth Galbraith and his wife. However, Panditji expressed a desire to host Mrs Kennedy for a couple of days and she gladly accepted his invitation. Panditji and especially Mrs Gandhi took a keen interest in making her stay pleasant and interesting.

The visit generated much excitement at the Prime Minister's House. Panditji and Mrs Gandhi were excellent hosts; they used to take care to ensure not only the comforts of their guests, but also kept in mind the details of their interests. Mrs Gandhi had heard of Jackie Kennedy's interest in the arts and knew of the First Lady's attempts to refurbish the White House according to its character.

Mrs Gandhi was keen to get some areas of Teen Murti House spruced up in preparation for Mrs Kennedy's stay. At this time contemporary yet Indian interior decoration had begun to be experimented with. Ratna Fabri, wife of the art scholar and critic Charles Fabri, was one of the pioneers in those days, so she was asked to help. Later Ratna Fabri got the assignment to do the interior of the Indian Pavilion at the New York World Fair.

Mrs Gandhi did not have flamboyant taste. Thus, without spending much, a quiet elegance was created for Mrs Kennedy's suite, with flowers and objets d'art adding to the ambience. Mrs Gandhi personally selected books on Indian art and culture and these were arranged in the room. I still remember Mrs Kennedy seated on the carpet browsing through the books piled all around her.

During her visit to Delhi, Mrs Kennedy announced a donation

of a mobile workshop for the Children's Museum at Bal Bhawan. As Mrs Gandhi was the chairperson of Bal Bhawan, she planned the presentation ceremony in the back garden of Teen Murti House. After the symbolic presentation, Mrs Gandhi in turn presented a collection of children's paintings as India's gift to the children of America. Mrs Gandhi also invited some artists, writers, and dancers to this function to meet Mrs Kennedy. The simple function was made charming with a beautiful Gujarati 'jhoola' (swing) placed at one end where the two attractive ladies posed for photographs.

Panditji hosted a dinner in honour of Mrs Kennedy to which her sister, the Galbraiths, and a few others were invited. In the early morning I received a telephone call at home from Mrs Gandhi asking me if a short cultural programme could be arranged before dinner that night. My heart sank at the short notice but replying in the negative was not part of the work culture of the Prime Minister's House. I promptly got in touch with Colonel Gupte, the director of the official Song and Drama Division, and we immediately chalked out the evening's programme. An open-air stage was set up in the garden with a floral curtain as the backdrop. Careful lighting created a charming atmosphere, and the guests were enchanted by the performances of Bharatnatyam and Manipuri dances.

The morning that Jackie Kennedy was leaving Teen Murti House happened to be the day of the Holi festival. Just before Mrs Kennedy got into her car, Panditji put a 'gulal tikka' (coloured powder dot) on her forehead to mark the occasion. Mrs Kennedy joined in the spirit of the revelry by doing the same on Panditji's forehead. All this caused a lot of merriment.

I cannot say that Mrs Kennedy was beautiful in a conventional sense. She had a rather angular face, but she was chic and was considered the epitome of fashion and style in that period. However, I remember a rather catty remark made by a lady at the American Embassy when I showed her the photographs taken of Mrs Kennedy's visit to the Prime Minister's House. She remarked to another: 'Didn't I say she was bow-legged!'

~

EIGHTEEN

A MOTHER'S ANXIETY

Mrs Gandhi was invited for a lecture tour to the USA in 1962. She gave a series of lectures in different places on India and mainly on political and cultural topics.

Whenever Mrs Gandhi used to travel outside Delhi, her mind used to be concerned about things back home. However, she used to be especially concerned about Sanjay, not necessarily because she was more fond of him, but because she thought that compared to Rajiv, who was more self-sufficient, Sanjay needed more attention and care. This is evident from the following letter dated 22 March that she wrote to me on the plane on her way to Bombay and then on to the USA.

Bombay
22nd March

My dear Usha,

Both you & Amie have worked overtime & very hard & earnestly these last weeks. You are so good to me that I become embarrassed & don't know how to thank you.

This time I have left Delhi with a very heavy heart. Sanjay's face looks so small & sad when I leave that it haunts me while I'm away. He does get very lonely. Please keep an eye on him & see that he goes regularly for his games & also either goes to other people's houses or asks his friends over. Especially on his off days i.e. Tuesdays & Saturdays. Saturdays he could go to a film. If there is a suitable play or other show he would like to see, please draw his attention to it & make the necessary arrangements.

Ask Swamiji to come & spend sometime with him whenever he is in town . . . He is a storehouse of stories from the ancient books.

Has Kapoor provisionally booked a cottage in Ranikhet? I think we should also have some provisional arrangement in Kashmir.

I believe PM is flying back from Bombay on the 29th. I have written to
Auntie Vakil informing her but please tell the PA accompanying PM to
phone her . . .
  With all good wishes

                                        Indira

Her anxiety about Sanjay again comes through in the following
letter she wrote from London on 31 March 1963, on her way to
New York.

                              9, Kensington Palace Gardens,
                              London, W 8
                              March 31, 1963

Dear Usha,

I'm better. I have had a message sent to New York. I am getting terribly
worried about the American programme. Now I have six major functions
with speeches plus the U.N. which I am told goes on until 2.30 or 3 a.m.
All in nine days. To say nothing of the travelling to & within the U.S. I hope
I shall return alive to describe the visit!

I have not written to Yunus. If I do, he will mention it to Adil [his son]
who will tell Sanjay & I think S will resent this very much. It is better for you
to speak to S & say Mummy does not want you to have friends coming to see
you or calling on the phone during lesson or homework time. If you or Amie
see Adil you could say it to him too. Teji [Bachchan] may be able to help
through Bunty—that is all the messages may be delivered by Bunty.

Tell Aunty [Vakil] I spoke to Jai [her daughter] on the phone. In her
own words she is 'as well as can be expected.'

Rosamund, the girl who was with the Tejas & came to see the folk dances
at P.M.H. telephoned to give her greetings to you all—Amie, Vimla & to ask
after everybody. She is going to Australia this summer & may stop in Delhi.
  Greetings to all

                                        Indu

Mrs Teja has had a daughter, 16 days or so ago—Anuradha.

Mrs Gandhi was a compulsive letter writer. Besides the official
and such letters, she must have written hundreds of letters in her

life—to her father, family, relatives, friends, acquaintances, and others. I think having been a lonely child, an introvert and a sensitive person, she found it easier to express her feelings and views in writing, which she often was unable to articulate. Written in a simple and non-fussy style, these letters conveyed her concerns, moods, and observations. She enjoyed letter writing, which I think helped release her tensions and emotional blocks. She could write at all odd hours and from all kinds of places, including while travelling on planes and helicopters. Later, especially after becoming the Prime Minister, due to lack of time and many involvements, her letters became shorter and to the point. Also, with growing confidence and with her family around her, the need to communicate through letters became less.

~

NINETEEN

DASH TO TEZPUR AND PANDITJI'S ILLNESS

The Chinese had been building up their troops on the border for quite some time, and on 20 October 1962 they struck with great force. On 19 November they started to march down the hill at speed and were expected on the outskirts of Tezpur at daybreak. This led to demoralization and an exodus from Tezpur. That is when Mrs Gandhi decided to visit Tezpur. She told Marie Seton who happened to be in the Prime Minister's House: 'I haven't told my father but I have been thinking of going to Tezpur. He will object, but . . .' Marie replied, 'You are remembering your childhood dreams that you may end as Joan of Arc.'

Mrs Gandhi rushed to Tezpur in a plane. Mr B.N. Mullik, Director, Intelligence Bureau, who was actively involved in the situation writes:

> I was anxious about Smt. Indira Gandhi's safety during her visit to Tezpur . . . I managed to get information . . . that she had arrived . . . and necessary security arrangements had been made for her and she had also visited several 'mohallas' in the town and also rural areas and her visit had been a great morale-booster. She was brave. She had planned this visit on the 20th when according to army estimates the Chinese were only 20 or 30 miles from Tezpur and were expected to reach the town before dawn and there was no inkling at the time that the Chinese would give a call for a ceasefire that night. Yet she was ready to brave the hazards of an unprotected town, deserted by the troops, the police and the civil administration and which might even have been occupied by the enemy.[1]

Mr Mullik continues:

> On the morning of the 22nd we . . . came to Tezpur. Here we heard that Smt. Indira Gandhi had been deeply moved by the hapless condition in

[1]B.N. Mullik, *My Years with Nehru*, pp. 442–43.

which the people had been left by the civil administration and she had gone back to Delhi that morning to protest to the Prime Minister against allowing the civil administration to withdraw. According to her if this order was not countermanded it would be impossible to heal the wounds that had been inflicted in the people's minds by the sudden and ignoble desertion of their protectors.[2]

Mrs Gandhi returned to Delhi for eight hours, made a short broadcast on AIR, and left for Tezpur again with material help.

Mrs Gandhi's courage in the face of a challenge and crisis was always tremendous. Her personality consisted of many elements—determination, insecurity, anxiety, and heroism. At the time of a challenge, the qualities of resoluteness and courage emerged uppermost.

Soon afterwards she started the Central Citizens Council to coordinate various kinds of activities to help the situation. Besides the collection of goods and materials to help the affected citizens, an important aim was to raise the morale of the people and to create more awareness regarding the challenges and the need for unity amongst the citizens. A programme of short films for this purpose was also undertaken. Romesh Thapar, a journalist who had moved from Bombay where he had also been associated with making short films, came into contact with Mrs Gandhi for the first time in this connection and was asked to help in this activity.

Besides the political impact of the Chinese aggression, the effect of the war had also started to take a toll on Panditji's health, leading to his illness in Bhubaneshwar, in January 1964. Marie Seton who was there writes: 'It seemed inevitable that great pressure was now going to be exerted on Indira. I hoped she would have the strength to be guided by her intuition.'[3] She then quotes Mrs Gandhi: 'Mercifully, I have got commonsense and I am prepared to trust my intuition. I thought the people coming to press me were self-interested and thought they could use any contact they had with me for their own benefit.'[4]

[2]B.N. Mullik, *My Years with Nehru*, pp. 442–43.
[3]Marie Seton, *Panditji*, pp. 397–98.
[4]Ibid., p. 403.

Mrs Gandhi was a person with sharp instincts and heightened perceptions. I feel that whenever she was guided by her own instincts and intuition, she rarely went wrong. When she allowed them to be clouded due to various factors or was under the influence of some people, she could falter, as she did in the case of the Emergency.

On his return from Bhubaneshwar, Panditji was confined to his room. After some time, he began to come down for a short stroll in the garden as physiotherapy, accompanied by a nurse. I could see from my window that his pride would not allow him to take the nurse's help and he would brush it aside.

We, the staff at the Prime Minister's House, were naturally very concerned about Panditji's health and sent him a card with the following text.

Dear Panditji,

> *We want you to live at least a hundred years. We have been watching for a long time your indifference and neglect towards your physical being and have been registering a silent protest. Now we feel the time has come for us to be more vocal and assertive.*

> *Offering you our warmest regards and love, we entreat you to be more fair to yourself now. If at any time we feel you are not, we hope you will forgive us if we take some positive action!*

> *The Staff*
> *Prime Minister's House*

January 14, 1964.

During this period, Anandmayi Ma, a Bengali spiritual guru with a beautiful smile and an inner luminosity, who had a large following, happened to be in Delhi. Because of Kamala Nehru's closeness to Ma, Mrs Gandhi also had a bond with her. Mrs Gandhi requested Ma to come to the Prime Minister's House. Her anxiety on account of her father must naturally have been at the back of her mind. Ma came but did not wish to go inside the house, so an 'asana' (seat) was placed for her in the back garden. Panditji came perhaps for Mrs Gandhi's sake; however, he seemed somewhat awkward and ill at ease. Panditji, I think, had a deeply spiritual side. He believed in the

93

essence of religions, not in religion as such or in rituals and gurus. Sunil Khilnani has observed in the 34th Jawaharlal Nehru Memorial Lecture which he delivered on 13 November 2002 that, 'If he [Nehru] was critical of organized religion, he did on the other hand have sympathy for the ethical and spiritual dimensions of religion.' I think that basically Mrs Gandhi also did not believe in rites and rituals. Later due to her increased burdens and difficulties, some interested people were able to play on her insecurities and influence her in this direction. She herself has said: 'Because of the political struggle, my own childhood was an abnormal one, full of loneliness and insecurity.'[5] I remember her mentioning that in her childhood, when her parents were together they used to read from the Gita in the morning.

Mrs Gandhi had been very close to her mother. Promilla Kalhan, Kamala Nehru's biographer, remarks:

> . . . according to close associates of the Nehru family, there is much of her mother in Indira . . . Both were sensitive and proud. They were reserved in the presence of all except those who gave them sincere warmth.[6]

Kamalaji must have been spiritually inclined and her personal sufferings drew her closer to various gurus for seeking guidance. Kamalaji took diksha (initiation) from Swami Sivananda of the Ramakrishna Mission in 1932.[7] Later Swami Abhayanand kept in touch with her and after her with Mrs Gandhi. He used to worry about Mrs Gandhi's health, and besides letters he used to send protein food items to her from time to time, even when she was the Prime Minister.

Padmaja Naidu, who was then the Governor of West Bengal, had come to be with Panditji during his illness. When she was returning to Calcutta, Panditji asked her rather unhappily, 'Am I going to see you again? Must you go?' Padmajaji could not bear to hear these words

[5]Indira Gandhi, *My Truth*, p. 55.
[6]Promilla Kalhan, *Kamala Nehru*, p. 72.
[7]Ibid., p. 86.

and left the room on some pretext. She did not see him alive again.

My last encounter with Panditji was in April. He was coming out of the dining room in the corridor. His gait was unsteady, his face puffy, and his smile kind yet sad. It was not possible for me to step aside, so I stopped and showed him the silver enamelled badge which we had got ready for our guides for the New York World Fair. He examined it, put his hand on my shoulder, and shook it affectionately. The customary spring in his step and his familiar animated expression were missing. In their place were tiredness and sadness. One sensed he knew his end was near.

~

TWENTY

JOURNEY WITH ASHES

On 27 May 1964, I came to the Prime Minister's House as usual around 9.00 a.m. and entered the downstairs office. Mr G.L. Nanda, who was then the Minister of Home, was on the telephone, looking grim, giving certain instructions (given during moments of crisis). Soon we became aware of the situation, and saw the movement of doctors and Mrs Gandhi in Panditji's wing. We were all in a state of tension. The head butler told me that they were all praying for Panditji's life. My father had died the previous year after lying paralysed and having lost his speech for three years. We had seen the tragedy of an active person becoming completely helpless. I was therefore praying silently to keep Panditji alive only if he could be brought back to good health, otherwise not. Rajiv was in the UK and Sanjay in Kashmir. A message was sent to Sanjay, and Mrs Gandhi asked me to go to the airport to meet him; he could not come by that flight. When I returned to the Prime Minister's House around 2.00 p.m. I learnt that Panditji had just passed away. I went straight to Panditji's room. He lay as if he was asleep, looking serene. Mrs Gandhi was sitting on the floor beside the bed, and the two doctors were standing near Panditji's feet, their faces downcast and sad.

As an only child, Mrs Gandhi had been used to taking charge of situations from her childhood. Sitting near Panditji's feet, Mrs Gandhi did not allow herself the luxury of indulging in personal sorrow. Many things had to be attended to and she alone had to take important decisions and face problems.

Soon she beckoned to me to go and help in the arrangements being made for the body to be kept for 'darshan'. H.C. Sarin, the then Defence Secretary, had arrived and we started with the planning. From time to time I would come up to tell Mrs Gandhi what we were planning and to take her instructions. By now the close associates and relations had begun to stream into Panditji's room. To keep the body in state on the front veranda, we got the beautifully carved front legs of a side table partly chopped to provide a slope so that Panditji's face could be visible to the people passing through the porch. The body was brought down in the evening and Mrs Gandhi sat beside it all the time until it was time for the cremation, except for a couple of hours in the early morning.

On the afternoon of 27 May, we had an amusing interlude. Marie Seton arrived looking very distraught as well as worried about Mrs Gandhi and the rest of us. She had brought a bottle of tranquilizer tablets and insisted on our taking them. I felt that this was a typically Western response in coping with tension. We were amused but appreciated her genuine concern for us. We tactfully explained to her that the tranquilizers were not necessary.

After the cremation, the large copper urn containing the ashes lay on the back lawn under a laburnum tree, which had been planted by Rajiv as a young boy. The tree was in full bloom and the flowers dropped silently on the urn as if to pay homage. After a week of prayer, recitations and the singing of devotional songs from different religions in the evenings, a special train carrying the ashes left for Allahabad.

I had noted my impressions of the journey which are given below, as I had jotted them:

7.6.'64
Reached Prime Minister House at 5.30 a.m. Kirtan going on near 'asthi-urn'. Very beautiful atmosphere. Anandmayi Ma's disciples, Pushpa, Chhabi and two others did very beautiful kirtan. Friends and relations stood sad and silent. I placed two rose buds on the urn to pay my homage. Rajiv and Sanjay carried the urn slowly, family and officials following—handed the urn to army-people near the gun carriage, who placed it on the stand. The carriage moved slowly, military band playing. Everyone's eyes were moist. Same house, same people, but the buoyant, charming and majestic personality who

97

drew people from everywhere—his ashes instead of him marching out.

Family followed in cars, but their cars went straight to station. I travelled with Rita[Dar], Raja[Hutheesing] and Rajan[Nehru]. Mrs Gandhi called me to her coupé next to the area where urn was kept.

Large compartment in which urn kept beautifully arranged. It is about 100' long all white from inside and outside. Urn stand in the middle—a small platform—a tri-colour on ceiling and a screen of 'motia' and red roses draped beautifully around it. In center, the beautifully carved copper urn-mouth covered with orange silk and flowers all around it—'motia', white roses and tuberoses etc.

A small basket lies near it. Very few people know it contains a few of Kamalaji's ashes, which Panditji had kept all this time in his cupboard. Indiraji has kept the basket near the urn to immerse them along with those of Panditji at the 'Sangam'. Panditji had also kept some of his father's ashes too. They will also be immersed together with others.

The carriage is also very beautifully decorated from inside—wreaths, garlands, white and red, 'bandanwars' etc. All windows have glass panes and green curtains.

So far, the train has stopped in Ghaziabad, Khurja, and Aligarh. The crowds have been tremendous, breaking all cordons. I don't know how many deep shouting 'Chacha Nehru Zindabad'. They can't believe this is his last journey—people on platforms showering petals—on other sides too—on ground, on pillars—on girders of roof—on top of stalls—hardly any place left. A long distance before and after the station is lined by people—old, young, women, men and children—perched on home tops, trees etc.

All kinds of people sitting in this coach. I am mainly in the bhajan party, we are singing away. I wonder if anyone is hearing or interested, but we go on singing 'Ramdhun', 'Vaishnavjan'—and other bhajans. Just now at Aligarh, Sheikh Abdullah joined us and we sang 'sare jahan se achha' and a ghazal. After we finish singing 'Shanti-path'.

Some of the people sitting on our side are Maniben, Smt. Jamna Lal Bajaj and family, K.C. Pant. On the other side are the close relations—Indiraji and sons, Mrs Pandit with three daughters and two sons-in-law. Mrs Hutheesing and 2 sons. Also Zakir Sahib. On four corners of platform are military people on duty, they change at every station. Hathras, Tundla and Ferozabad had also passed. Crowds instead of decreasing are increasing. At stations, people sometimes have passed from one side to the other under the carriage. Along with flowers, people were also throwing coins and notes. From handkerchief, we have now a tablecloth to tie the money. Indiraji rushes from one window to others to greet the people. Even the boys, Rajiv and Sanjay are most responsible helping pick the flowers, shaking hands with people. When the train leaves the station, people run along with the train. Maniben and Brijkrishenji are busy spinning. Have passed Shikohabad and are at Etawah now. Crowds are pressing—everyone who wants to have a view rushes towards this coach. At platforms some windows are opened—there is a terrible stink of sweat—mass of humanity and faces with anxiety and tears.

Kanpur. There is no end to crowds, police has no control—it seems even they are so keen to have 'darshan' that they have joined the crowds. One of the main glass panes on one side of urn is cracked with pressure. Mehta and Mehra, [security officer,] are trying hard to prevent its breaking. I wonder how long they will be able to prevent it. It is said there are about 5 lakhs of people. Engine is being changed so the train can't move.

Everyone is restless and afraid. It is said there are lakhs of people outside the station and it would be a terrible thing if a stampede starts. Beautiful wreaths and bouquets have been presented and people came with garland or a few petals even. Some women fainted, were brought into the carriage. I wonder when the train is going to move. There is a sea of people. When Mrs Gandhi peeps out they clap and shout.

We are all sweating like in a Turkish bath. People look like nothing on earth—dishevelled, grimy and wet with perspiration. First there were home-guards on duty—more police has been called and there is mild lathi-charge even. One small pane did break. After a lot of delay and restlessness, the train started much later than scheduled.

I had a little nap in the main carriage just before Fatehabad. Mrs Gandhi had gone to her coupé—told me if she falls asleep to wake her before next station. When the train slowed down before next station, I peeped in—she was asleep—must have been exhausted—hated to disturb—knowing her sense of duty, woke her reluctantly told her so. She remarked—when people come from far at late hour, she must be present to acknowledge their sentiments. Crowd was less but very orderly. Afterwards Mrs Gandhi, Teji and a few of us took away the old withered flowers. We rearranged the central platform. At 3.30 had just dozed off when the person in-charge woke me up to have a cold drink. Got ready just in time to reach Allahabad.

8.6.'64

Reached Allahabad at 5.00 a.m. very good arrangements—Dalai Lama was also present. We are moving in cars to Anand Bhavan. Barricades on either side of road—people very orderly and solemn. Here people have really felt deeply—Panditji belonged to this city. After wending our way slowly in procession, we finally reached Anand Bhavan. Spacious grounds, some good trees and a number of crotons. Had seen the home in pictures—felt strange and sad to enter it for the first time on an occasion like this.

Rajiv and Sanjay carried the urn first into the house and then brought it out and kept it on a round platform under a big spreading and flowering gulmohar tree, very near it stood a tall Ashok tree. The staff of Anand Bhavan, Kamala Nehru Memorial Hospital and Children's National Institute in Swaraj Bhavan came and paid their homage with flowers, the scene was touching. His mortal remains instead of his bright charming living self.

I stood at a distance for some time and then gradually moved near the house. Somebody said that Indiraji was looking for me, met her in the hall and told her sadly what an occasion to come to Anand Bhavan. She asked me to have a cup of tea. It was badly needed as the previous day's journey, emotional scenes and no sleep had had quite an effect—found myself swaying in the morning.

Indiraji said that as the bhajan party was lost in the way, she wanted

me to do the 'Shanti-path'. I did not know it so well and hesitated—
then started learning it from Vimla. After a short while, Indiraji came
and said their Pandit who was reciting the Geeta, will do the 'Shanti-
path'. I felt relieved.

The procession started forming again. When I reached the car in
which I had come, I found it completely packed. Sitting on Vimla's
lap I went on learning 'Shanti-path' and read 'Nava-Mahala', a Chapter
from the Guru Granth Sahib as well. Flying Club planes showered
flowers and a helicopter hovered above taking photos.

Gradually we reached the Fort, near 'Sangam'. Some distance away
from the bank, everyone got down and Rajiv and Sanjay started to
carry the urn towards the 'duck'(boat). A small pontoon bridge had
been made to reach the duck. As the boat began to move—we
started returning to cars. I heard someone shouting my name, it was
Mehta, the security officer. The boat was returning—I rushed and
found that Indiraji had sent for me. While the boat was moving, I was
asked to sing and I sang a Mira Bhajan. Was filled with gratitude that
I could be present at the journey to 'Sangam' also. The duck moved
towards 'Sangam' and Jamuna and Ganga could be seen clearly—
the blue Jamuna and the muddy Ganga. At the 'Sangam' Rajiv and
Sanjay poured the ashes from the urn, Indiraji dropped Kamalaji's
and Motilalji's ashes Panditji had kept, into the 'Sangam' also.

TWENTY-ONE

MINISTER FOR INFORMATION AND BROADCASTING

When Lal Bahadur Shastri became the prime minister, he was not keen to shift to Teen Murti House, so the idea of converting the Prime Minister's House into the Nehru Museum came up. Mrs Gandhi wrote to a few leading people regarding the proposal. As far as I remember, Rajaji (Mr Rajagopalachari) was not in favour of the proposal on principle. After it was decided that the house would become a museum, it naturally could not be termed the Prime Minister's House. Mrs Gandhi asked various people to suggest alternate names. Teen Murti House, the suggestion of Asok Mitra (ICS), was selected. The reference was to the three statues of soldiers in the round park in front of the house, which before Independence had been the residence of the commander-in-chief.

After a couple of months, it was time to move from the Prime Minister's House, and I am sure it must have been traumatic for Mrs Gandhi as so many memories were associated with the house in which they had stayed for twelve years. Some houses were suggested and I was sent on survey missions. I would report back, sometimes with sketches. Mrs Gandhi finally opted for 1 Safdarjang Road. It was nearest to the Prime Minister's House and thus perhaps unconsciously an emotional link was maintained. The bungalow was small, generally meant for senior bureaucrats. As she was the Minister of Information and Broadcasting and since both the boys were studying abroad, it was sufficient for her needs. Who would have guessed then that one day this house would be converted into the Prime Minister's House.

In the new house she was quite lonely. Adjusting emotionally to the situation also must have been difficult. After having had a large staff, she now had very little help. One evening when I dropped in, I found her indisposed and with no help, so I made an egg and toast for her.

During this time, the so-called 'kitchen cabinet' had started to come up, consisting mainly of Dinesh Singh, Romesh Thapar, and I.K. Gujral. Being new to the power game and somewhat insecure and diffident, perhaps Mrs Gandhi could communicate better with them and through them to others. The trio enjoyed the importance this gave them. Dinesh Singh and Gujral had their own political ambitions and were only too ready to help. Romesh Thapar was interested in the political scene and developments but I do not think he himself had personal ambition. He was too forthright, which created problems later on.

When Shastriji became the prime minister, he came to meet Mrs Gandhi. Mrs Krishna Hutheesing has written movingly about the incident:

> On the ninth day after my brothers' death . . . Mr. Shastri came to ask Indira to become Foreign Minister . . . That was the first time . . . that Indira broke down, weeping she told Mr. Shastri that she does not want any place in the Government; she only wanted to work for the memorial to her father . . . 'I would like to have six months of quietness before I take any job in the Government.' They (Ministers and others) all arrived and tried to persuade her and in the end she gave in and took a small job . . . Minister of I & B.[1]

Mrs Gandhi brought a breath of fresh air to the Ministry. She welcomed creative people and was open to new suggestions. Romesh Thapar played an active role during this time in giving advice and suggestions because of his involvement in the media and related subjects.

Another view of Mrs Gandhi's style of functioning was:

> She approached her work as a Minister with customary vigour . . . She also encouraged democracy by opening the air-waves to the opposition

[1]Krishna Hutheesing, *We Nehrus*, p. 324.

parties and independent commentators . . . Indira was bigger than the job, however, and needed other challenges.[2]

As Minister of I & B, Mrs Gandhi could have only a small personal staff. N.K. Seshan had been working with Panditji since the days of the Interim Government. He was a fine person and Mrs Gandhi took him as her private secretary. She could have two PAs. Yashpal Kapoor and Amie Crishna were taken for the posts. My assignment of the New York World Fair was still continuing, so she could have four people instead of three. Because of my interest in cultural matters and films, I was also helping Mrs Gandhi with the work of the Ministry. It was embarrassing though to find that in the new setup I was in the lowest grade. I had not cared what position I held earlier while Mrs Gandhi worked in an unofficial capacity. In the bureaucratic hierarchy, however, one's merit is measured by the position one holds. I realized that Mrs Gandhi could not comprehend this anomaly. I found it embarrassing to talk about it, and as my assignment for the New York World Fair was due to end soon I left a note for her:

10.11.64

Dear Indiraji,

For quite some time I have been thinking of talking to you, but have given up the idea as it embarrasses me terribly to talk about myself and also I am not especially good at expressing myself verbally.

Over the last few months, the pattern of work has changed considerably. In the new pattern I find myself in a nebulous and rather superfluous position which demoralises and does not provide enough incentive for work. It is not necessary that all the people are required all the time and this should not cause any embarrassment or misunderstanding.

I hate to write all this, but feel that a point arrives when if you do not express yourself, you are fair neither to yourself nor to the other person.

Not being a very clever person, I am putting down my feelings in a straightforward manner. I hope I am not misunderstood.

Love
Usha

[2]Jad Adams and Phillip Whitehead, *The Dynasty*, p. 193–94.

Her deeply felt and moving reply to me was:

Dec 6.1964

My dear Usha,

I have been deeply hurt by your letter at a time when the anaesthetic effect of the numbness of shock is wearing off and all the agony of the old wounds is making itself manifest in an excruciating manner.

If you don't want to stay how can I even ask you to do so? That is a decision you must make for yourself. If you feel you are wasting your time here, you should certainly take up whatever seems more worthwhile. I am not conceited enough to blame you for that or to feel hurt at such an attitude. What did hurt me is that, after being with me for so many years, you should even think that I don't care about you. You are a person of quality—which is rare enough anywhere in the world. That is why I find myself unable to treat you just like anybody else. [I do not, of course, want to make comparisons, for everyone has been so loyal, hardworking & tremendously helpful in extremely difficult conditions.] To have you around has meant a great deal to me. I don't ask as much of you as I might because I don't want to intrude on your privacy.

Amie hinted that you wondered why you were not absorbed in the ministry. Quite frankly, I did not think you would wish to be just another clog [sic] in the bureaucratic machine. In fact I think you told me so yourself some years ago. I have been trying to find something for you which would enable you to express yourself more fully, to open out the qualities which one can only guess at & to make a contribution which would be worthwhile for the work itself & for you personally.

My own preference was for you to be associated with the Memorial Museum because of my trust in your taste and attitudes. You would have the freedom to develop programmes, you would work closely with me & would be able to help me in a variety of ways, should the need arise. As a matter of fact I was even wondering if you would sometimes come & stay with me. Who can I trust with my father's letters & the papers? And how can I possibly find the time to deal with them myself? If some one else takes the museum job, it will virtually mean my being cut off from it, for naturally the person will be under the Minister of Ed [Education]. I can make suggestions only up to a point.

Even at present, your contacts with the world of music, art & cinema have been of enormous help to me. Exhibitions of different kinds, children's programmes will always be a part of my life—it is not the work of my ministry but I get involved.

What more can I say?

Indira

We had a strange relationship, sometimes full of understanding and sometimes not being able to comprehend each other.

I continued working and in the meantime Mrs Gandhi asked Seshan to look around for some slot for me. One or two suggestions were made, including that of the administrative secretary of the Nehru Memorial Fund which had just been set up. As my interests were more in creative happenings and less in administrative areas, I thought it better not to accept something that I might regret later. I, therefore, politely declined. I also felt that Mrs Gandhi should not feel that she had to accommodate me somewhere.

The day my assignment was ending, in September 1965, I felt it easier to leave a short note for her rather than conveying it verbally. The next day I received the following letter from her:

Minister
Information & Broadcasting
India

11.9.1965

My dear Usha,

I did not realize that today was your last day here or that you were leaving before lunchtime. You have been so long with me, so involved in all my ventures that the house will seem strange without you. As Prof Higgins said—'I have grown accustomed to your face'!

I hope we shall continue to meet occasionally and that I can call upon your help when needed. However, as this is the end of a particular chapter, I should like to express my deep gratitude for the help and loyalty & above all for the companionship which you have given me over the years. This has been invaluable as the period has been of steadily increasing responsibility, difficulty and loneliness.

Wherever you are & whatever you choose to do, you will have my good wishes. I sincerely hope you can find something which will give you fulfillment and which will give your talent opportunity to grow & blossom.

If ever there is anything I can do, I hope you will not hesitate to say so.

With every good wish,
Indira

I was very touched by her letter but felt it was time to move on. However, I used to go from time to time if there was work. It was her birthday in a couple of months, which used to be quite an event in those days. I went to greet her and help. After the rush was over, Amie and I sat down for a quiet cup of coffee. Mrs Gandhi walked in and joined us. She had been to East Africa and was accompanied by Dinesh Singh. While referring to her visit, she commented on the polite demeanor of Dinesh Singh. I kept quiet for sometime but could not help adding, 'Perhaps too polite.'

In 1965, one began hearing about Mrs Gandhi's unhappiness. P.N. Dhar writes:

> She [Indira Gandhi] made several such comments which indicated that there was no rapport between her and Prime Minister Lal Bahadur Shastri . . . What seemed to have hurt her personally was a belief that he had positioned her in his cabinet more as a political necessity than as a valued colleague.[3]

One afternoon in December, a car stopped outside my house and Mrs Crishna, who was still working with Mrs Gandhi, came in and told me that as Mrs Gandhi was quite depressed, she had brought her out for a drive and then suggested that they come to my home. It was a pleasant surprise and I quickly made some tea for them.

During those days, Sunil Janah, the well-known photographer whose photographs especially of tribals were famous, was holding an exhibition of his work. I persuaded Mrs Gandhi to visit the exhibition, which she enjoyed. Janah told me that he wished to do a portrait of

[3]P.N. Dhar, *Indira Gandhi, the 'Emergency' and Indian Democracy*, pp. 102–03.

Mrs Gandhi. Although he took photographs a month before Mrs Gandhi became the prime minister, they had the bearing of a prime minister and were used to a great extent after she assumed office. In the meantime, I had joined an NGO and I remember the first day I went to work was 10 January 1966. That same night Shastriji died in Tashkent.

~

TWENTY-TWO

THE PRIME MINISTER

Shastriji's sudden death not only shocked the nation but also created uncertainty once again about the political future of the country less than two years after Panditji's death. This led to frantic political activity and a tussle for leadership, with Mrs Gandhi emerging as the prime minister.

That Mrs Vijaya Lakshmi Pandit also had ambitions in this direction is revealed by her sister, Mrs Krishna Hutheesing. On learning of Shastriji's death she writes:

> My sister cancelled her lecture tour and came tearing home from America. Having been Indian Ambassador to Russia, the U.S. and High Commissioner in London and world figure because of her presidency of the U.N., I believe, she thought she had a chance. But . . . Mr. Kamaraj had not even thought of her, because though she was popular abroad, she had been away from India too much . . . His (Kamaraj) choice fell on Indira . . . he felt she was the one who would be the most acceptable to the Indian people and therefore would be a unifying influence.[1]

Mrs Pandit's greeting to Mrs Gandhi was also tongue in cheek: 'Mrs. Gandhi has the qualities. Now she needs experience. With a little experience she will make as fine a Prime Minister as we could wish for . . . She is in very frail health indeed. But with the help of her colleagues, she will manage.'[2] Regarding Mrs Gandhi's frailty, Katherine Frank writes: 'Though she often appeared frail and vulnerable,

[1]Krishna Hutheesing, *We Nehrus*, p. 337.
[2]Zareer Masani, *Indira Gandhi: A Biography*, p. 140.

there was a hard and resilient core within her: she never collapsed.'[3]

When Mrs Gandhi was elected prime minister, I went to congratulate her. I still remember that her face had a glow of an inner radiance. Perhaps for the first time she felt a sense of personal fulfilment. Most of her life she had done things for others or because of others, which had constrained or restricted her, without giving any fulfilment. Perhaps she suddenly felt free of those feelings. In the first decade that I knew Mrs Gandhi, she was frequently moody, irritable, and often ailing. When she became the prime minister and faced challenges on her own, I feel this brought out her potential, creative energy, and inner reserves, and she gained in confidence and her sense of well-being was enhanced. As Mary C. Carras writes: 'It [the job] also offered her a degree of challenge that suited her personality and the opportunity to exercise skills and develop capabilities—thus satisfying [her] need for self-fulfillment.'[4]

In the meantime, I continued to work for the NGO. In late 1965, a job was advertised for a person to look after SONA, a shop of handicrafts, which had opened in New York, due to the interest generated in the arts and crafts because of the New York World Fair. This field had always interested me, so I applied for the job and was invited for an interview. Before the interview could be held in early February 1966, Mrs Gandhi had become the prime minister. The interview was an annoying as well as an amusing experience. Most of the people on the interview panel, including Mrs Pupul Jayakar, knew me. When I entered I found all the faces looking very embarrassed. They would look to the other to ask me questions. Perhaps they felt that as Mrs Gandhi had become the prime minister and may need me, they did not wish to create an awkward situation. Naturally, I was not selected. Perhaps the interviewers were right, as three or four days after that I received short handwritten notes from Mrs Gandhi asking me to do some errands for her, as well as asking me to rejoin her.

[3]Katherine Frank, *Indira*, p. 112.
[4]Mary C. Carras, *Indira Gandhi*, p. 27.

NOTE NO. 1

Usha. Would you like to join my staff? You know how very much I should like to have you.

ING

NOTE NO. 2

Usha—

If you have a moment, will you please have a look at Travancore House. I don't even know where it is or for what it is being used.

[Maybe someone suggested it to her as a possibility for the Prime Minister's House.]

ING

NOTE NO. 3

Saris—Amie has done some preliminary selection. Would you please have a look and give a connoisseur's point of view?

ING

8.2.66

NOTE NO. 4

URGENT

Usha—

Marie Seton is writing on me for the Reader's Digest. As you know it is being read all over the world. Could Pupul or anyone help with points which should be made? One point which strikes me is that I have held one of the toughest jobs, that of Congress President, dealing with many intricate & . . . problems. All newspapers requesting me to continue had commented that it was the year when Congress became best organized and effective.

She also mentioned that if I had any reservations (regarding the job) I should come and see her. Due to my experience in the past, I did have reservations regarding the functioning. After doing the errands she had asked me to do, I thought it would be easier to send my reservations in writing. I did not hear from her and went on working at the NGO. I would be sent for a particular job, which I would readily do. The letter below is regarding the dinner she hosted for General Ne Win, President of Burma, and his wife at her home.

Prime Minister's House,
New Delhi
February 18, 1966

Usha—

Just a line to thank you for all the trouble you took over last evening's arrangements. I wish you could have seen the flower arrangements! Without them the house would not have looked presentable. Perhaps Amie has told you that the dinner was a great success.

ING

As Mrs Gandhi felt diffident about discussing the matter regarding working with her personally, she spoke to mutual friends to find out my reservations. I received calls from Mrs Jayakar, Romesh Thapar, and I.K. Gujral, but did not wish to discuss the matter through intermediaries as invariably things get misinterpreted.

One morning in May I went to Safdarjang Road to give the invitation card for my brother's wedding. She was meeting the public and when free, she sent for me in her room. After I handed her the card, she suddenly asked me about my reservations. I told her in brief. I am not sure whether she fully understood them, but she seemed keen that I join. Looking back now, I realize that perhaps the problems lay with me. I think I was a square peg in a round hole. Power and ambition did not attract me. My interests lay in having an area of work in which I could find self-expression and self-fulfillment, which was perhaps difficult to achieve in the nature of the work in the Prime Minister's House. In 1953, when I joined Mrs Gandhi I was a one-person Secretariat. I could not have even dreamed that she would one day become the prime minister. If I had, I may not have joined her! As the charge report for my joining was waiting in the Prime Minister's Secretariat and destiny was beckoning me in that direction, I again joined Mrs Gandhi in May 1966.

~

TWENTY-THREE

THE AICC SESSION IN BOMBAY

A few days after I joined, Mrs Gandhi went to Bombay to attend the AICC session and took me along with her. I jotted down some notes of the visit which are reproduced below:

20th May 1966
Travelled to Bombay by IAF Viscount. Others (on the plane), Subramaniam, L.K. Jha, Dinesh Singh, Gujral, V.C. Shukla, etc. Large crowd on arrival. Prime Minister extremely nice and extra considerate and very friendly (to me).
Went (with her) to private viewing of *Dr Zhivago* at night.

21st...
Accompanied Prime Minister to youth rally and then to AICC session. She spoke well at Rally—has a wider horizon of the subject matter on whole. AICC session strange conglomeration and atmosphere. Vast stage, vast hall, people lying and sitting listlessly. Lot of movement. Wondered who listened to speeches.
Went to see Moinuddin Dagar (Dhrupad singer, whom I knew) in hospital, lying seriously ill, took flowers from Prime Minister (he died the next day).
Dinesh Singh came after dinner time, discussed politics, displays much more confidence. Mrs Gandhi walked and looked at sea. She said sea is relaxing and mountains stimulating.

22nd
Nargis came in morning. Soonoo Godrej [a friend who was with Mrs Gandhi in Mrs Vakil's school in Poona in the early 1930s] and I went with Prime Minister to Social Education crash programme arranged in a theatre hall and same old speeches. Functions lack imagination.

After lunch went with Prime Minister to the AICC Women Department's programme at Metro. Packed hall, good arrangement, all kinds of women, foreign also. Kamraj called her the 'jewel amongst women' on whose shoulders they have put heavy burden. One never knows how much politicians can be believed. Maniben accompanied Kapur and me to AICC—a frustrated woman—asked all kinds of pointed questions about Prime Minister. Met Krishna Menon at session—seems to miss late Prime Minister whose support and confidence he had. Now seems lost.

On return, had to face lots of people waiting for Prime Minister—Feroze's niece and husband, Harin Chattopadyaya, Lady Rama Rau, Pepsi Wadia and Mrs JRD Tata. Prime Minister arrived late. Had to entertain them.

Prime Minister said she missed me while returning as large crowds on way, said crowds bring tears to her eyes. She has had a very hectic day, from 8.00 a.m. continuously. After an hour's stay at dinner time, she went to attend Working Committee meeting at 10.00 p.m.

The Point bungalow (Jal Chintan) at a most glorious place in Raj Bhavan. Mrs JRD Tata said best in the world. Cottage situated on a rocky spur into sea. Am staying in the room generally occupied by late Prime Minister (Nehru). A verandah outside, then a drop—large black boulders below and sea lashing. Lovely breeze all day. Absolutely heavenly. Mrs Gandhi did not wish to stay there as it does not have an A.C.

Before returning to Delhi, Mrs Gandhi stopped in Poona for a few hours. This was the first time that I travelled in the prime minister's car cavalcade, and watching the crowd, their faces and response, I jotted down my impressions. Some excerpts:

The plane lands in Poona—crowds, flowers, cars lined up. Motorcade begins. Streets lined with crowds—children, joyous and clapping—young and eager faces. Women, young and old in colourful sarees—shy, beaming, and proud faces. Nurses in uniforms, students with books. Old couples in night clothes, stooping but moist-eyed. Crowds interspersed with 'gulmohars', ashoks, jacarandas, and abundant sprays of bougainvillea. Traditional arches called 'kamans' all the way—beautiful motifs on green, yellow ochre, and Indian red cloth. Welcome with 'dudunbhi', 'nagara', and 'kumkum'. In response to greetings, almost continuous waving of arm by PM. A few halts to exchange flowers with children and old people.

After a few minutes respite at Raj Bhawan, start on a 48-mile winding dusty road to the scarcity areas. Rolling countryside, large spreading banyan trees on the roadside. Rich loamy brown-black soil, but parched. At places thin soil on rocky slopes—elsewhere big black rounded igneous boulders studded like jewels on hillocks.

Saw people's courage and determination to face nature's non-cooperation. People busy with 'bunding' to conserve soil and water. A lift-water scheme run on a cooperative basis showing corn yield results three times the normal. A dramatic view of a percolation tank in a gorge to conserve water—rows of men and women digging and transporting earth in quick and rhythmic movement, greeting and shouting slogans.

Refreshments and a few minutes' rest at a nearby rest house. Cool drinks and delicious Poona figs. An opportunity to cross-examine officials and non-officials regarding the food situation and plans.

In the afternoon, we returned to Delhi in the Air Force Viscount. I was sitting with Mrs Gandhi in a separate compartment. Due to the heat and dust, the flight was a little bumpy, and the sign 'Fasten seat belt' lit up. I quickly fastened my seat belt but saw that Mrs Gandhi had not done so and was moving around. Not being an experienced flier, I felt embarrassed at being too safety conscious and undid the belt. That evening the ceremony for the National Film Award was to be held, and Mrs Gandhi was to present the awards. She asked me to suggest some points. As I was jotting them down the plane went into convulsions and I said my last prayers. The pilot said later that due to the dust haze, he could not see a bird until too late, and to avoid it he had to suddenly drop the altitude. When the plane stabilized, flowers and other things were strewn here and there and coffee was flowing from the pantry. G.C. Dutt, the security person, and B.G. Verghese, who was then the information adviser, rushed into our compartment and worriedly looked at Mrs Gandhi, whom I found sitting in another seat. (She told me later that she had fallen down and had scrambled on to the other seat.) She signalled towards me, saying that I was bleeding. As I did not have the belt on, I was thrown up and my head hit something. To everyone's utter amazement, there was no first aid box on the Air Force plane, nor water in the toilet. (It was after this accident that a doctor started to travel with the prime minister.)

After twenty minutes, when the plane landed, I was taken to the Willingdon Hospital. Luckily the injury was of the scalp and required ten stitches. But I had to remain in the hospital for a week under observation. Mrs Gandhi and Mr Verghese came to see me straight from Vigyan Bhavan. Amongst other visitors who came to see me were the Thapars, and Romesh told me in his characteristic style that I being the most relaxed person was thrown up while the others had fallen down!

This mishap during the flight turned out to be perhaps an initiation, as from then onwards I accompanied Mrs Gandhi during many tours abroad. However, since then I always kept my seat belt fastened during flights, in spite of jokes from Sanjay and others.

~

THE EARLY DAYS

Mrs Gandhi as well as the rest of us took some time to adjust to the new work and responsibilities. There were new challenges, and confusion, yet excitement too. For the first couple of years, speech writing was quite a bugbear. Besides the material supplied by the office, a few friends were asked for their suggestions and ideas as well. Being fastidious and meticulous, Mrs Gandhi used to work long hours late into the night giving shape to the speeches. When the first volume of her speeches was published and some copies sent to her, she inscribed a few of them. The copy for me said:

I remember the first speech she had to broadcast on AIR soon after becoming the prime minister. She had to go to the radio station to make a live presentation. The time had been fixed. The speech was still being finalized and was being translated into Hindi and typed. Mrs Gandhi left for AIR with some pages while I waited for the last pages to be typed and then rushed to the station afterwards. Gradually, she became more confident both in handling her affairs as well as in writing her speeches. She would take less time and became more relaxed. Of course, when Mr Sharada Prasad took over as Information Advisor, he became the mainstay in this sphere and used to work diligently and unobtrusively in preparing the drafts.

When Mrs Gandhi moved to 1 Safdarjang Road as Minister of I & B in 1964, it was quite sufficient for her needs. After she became the Prime Minister, the house started bursting at the seams. The public would fill the small front lawn, trampling on the grass and plants. A 'shamiana' was installed to protect people from the heat, cold, and rain, giving the place a shoddy look. People also flowed in and out of the front veranda and the rooms, and there was hardly any privacy.

The idea of moving to a bigger house was mooted. Some people seriously suggested moving back to Teen Murti House and I had a feeling that Mrs Gandhi was not averse to it, although nothing was mentioned. Fortunately, Padmaja Naidu and a few others took strong exception to the idea as it meant dismantling the Nehru Museum, and the idea was not pursued. Then a suggestion was made to build a Prime Minister's House in the vast grounds of Rashtrapati Bhavan, but that idea did not take off either.

A search for existing suitable premises was then made. I was sent on survey missions and saw the building now occupied by the National Defence College, the bungalow at 10 Janpath, as well as a few other places. However, for security considerations and other reasons, these buildings were not approved. After these exercises, it was decided that 1 Akbar Road, adjoining 1 Safdarjang Road, should be acquired for meeting the public and other such purposes. This was not a very satisfactory arrangement, but it did help to decongest the house at 1 Safdarjang Road and give more privacy to the Prime Minister and her family.

In the early years of her tenure as prime minister, when the burden of politics did not hang so heavily on her, Mrs Gandhi wished to meet interesting groups of people, to interact with them and to learn about their problems.

I should like to try to meet groups of people — small groups. Who & whom do you suggest?

UB

She added: 1. Bright young people—mixed artists, students, 2. Social workers, 3. Lawyers, senior citizens, and 4. Architects.

When she met a group of Hindi writers, I was a little apprehensive. The spoken Hindustani of the Nehrus was excellent, but Mrs Gandhi had not done much reading in Hindi, unlike English. That is why, after becoming the prime minister, for some time she was not very fluent in reading speeches written in Hindi. (I was audacious enough to suggest that she scan Hindi newspapers as well.) However, the dialogue with the Hindi writers went off very well. While the discussions were about literature and related matters, it was amusing to note that a number of these intellectuals seemed quite desirous of state patronage. It was refreshing to see rebel streaks in two young poets, but one of them, over a period of time, cultivated a person in the prime minister's personal office and eventually managed to become an MP. She met another group of Hindi writers and poets in 1980 which included Namvar Singh, Kedarnath Singh, Ashok Vajpayee and others. The exchange was more interesting and had a certain candour.

In early 1969, after chairing the meeting held for the commemoration of the 50th anniversary of Jallianwala Bagh, Mrs Gandhi told me that something interesting and meaningful should be organized for the occasion. We invited Amrita Pritam, the well-know Punjabi poet and the playwright Mohan Rakesh, along with I & B Minister I.K. Gujral, for discussion. It was decided that Amritaji and Mohan Rakesh would write a script and rather than a live programme, a son-e-lumière would be organized in Jallianwala Bagh. Thus, the place itself would speak out its tragic history, which would be more poignant. Col. Gupte, Director, Song & Drama Division of I & B Ministry was given the responsibility of mounting the show. The programme was a great success and it enthused Col. Gupte to use the same pattern for the 500th anniversary celebration of Guru Nanak.

Both Amritaji and Indiraji being sensitive had a soft corner for each other. Amritaji and Basu Bhattacharya, a film-maker, wanted to shoot some sequences with Amritaji in conversation with Indiraji, at different locations. Some unusual sequences were shot. When they wanted to shoot at midnight at India Gate, Mrs Gandhi did not think it proper. Later, perhaps due to some differences between Amritaji and Basu Bhattacharya, the project did not continue. I wonder what happened to the footage they shot—it would be quite interesting to see it now.

<u>UB</u> I told
Amelia that you would
phone/her re appt *(this afternoon)*
with Bosh B <u>tomorrow</u>.
As you know, they want
midnight India gold
shots. To me this
doesn't seem very
dignified. What is
your view?

TWENTY-FIVE

~

THE SURPRISE BIRTHDAY PARTY

On Mrs Gandhi's birthday, I think in 1967, Raj Thapar and I planned a surprise dinner at the Prime Minister's House. I remembered the surprise party for Aunty Gauba in 1959, which was a pleasant experience, but this one turned out to be a fiasco. We roped in the Karan Singhs and Pupul Jayakar, and they both and the Thapars were to bring some dishes. I had arranged for their entry from the side entrance straight into the dining room. Raj and I were excited because we thought that our venture would be a pleasant surprise for Mrs Gandhi. Mrs Gandhi used to come to the dining room only at dinner time. On that day while I was supervising the table arrangements, she suddenly entered. She looked at me and I had to confess our 'surprise'. She became very angry, saying she would not come to the table and walked out. Soon after, the guests started to arrive from the side entrance with the dishes of food. When I told them what had transpired, their faces fell with embarrassment and we thought of moving to the Thapars' house. Mrs Gandhi must have realized the awkward situation created and sent word that she would join the dinner. She came after some time but naturally both the atmosphere and the conversation were forced and lacked spontaneity. Raj Thapar writes that they received a letter the next day from Mrs Gandhi apologizing for her ungracious behaviour.[1]

When I tried to compare the two surprise parties, I realized that the main reason for the failure of the second party was that Mrs Gandhi was now the Prime Minister and perhaps did not like to be taken for granted, nor did she like liberties taken with her. It was a lesson well learnt.

[1]Raj Thapar, *All These Years*, p. 277.

In February 1967 Mrs Gandhi was on a tour of Orissa, and while she was giving a speech in Bhubaneshwar some rowdy young people threw stones to disturb the meeting. A stone hit Mrs Gandhi on the face and a nasal bone was cracked. When she returned to Delhi, she looked quite a sight and had to be in hospital for a couple of days. Her vanity had been hurt by the injury, and being always conscious of her long nose, she wrote to Dorothy Norman half in jest:

> Ever since plastic surgery was heard of, I have been wanting to get something done to my nose . . . I thought the only way it could be done without the usual hoo-ha was first to have some slight accident which would enable me to have it put right. But as you know, things never happen the way one wants them to.[2]

It is strange how Orissa and Bhubaneshwar cast dark shadows in her life through accidents and other mishaps. The first mishap occurred when Panditji fell ill during the AICC session in Bhubaneshwar in 1964. Then the incident in 1967 referred to above. There was a plane mishap in 1971, and in her reply to Dorothy Norman's enquiry, Mrs Gandhi wrote in a letter dated 23 April 1971: 'Is it not strange that something happens every time I go to Orissa?' She was again in Orissa on 29 and 30 October 1984 where, almost with a premonition of her end, she said in her speech in Bhubaneshwar on 30 October: 'I am here today, I may not be here tomorrow . . . I do not care whether I live or die.' And she was no more the next day.

[2]Dorothy Norman, *Indira Gandhi*, p. 117.

~

TWENTY-SIX

RAJIV AND SONIA'S WEDDING

Rajiv returned from the UK to India in 1967. Although he studied engineering there, he decided to become a pilot. When he started the flying lessons, I was very worried and would say that flying as a hobby is all right, but as a profession it is dangerous. He would smile and say that something can happen even while crossing a road.

Rajiv and Sonia had met in Cambridge, England. Their friendship had developed into a serious relationship. Rajiv had introduced Sonia to Mrs Gandhi when she went to London in 1965 for the Nehru Exhibition. Sonia and Rajiv had made up their mind to marry; Mrs Gandhi felt that Sonia should come to India for a few months to see things for herself before taking the final decision. Sonia's father was not particularly keen on Sonia marrying Rajiv, not because he did not like Rajiv, but his daughter going to a distant land and culture must have worried him. I think he was also concerned at Rajiv being the Prime Minister's son. Nobody could have imagined then the situations which developed later. Unconsciously perhaps the father's concern had a point. Sonia thus waited to complete her twenty-first birthday in December 1967 and arrived in Delhi in early January 1968. She was put up with the Bachchans at their Willingdon Crescent House, though she spent the day at 1 Safdarjang Road. After a week or two, Mrs Gandhi realized that both were very serious and there was not much point in waiting; their going around would only encourage gossip. Towards the end of January, their engagement took place and the wedding was fixed for 25 February. Although it was a simple civil marriage, Mrs Gandhi took an interest in the minute details of all arrangements for both the sides, the bride's and the bridegroom's. The following slip I found with her instructions conveys this:

Usha,

1. Invitation
2. Music–wedding and reception
   (a) Wedding March (Mendelsohn or Lohengrin) during bride's entry
   Then selection of classical Western and Indian music. Someone to sing?
3. Décor—1 Safdarjang and Hyd House
   Flowers
   Plants
   Jasmine screen
   Alpana
   Two types of shlokas—one for invitation card and the other for chanting at wedding.

Author slip said:

1. Will it do to have a garba dance immediately after the wedding here?
2. Music, before and after? At dinner?

Sonia's father did not come but her mother, sister, and maternal uncle arrived a day or two before the wedding and they had to be looked after, too. The 'mehendi' ceremony was held at the Bachchans' house. The marriage, a simple and elegant civil ceremony, took place in the back garden of the PM's home, against a floral backdrop. The only untoward thing which happened was that on learning that there were a couple of journalists present amongst the gathering, Rajiv became furious and refused to come out. Mrs Gandhi had to cajole him and brought him out with difficulty for the ceremony! A reception was held the next day at Hyderabad House.

After the wedding, Rajiv would go off on his flying duty and Mrs Gandhi to her office. Sonia was lonely as she had no relations or friends in India and was new to the country. Very often she would come and sit in our office where she could talk freely and perhaps also gain insights into things Indian. My colleague Amie Crishna would tease her that instead of one, she had three mothers-in-law. As I myself had noticed earlier, Mrs Gandhi took quite some time to be

125

free with people. It was so with Sonia, too. One day Mrs Gandhi left a long letter for Sonia expressing her views, some critical, on certain things. Sonia arrived in our room very distressed, and almost in tears; she could not understand why Mrs Gandhi could not talk to her rather than write a letter. I told Sonia that Mrs Gandhi often found it difficult to communicate and said that if she had left letters for her father and husband as well, Sonia should not mind this form of communication. For quite a long time Sonia was very shy and most reluctant to go before or mix with people whom she did not know. It used to be quite a job to persuade her.

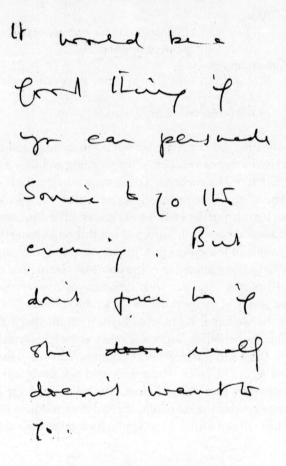

It would be a good thing if yr can persuade Sonia to go this evening. But don't force her if she doesn't want to go.

I think it took Sonia some time to get accustomed to things but she was a quick learner and gradually started gaining Mrs Gandhi's confidence and created a place for herself in the family. One could see that Sonia was an organized person, knew her mind, and was the stronger of the two. She was low key but knew what she wanted. Mrs Gandhi was keen that Sonia learn Hindi. A teacher was arranged for her but Sonia was not interested in learning the language academically. The attempt was given up and she gradually picked it up by listening and speaking.

Please do conversational Hindi with Sonia. The proper with the Hindi teacher seem to be non-existent. His method is also rather out of date.

I.B.

Rajiv was gentle, good natured, and accommodating. However, he had a streak of temper. He was a very meticulous person and expected the same standards from others. Once in the 1970s he was dissatisfied with the work of the PWD in the house and sent for their senior officer. He really lashed out at him. Later I spoke to Rajiv regarding his manner of reprimanding as it reflected on his mother too. I do not think he took this kindly. I realized that he was no longer my 'student' and that I should not intervene in his affairs.

The birth of Rahul and Priyanka, with an age difference of one and a half years, made the family complete. When Rahul was born, Mrs Gandhi was on tour and I rang her in Patna to give the happy news. The children added joy to Mrs Gandhi's life and she loved to fuss over them. She would think of their needs and comforts and send messages even from her office. As the children were growing up, I could see the difference between them. Rahul was naïve and carefree, while Priyanka knew her mind and was very poised from the beginning. She would hardly get into trouble, but Rahul often did; the grandmother then was very protective towards him. I used to enjoy watching her with her grandchildren.

~

TWENTY-SEVEN

THE THIMPHU EPISODE

In early May 1968, Mrs Gandhi was to visit Bhutan and decided to take Sonia with her. She had recently been married; to keep Sonia company Preeti, Mr T.N. Kaul's daughter, also came. Mr Kaul was accompanying Mrs Gandhi as Foreign Secretary.

The plane reached Hashimara from where the Prime Minister's party was to go to Thimphu in helicopters. It was drizzling and we had to wait for more than an hour. When we reached Thimphu, King Jigme Dorji Wangchuk, father of the present ruler, was at the helipad to receive Mrs Gandhi. He told her that he had requested the Head Lama to pray for good weather and it was sunny when we reached there.

We drove towards Tashichhodzong, the imposing monastery which towered in the landscape. The masked dancers danced their ritual dance in front of Mrs Gandhi's car. As we began to climb the entrance staircase, Mrs Gandhi looked back and said all should climb slowly as Thimphu is located at a height of approximately 8,000 feet above sea level. There were no continuous stairs, but quite a few flights, with courtyards in between. Later I counted nearly ninety steps in all to reach the Throne Room. One part of the monastery was used for administrative purposes. Adjoining the Throne Room, with an impressive altar of the Buddha, were the private quarters of the king, consisting of three rooms. As Thimphu was then a very small place with hardly any suitable place for accommodating Mrs Gandhi, the King vacated his quarters for her. She was given the King's room with an attached bathroom and Sonia, Preeti, and I were given the other rooms. We three were supposed to use a bathroom downstairs, to reach which we had to pass through the Throne Room. Mrs Gandhi overruled this, saying that we would all use her bathroom. The King himself showed us to our rooms, and after he left, our Political Officer (ambassadors were appointed later) took me into my room, pulled away a rug, and showed me a trapdoor, just for my information. Soon after, Sonia came to my room, and I casually mentioned the trapdoor. Being young, she got very excited, brought along Preeti, and they both started looking for the trapdoor. I got very worried and shooed them from the room. A little later Mrs Gandhi along with the two girls went to the dinner given by the King. The official dinner did not take long and we saw Mrs Gandhi and the others pass by the room where the rest of us were having dinner. When I came up, there was no light in my room and I heard giggles from the girls' room. As I entered to find out what was amusing them, their giggles became uncontrollable. On prodding them, I was horrified to learn that on their return they had gone to my room to look for the trapdoor, found it, and tried to open it. When a torchlight flashed from below, they quickly dropped the door, and ran out of the room. We later learnt that the King had moved downstairs.

On hearing about the pranks of the girls, I was extremely upset as this had happened in the room I was occupying. It was a foreign country and this incident could lead to misapprehensions. I walked into Mrs Gandhi's room. She was going to retire, and I told her agitatedly about what had transpired. She looked up with a smile and asked me not to get so worked up, and instead to ask our security official to come up, to explain the matter to him, and to ask him to convey it to their security officer. I wonder if Mrs Gandhi's reaction would have been the same had there been someone else in the place of these young girls! With the help of the security officer, I placed a table over the trapdoor so that I could sleep peacefully. On our return journey, Mr T.N. Kaul made a remark with a mischievous smile about the trapdoor being in my room. I replied in the same vein, adding that the girls had spoilt the chance!

From Thimphu in Bhutan, Mrs Gandhi and her party went by helicopter to Gangtok in Sikkim for a a day's visit. Mrs Gandhi, both the girls, and I were the guests of the Chogyal and the Gyalmo (Hope Cooke) at their palace. At night when Mrs Gandhi had retired, and Sonia, Preeti, and I were together in a room, the Gyalmo came in her shuffling style and brought some smoked salmon and other delicacies for us.

~

TWENTY-EIGHT

FROM BRAZIL TO BOROBUDUR

After Mrs Gandhi became the Prime Minister in 1966, her first official visit was to the USA in March. I joined her only in May. Her next visit was in July, to Egypt, Yugoslavia, and the USSR. Both President Nasser in Egypt and President Tito in Yugoslavia welcomed her warmly because of their close bonds with Panditji. President Tito, I think, was one of the best hosts. It is said that he took a personal interest in all arrangements, including the flowers, linen, and food. President Brezhnev and Prime Minister Kosygin welcomed Mrs Gandhi in Moscow. After the banquet at the Kremlin, the convention of segregating the men and the women for coffee was still observed. However, it was amusing to observe that Mrs Gandhi being the chief guest was included in the men's group. An overnight stay in a dacha in the woods on the outskirts of Moscow was a pleasant experience.

In 1967 October, Mrs Gandhi again visited eastern Europe—Poland, Yugoslavia, Bulgaria, and Romania—as well as the UAR. In Warsaw she stayed in an old hunting villa. Warsaw had been almost completely damaged during the war. A few members of our party visited the beautiful old city centre. We were told that when plans for the reconstruction of Warsaw were being drawn up, there was a consensus that before beginning the work on the functional buildings, the city centre should be remade first according to the old design, as it was a source of pride for the residents.

In east European countries, due to the encouragement of folk art or people's art by the government, folk dance ensembles were presented as official cultural programmes. In Bulgaria the welcome was very warm; Slavs are an effusive people. In addition to Sofia in Bulgaria, the Prime Minister was taken to Varna, a sea resort on the Black Sea, and she also visited an old Roman site nearby.

Romania being more Latin, the welcome was comparatively restrained. Mrs Gandhi was taken to an oil refinery and a petrochemical works outside Bucharest and afterwards for lunch to what had once been a monastery now converted to a wine-producing unit. As a special gesture, a wine-tasting session had been arranged before lunch. Mrs Gandhi, of course, did not taste the wine, but I believe in the saying 'When in Rome do as the Romans do.' So I tried to do dutifully what I was supposed to do until my head started to whirl. Mrs Gandhi watched me with amusement.

It was rewarding to see the Village Museum in Bucharest. To display the folk culture of the country, actual small wooden huts, with their artifacts had been transported from different regions of Romania and had been set up in a park as a museum. Some folk dances were also arranged. We were impressed with the idea and carried it to India; but somehow it did not take root. The remnant of the experiment is visible as the Village Complex in the Crafts Museum in New Delhi.

Sometime after the Bhutan visit in 1968, Mrs Gandhi told me that she may be going to Latin America and also to Japan. She asked me where I would like to go. I kept quiet for a few seconds and then was audacious enough to reply, 'If possible to both, otherwise Latin America.' She smiled and eventually I went to both countries.

In 1968 times were a little quieter politically, so in September Mrs Gandhi left for a four-week tour of Latin America. This was the first time that a Prime Minister of India was visiting the distant South American continent. The countries visited were Brazil, Uruguay, Argentina, Chile, Columbia, Venezuela, Guyana, and Trinidad and Tobago. The whole trip was quite an experience. However, what used to upset me was that the original inhabitants were hardly visible and the people and the governments we were dealing with were all of Spanish and Portuguese descent, erstwhile colonialists who had centuries ago occupied these areas, vanquishing or pushing back the natives, and had become the rulers of the continent.

From New York, we flew directly to Rio de Janeiro in Brazil. I met a grand-uncle who in the 1920s had run away from Rawalpindi to Bombay, then made his way to Iraq and Rome, and from there had migrated to Brazil. He came to meet me with his wife, a Polish émigré. Brazil is a large country and the new capital, Brasilia, which was our next stop was almost complete. Mrs Gandhi laid the foundation stone of the Indian Embassy. There were four Ministry of External Affairs officials in the party: Mr Rajeshwar Dayal, Foreign Secretary; Jagat Mehta, Joint Secretary; S.K. Singh and Natwar Singh, both Deputy Secretaries. While leaving for Sao Paulo, S.K. Singh was almost left behind due to his love of siesta after lunch. In Uruguay, the next stop, Mrs Gandhi had to attend an official stag lunch!

In Argentina, Madame Victoria Ocampo, the eminent writer and intellectual with whom Rabindranath Tagore had stayed during his visit to the country in 1924, hosted a lunch for Mrs Gandhi in her beautiful sprawling estate in San Isidro. Over forty eminent intellectuals—writers, artistes from the fields of music, fine arts, theatre, films, scientists, journalists, and others—were invited. We saw the bench on which Tagore often used to sit. Madame Ocampo had been awarded the 'Desikottama' by the Visva Bharati, Santiniketan, the university's highest honour. Mrs Gandhi presented the award to Madame Ocampo at a function held in the Indian Embassy.

At a women's reception in Chile, as Mrs Gandhi entered the room, a woman standing next to me gasped and exclaimed, 'Oh, she looks so delicate. We had thought she would look like Golda Meir.' A Sindhi family settled in the southern tip of Chile, almost near the Straits of Magellan, came to see Mrs Gandhi. I marvelled at the enterprise of the Sindhis.

While still in Santiago, we heard that there had been a coup in Peru, our next stop, and that the President, a General, had escaped via Chile. We were thus deprived of the opportunity to visit Peru, as the new government had to be officially recognized before Mrs Gandhi could visit the country. Both Mrs Gandhi and I were very disappointed, because at her request a visit to Machu Pichu had been included in our itinerary and we had been reading about pre-Columbian art and the Incas and were looking forward to the visit with much excitement.

The Chilean government had to host us for the extra days originally meant for the visit to Peru and sent us to Viña del Mar, a sea resort on the Pacific. Mrs Gandhi rested and read most of the time. An architect and his artist wife invited me to their home, where I saw a portrait of Chè Guevara, who had died shortly before. The portrait was on a collage of press clippings from different newspapers about the revolutionary leader's death. The couple was obviously leftist, and I worried about them when the post-Allende regime came to power soon after. My hosts took me for a meal to Valparaiso, a port, and the twin town of Viña, and then to a bohemian café, where Pablo Neruda often used to drop in. He was expected but did not come that evening. Thus I was deprived of meeting him.

Our next stop after Chile was Colombia, but as we were travelling by a commercial flight the plane had to touch Lima, Peru. The chief of protocol and other officials were at the airport to request Mrs Gandhi to come to the airport terminal. Our officials argued against it due to the diplomatic procedures. When Mrs Gandhi saw my disappointment, she urged us to go. As the ambassador's wife, Sakina Mehta, and I started to descend from the back exit, the cameramen and photographers rushed towards us and started clicking, evidently thinking that Mrs Gandhi was giving them the slip. We had to wave them away. Mrs Gandhi was finally persuaded to come down to inaugurate the Indo-Peruvian Friendship Association, which was a part of the original itinerary; the members had assembled in the terminal building for the inauguration.

In Bogota, Colombia, arrangements for Mrs Gandhi's stay were made in the Club Militar, in the suite which had earlier been done up for the visit of the de Gaulles. Mrs Gandhi was to stay in Madame de Gaulle's spacious room, with its feminine and somewhat jazzy décor, and I was to occupy General de Gaulle's room, which was smaller, staid, wood-panelled with maroon velvet furnishings. For some reason Mrs Gandhi preferred the General's room, and I had to stay in Madame de Gaulle's luxurious and opulent room. The Colombians, I found, had an old world charm and culture. Their memorial for Simon Bolivar was a quiet place in a natural setting and had ambience compared to the massive and imposing building of the Bolivar Memorial in Caracas, Venezuela.

Latin America is a continent known for its meat, especially beef. To avoid any problems, our standard menu in all the countries was soup, fish, chicken, and dessert. Towards the end of the visit Mr Natwar Singh, a member of our party, remarked that he had had so many chickens that he thought he could start laying eggs! At the end of our four-week visit, when the Air India flight came to pick us up from the last stop, Port of Spain, everyone wanted vegetarian Indian food, pickles, and chutneys to revive our tastebuds.

In 1969 Mrs Gandhi visited Japan. In addition to the official visit to Tokyo, she also went by the bullet train to Osaka for the Shinto ground-digging ceremony for the Indian pavilion which was to come up for the Osaka Expo 1970. She met a group of writers, musicians, and other artists in Tokyo as well.

From Japan the next visit was to Indonesia. Besides Jakarta, we were also able to visit the famous and imposing Borobudur temple at Jogjakarta which was then being renovated by UNESCO.

Back in India, I think it was a lull before the storm.

~

INTERLUDE

~

INDIRAJI: AN ENIGMATIC AND COMPLEX PERSONALITY

Mrs Gandhi was a multi-faceted person, who could at the same time be complex and simple, familiar and aloof, haughty and humble, sociable and lonely, tough and vulnerable, gentle and harsh, and many other things.

In a letter to Dorothy Norman dated 20 September 1959, Mrs Gandhi wrote:

> Are most people not just a split personality but several personalities? I feel I am and I have learnt to make all the separate personalities quite friendly with each other. But I still don't know how to present them to the world. Different people see different me-s![1]

I am not sure if these traits were as friendly to each other as Mrs Gandhi claims. However, interaction with different people brought out different aspects of her personality, and they assessed her accordingly.

She had an inner quality which remained untouched by the outer turmoil she faced, and there was a tremendous amount of turmoil in her life. Armed with this inner strength, she withstood many storms, both political and personal. At the same time she could be very vulnerable, too. These were the many paradoxes in her life and personality. She was a loner; she shut herself in but didn't shut others out. Actually, she had a wide circle of contacts and maintained relationships even with distant relatives and friends from her school days, and she participated in their joys and sorrows.

While Mrs Gandhi could talk quite intimately with people, and this led some to form an impression that she was close to them, this

---

[1]Dorothy Norman, *Indira Gandhi*, p. 59.

was not necessarily so; an inner distance was always maintained. Another of her traits was that sometimes, when meeting a person with whom she was diffident about interacting, she would keep quiet and make notes or doodles. I remember once Krishna Menon came out quite exasperated after meeting her, and seeing me in the corridor he pulled me by the arm while walking out and said, 'I come to talk to her on important matters and she just sits and doodles.' Knowing her as I did, I knew this was merely a stance on her part; she must have taken in every word. She generally kept her views close to her chest, and in this case perhaps having different views, she did not wish to argue with a senior person like Mr Menon whom she had known since she was a student in England.

She was not a feminist, but proved the point through actions rather than words. Any reference to her as a woman prime minister used to irritate her. She herself had stated: 'I'm no feminist, I'm a human being. I don't think of myself as a woman when I do my job.'[2] She felt, however, that a woman has to work twice as hard as a man to prove her merit. Mary Carras offers an interesting insight:

> In her political demeanour [Mrs.] Gandhi rarely revealed any of the 'feminine' traits ascribed to women . . . In her public persona, she did not fit the female model as 'nurturer' or peacemaker. But in her dress and . . . bearing, she was very feminine . . . In the privacy of her home, with her children and especially grandchildren, she was decidedly a 'nurturer'.[3]

An article in *The Statesman* (6 June 1981) mentions:

> I have experienced an identity crisis at work. There are expectations and temptations to be like men, the 'one of the lads' syndrome. How feminine should I be . . . ? The release of tension when I decided to be 'me' was enormous. I've my own personality and that I will not trade for my career.

[2]Indira Gandhi, *My Truth*, p. 113.
[3]Mary C. Carras, 'Indira Gandhi: Gender and Foreign Policy', in Francine D'Amico with Peter R. Beckman, eds., *Women and World Politics: An Introduction*.

Knowing that Mrs Gandhi would find it interesting, I put up the article to her; it came back with the comment: 'Because I have always remained 'me', I have avoided tension.'

An important aspect of her personality, and so naturally of her work, was her quiet, subtle and unostentatious way of working. This was also reflected in the simple, natural, and yet aesthetic environment of her surroundings. Simplicity and economy were the keys to her personality. One was reminded of Japanese art, which though understated, suggests a greater non-expressed depth. Her capacity for economy was visible in all aspects of her character and personality, even in her body movements and the way she packed for travel. She was often dissatisfied and irritated with the packing done by others because she felt they wasted space. She often took out everything and repacked the bag herself in such a way that many more things could be accommodated.

The quality of economy was especially evident in her writing. She had the ability to grasp the essence and weed out the superfluous. She would have made a good editor. I noticed this right away when I started to work for her and was a one-person secretariat! A draft put up to her would come back chiselled, sharper in focus, with all verbosity slashed away. She was quite allergic to pompous, verbose and flowery language, which she felt generally diffused the meaning and power of the language. She liked to be provided the basic material, the inputs and the draft, but she then used them as raw material, as the craftsperson does to mould and shape the text to her own liking. She often rejected suggestions but negating them would often ignite her own creativity and expression. She worked on revising her special speeches and letters, even to children, until she was fully satisfied. In some cases this would take hours and sometimes even days.

A girl from Germany whose hobby was to collect poems from important people wrote to Mrs Gandhi in September 1984, asking her to send a poem she liked. Mrs Gandhi asked for a translation of Tagore's 'Ekla chalo re'. However, the translation provided did not satisfy her. Instead, she herself worked on the translation for days, and it was finally sent around the middle of October, significantly only a short time before her fateful end. Excerpts from the letter and the translation reveal her thoughts:

> There are many poems which inspire one at different moments. One of them is: 'Walk Alone' by our well-known poet Rabindranath Tagore. The translation below is not literal, but I have attempted to put it in words which capture the spirit of the poem.

> If no one listens to your call,
> Walk alone.
> If in fear, they cower mutely facing the wall,
> O hapless one,
> Open your mind and speak out alone.
> If, as you cross the wilderness, they turn away and desert you,
> O hapless one,
> Tread firmly on the thorns along the blood-lined track,
> And travel alone.
> If, in the storm-troubled night, they dare not hold aloft the light
> O hapless one,
> Ignite your own heart with the lightning and pain,
> And yourself become the guiding light.

She was a quick reader and went through official papers and books at quite a speed. At the same time one felt that her reading was not superficial and that she had comprehended the essential points. Intrigued, I once asked her how she managed to do this. She said that first she skimmed over the words to get the sense. If the ideas or the language interested her, she then went over the text more slowly.

Although the scope and amount of her work changed over the years, her style of work more or less remained the same. Work, leisure and family duties were never compartmentalized, but they flowed into each other. In Teen Murti House her work table was in her bedroom, and even at 1 Safdarjang Road she continued working in a very informal setting, in a study in an enclosed veranda adjoining her bedroom. She worked best when a number of streams of activity interacted with each other, and while working on one task she could attend to numerous other activities as well. Her faculties worked simultaneously, which was perhaps the secret which enabled her to attend to so much more work than other people. It was a rare quality, which I have not seen in others. For her, work and relaxation were intertwined, and she did not need separate periods to rest and relax. However, relaxation did not mean long periods of doing nothing. It was really doing something different, even if this was for a short time, such as reading, arranging flowers, sorting books or clothes, or talking to her family. She sometimes worked while listening to music or even watching television. While having lunch she often did crossword puzzles, which also perhaps helped her to defuse the tension, to relax, and to sort out her ideas.

Her day and her work did not have strict divisions. How much she could do in a day was amazing. One of her favourite maxims was that the more you do, the more you can do. With her organized and disciplined mind and her ability to grasp the essential without wasting time or energy, she could do much more in twenty-four hours than most people generally manage to do. She also followed an exercise regimen. If she did not get the time in the morning, she would do it on her return from the office in the evening. When she came home for lunch, as far as possible she would rest for fifteen-twenty minutes. This regularity and discipline is what kept her going.

Mrs Gandhi was a very frugal eater. She used to have coffee, toast with honey, and fruit for breakfast while working in her room. Lunch consisted of simple Indian food in a 'thali', eaten with the family in the dining room. Dinner was again light—fish or egg, steamed or baked vegetables—often in her room unless the whole family was eating together. She was not keen on desserts and watched her weight. This does not imply that she did not enjoy good food—Indian, Continental, and regional. Sheikh Abdullah when he came from Kashmir often brought 'gushtava' and other tasty but rich Kashmiri delicacies. A Congress leader from Chandni Chowk would sometimes bring Delhi delicacies such as 'kachoris' and sweets. Mrs Gandhi would have a good fill, and then later complain that we did not stop her from overeating.

She used to travel all over India and was unhappy about the sameness of the food served to her, a kind of north Indian cuisine. She then

AC/UB

PD must go back to old food regime. Please tell servants No sugar, sweets puddings etc.

issued instructions that she should be served the food of the region. What used to amuse me sometimes was that while referring to a particular dish, she would say that 'We don't cook like this' or 'We don't put certain spices.' The 'we' referred to the Kashmiris. Her pride in her ancestry was revealed by such remarks. She would also observe Navreh, the Kashmiri New Year. On Basant Panchami (spring festival), she would not only wear a yellow sari but would also instruct the 'mali' to arrange yellow flowers in the house. She was a good blend of the traditional and the contemporary.

As Mrs Gandhi's mind worked all the time and since it was sometimes not possible for her to convey her instructions and comments personally to the persons concerned, she would often leave slips of paper for them. Some of her slips to me are reproduced here; they convey her personality, style of functioning, humour, and eye for detail. When thinking and talking, she would sometimes doodle, drawing faces, patterns, and so on, some of which are reproduced in this book.

Her interest in books stayed with her from her childhood till the end. She was happy in their company and liked to be in touch with the latest thoughts and writings. Even if she travelled out of Delhi for a day, books would accompany her. Books and journals would collect in her room over a period of time. To help sort them, she would sometimes ask me to come over on a Sunday morning (perhaps she thought me to be somewhat literate). She really enjoyed browsing through them, keeping some and discarding others. Once we came across a paperback of Charles Reich's *The Greening of America*. She had met him in New York where he had presented her a hardcover copy. As this was a duplicate, I asked a little hesitantly if I could have it. She did not say anything nor did she give me the book. I felt embarrassed. But the next day I found the book in my tray, and it was inscribed by her:

To Usha,
> *Who is herself concerned with the greening of India.*
>> *Indira Gandhi*
>> *18.7.71*

These quiet ways of hers were quite charming.

In 1972, an American woman wrote to Mrs Gandhi enquiring about the kind of books which interested her. Mrs Gandhi's reply to her, of which I have a copy, mentions,

The very first and probably lasting influences of literature on me were of the great Indian epics, 'The Ramayana' and 'The Mahabharata' . . .

As a child I was a compulsive reader. I just could not resist books, even those which I did not fully comprehend. Sometimes understanding dawned months, even years, later!

Since my family was deeply immersed in the political fight for

India's freedom, I was naturally attracted to the heroes of freedom movements everywhere. Books on Joan of Arc, William Tell, Garibaldi, Juarez, and others . . .

A poem which impressed me was Oscar Wilde's 'Ballad of Reading Gaol.' . . . I was deeply moved by Victor Hugo's 'Les Miserables'.

Entirely different types of books, for instance, the Faber Book of Insects and Maeterlinck's books on Bees, Ants . . . also contributed to the shaping of my personality. They inculcated the habit of close observations of everything around and reinforced what my mother used to tell me of the links between all creatures. My father's letters had explained how rocks, stones and trees told not only their own story but those of the people and creatures who lived amongst them. Very early I became a conservationist with a strong feeling of companionship and kinship with all living beings . . .

Tagore's poetry opened out a new world. My reading ranged . . . [from] biography, science, adventure as well as fairy tales, poetry and plays. As a child I also loved the Alice books—'Alice in Wonderland' and 'Alice through the Looking Glass'.

Besides books, on some holiday's she would sometimes become involved in sorting and revamping other things. When she would get into this mood, it could go on for hours. I have a feeling that this helped her unconsciously to rearrange and discard ideas as well. A couple of times it so happened that the day after a session of cleaning up, there was a reshuffle of the cabinet. So whenever she would get into this mood, there was a standing joke between my colleague Amie Crishna and me that there was a cabinet reshuffle in the offing!

Mrs Gandhi's powers of observation were quite extraordinary. In a reply to a journalist, she once remarked: 'Whenever I enter a room I instantly note the colours, the placement of the furniture . . . and can tell you about them even afterwards. This is due to a lifetime's habit of observation. We in India are not taught to observe, but I learnt it from my schooling in Switzerland.'[4]

Even when her mind was involved in serious business, she never failed to observe minute details of the people and the environment

[4]*Eve's Weekly*, 22 November 1967.

around her. Sometimes we would be together at a place and on our return she would refer to many points of interest which, to my embarrassment, I had not noticed.

Her sense of humour was subtle, often going above the heads of others. Sometimes when she was in the mood, she would come out with amusing and interesting anecdotes, at the dinner table, or when among friends, and even at formal parties. Sometimes small slips of paper would arrive from her while attending cabinet or other meetings, bearing really amusing remarks or comments.

Once a man from Switzerland wrote to Mrs Gandhi: 'I confess you that your beauty has been so great and brilliant that I even dreamt to be married with you. Please be so kind to consider it as a compliment from a small earth being.' Knowing this would amuse Mrs Gandhi, I put up the letter to her, marking the paragraph with an exclamation mark. It came back to me marked 'private', and with the remark: 'In true Rama's style—shall I refer him to you?' (This is

147

regarding the incident in the Ramayana, when Shurpanakha, Ravana's sister, on seeing Rama in the forest becomes enamoured with his charm and beauty and pursues him to marry her. Rama, with Sita beside him, tells Shurpanakaha that he is already married and points, perhaps a little mischievously, to his brother Lakshmana.) These small and light-hearted gestures must no doubt have relaxed her mind for a few moments during serious meetings.

However, to say that Mrs Gandhi was always pleasant and good-humoured would not be true. There were many rough edges to her personality. The pressures she faced often produced irritation and eruptions of temper. While Panditji also used to lose his temper, with him it was like a cloudburst which subsided immediately and there was a blue sky thereafter. It was not always so with Mrs Gandhi. She could nurse grudges for quite a long time and some lasted all her life. Sometimes she would become cool towards a person who would often be unaware of having given cause for offense, thus leading to an uncomfortable atmosphere. One learnt to give her time and space.

After she became the prime minister, however, such moods decreased because she became completely involved in many activities in her own right. This gave her not only a sense of fulfilment but also left her with less time to brood over hurts and grievances. Still, the tendency did not disappear, and though it was not always visible, it was sometimes reflected in her behaviour in the political field as well.

Mrs Gandhi was humane, compassionate, and sensitive, but she did not find it easy to be large-hearted and generous. Possibly that is why she especially admired her grandfather, Motilal Nehru, who had these qualities in abundance.

She took her work—political and official—in her stride and it did not submerge the feminine side of her personality, which extended to different areas, ranging from her interest in hospitality and interior decoration to personal grooming. While living at Teen Murti House, when important dignitaries such as Madame Sun Yat Sen and Jacqueline Kennedy stayed there, Mrs Gandhi looked into the minutest details of their comfort, as well as the particular interests of each individual guest. Later, as prime minister, she took a keen interest in supervising different aspects of state banquets and official meals, for instance, looking over guest lists, menus, flower arrangements, and cultural programmes. She would often make changes in the guest lists and table plans submitted to her with the aim of encouraging more interesting conversation and interaction among the guests.

The gifts presented to the VIPs during state visits also did not escape her eye. We would do the preliminary selection and the objects were brought for her final approval; they could be beautiful speciments of handicrafts, paintings, carpets, books, etc. When she went to Brazil in 1968, an ivory chess set (this is before ivory was banned) was presented to the President. He told Mrs Gandhi the next day that he was so enamoured by the excellently carved pieces that he could not stop looking at them again and again.

In spite of her tremendous work schedule, Mrs Gandhi managed to retain her grace and elegance, which had both external and internal aspects. There was nothing sloppy about her. No doubt she had an eye for beautiful saris but she also possessed the ability to carry them off with élan, which many women do not have. Mrs Gandhi liked all colours except mauve. She preferred shades which were clear and luminous, not pastel or dull. She was attracted more to autumn colours such as yellow, orange, red, brown and also shades of green. It was difficult for her to go to the shops herself. Keeping her preferences in view, we would bring saris on approval and she was quick to choose the ones she liked. She looked as elegant in a simple white khadi sari as she did in a heavy 'tanchoi'. Personally I think simplicity enhanced her personality. My mother once remarked, 'She always looks fresh, as if she has just come out of her bath.' She chose her clothes to reflect the traditions of the different regions of the country. Thus she not only made a fashion statement but also gave an impetus to the development of the khadi and handloom sectors in India. She also liked to wear regional costumes with the aim of conveying the message that the sari is not the only garment worn by Indian women.

She did not spend much time on her hair and the hairdresser came only to trim her hair. However, on special occasions abroad, for banquets etc. a hairdresser added to her overall elegance.

No one ever
noticed my
hair do !

During her visits abroad, Mrs Gandhi's dress sense and her well-turned-out appearance were admired. She, of course, had a natural elegance, but for the trips abroad much planning was involved behind the scene. A chart was prepared indicating the different occasions she would be attending. Mrs Gandhi's saris and accessories were decided upon with great care with her concurrence, and these were then entered into the chart in different columns. This resulted in no wastage of time, as everything was planned ahead and her clothes and accessories were kept ready for her rushed schedule.

She had an innate sense of beauty and experienced it not only in formal expressions of art, but even in ordinary things such as the shape of a leaf, the texture of a stone, or the colour of a seashell. She felt closest to unspoilt nature and the mountains and was happiest amongst them. Left to herself she would perhaps have been quite happy to live alone in that environment. The preservation of the environment and wildlife and conservation of India's cultural heritage were issues close to her heart, and she frequently came to the rescue of endangered areas such as the ecologically and genetically rich Silent Valley in Kerala in the late 1970s. An SOS to her on such matters usually elicited a quick response. Once the well-known dancer, Mrinalini Sarabhai, rang up from Ahmedabad to convey the citizens' concern regarding plans to demolish a *pol* (old city gate) to widen a road. Mrs Gandhi immediately spoke to the chief minister of Gujarat on the matter. She also took a keen interest in the setting up of Project Tiger, the Delhi Urban Arts Commission, and many other heritage preservation projects.

In the fifties, Mrs Gandhi was a member of the Bird Watching Society and would often recognize the bird by its sound. She and Mr Malcolm McDonald, the then British High Commissioner and a keen bird watcher, would sit quietly observing the birds in the back garden of the prime minister's home. She was close to Mr Salim Ali, the well-known ornithologist, and helped him whenever he needed it. Mrs Gandhi was also involved in the film society movement in its early stages.

Folk arts and crafts were another area in which Mrs Gandhi was interested. In 1952 she took the initiative in starting the folk dance festival during the Republic Day celebrations. She told Dorothy Norman in 1952:

> Right now I am helping to arrange for the performance of tribal dances at the Republic Day celebrations. Great numbers (of urban people) will be able to see ceremonials they could not otherwise witness and villagers from remote areas will have an opportunity to meet others from different parts of the country. When I go to villages I love to join in tribal dances.[5]

Mrs Gandhi had a special affinity with the tribals because they are unaffected, spontaneous, and close to nature. She had once mentioned that she would have liked to be an anthropologist.

Due to her interest in folk dances an experimental Folk Dance Ensemble was started in the seventies, but for various reasons it did not take off.

In 1955, in a letter to Dorothy Norman she wrote:

> My most favourite—folk dancing—is merrily on its way and able to fend for itself. The current favourite—'community singing'.[6]

She was keen to popularize community singing as it would preserve traditional songs and inculcate the joy of singing together, and national integration. The project could only take off in the early 1980s when the movement began to spread among students in different parts of the country. Unfortunately, the project ended with Mrs Gandhi's demise.

Mrs Gandhi's concerns reflected her interest in different fields such as the preservation of Vedic chants as evident in the slip on the next page. The UNESCO subsequently recognized Vedic chants as an intangible cultural heritage.

[5]Dorothy Norman, *Indira Gandhi*, p. 20.
[6]Ibid., p. 28.

I spoke to Shivaramamurti
in your presence re
taping or recording of
vedic chants before
the old clergy (with the
correct knowledge &
~~pronunciation~~ ~~pronun~~
pronunciation) pass
away. Is he doing
something about it?

OSD

19.8.81

How does one sum up Mrs Gandhi's personality? According to Mary Carras she mirrored India in many ways: in the contradictions within her personality, her penchant for synthesis, and her singular ability to evoke both hate and love—to alienate and to charm, to frustrate and simultaneously to delight. Carras adds that the motivation of her personality blended in unique ways with opportunities offered, by her culture and that only in the interaction between her environment and her personality can her political behaviour and outlook be understood.[7]

Of course, this is only one interpretation. Mrs Gandhi was an enigmatic and complex person, and there are bound to be many different interpretations concerning her.

[7]Mary Carras, *Indira Gandhi*, pp. 1–2.

~

NOTES FROM INDIRAJI

Some of the notes and slips Mrs Gandhi used to leave for me have been integrated in the text. However, to convey many of her diverse interests and other facets such as keen observations, eye for detail and humour, a few more slips have been included in this section.

PRIME MINISTER'S HOUSE,
NEW DELHI.

To Aunty Usha

"An un – birthday present"
As Humpty Dumpty told Alice.

Rajiv
Sanjay

P. S. We're so sorry we
forgot your birthday — so Rajiv
thought he would share
his.
I.I.

15. 8. 57

For foreign mail we
should try to use
the nicer stamps —
Beethoven for example
or the miniatures.

I M

26 . J.

UB — for
information
I am not
biting my
nails in the
Leh photograph
but eating the
small Ladakhi
almonds !

This was sent to me with a photograph taken in Leh, Ladakh.

उषा — मीटिंग के बाद जब बापू की फोटो में से हार हटा दिया जाता है — बहुत खराब और inappropriate लगता है —

[Usha—when the meeting ends have the garland removed from Papu's picture—looks very bad and inappropriate]

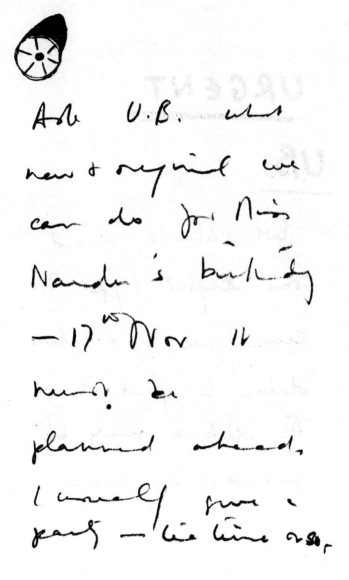

Ask U.B. what
new & original we
can do for Miss
Naidu's birthday
— 17th Nov. It
must be
planned ahead.
I would give a
party — like time ago.

Padmaja Naidu was like a family member.

URGENT

U.B.

We shall need some *tight* type of Kum Kum & a silver 'dibia' to put it in. The dibia may be found in the house.

This I think pertains to the engagement ceremony of Sanjay and Maneka.

Garden

To have the roof
cleaned - Dried branches,
bits of broken glass etc
are lying there
—

Either steps for steps
leading up to roof.
—

Path in garden - The
rain has caused some
steps to sink   Some one
may stumble at night.

TOP- SECRET

U.B.

I wonder if it necessary
to send measurements.
However since you posed
the question, I thought
I had better get the
latest! 35 . 27 . 35½

All it indicates is
that the centre figure
must be reduced by 1½
inch at least.

18 . 8 . 72

The measurements were required for the wax model being made by Madame Tussaud's Gallery in London.

Usha.

I must apologize
for dampening your
enthusiasm regarding
the hailstorm + not
giving full credence
to your description
regarding the size +
quantity of the
hailstones !!

11.3.76

I had talked to her excitedly about the hailstorm and the large size of the hailstones

Re paintings

A. Library.

1) Singapore one goes over the other door

2) My portrait comes down under the corner or whatever it is called

3) The bend is too low

4) The carved wood is too high

5) Can the lift be accommodated in my bedroom?

Mrs Gandhi used to love to reshuffle paintings.

Hussein wants a
message, for his
exhibition (a real
participation) -

at Sao Paulo Biennale.

He also wants his &
the other Indian
artists fares paid
How many & how
much ?

May 1971

UB

Priyanka comes home
for school at 1.30 or
so. She will be at
home except for
3.45 & 5.15 when
she goes to her dancing
class. Could you
please stay until
~~Rajiv~~ ~~comes~~ Rajiv returns
at 7 ? You can bring
your work here.
CT 27.9.84

Written about a month before the fateful end in October 1984.

~

LETTERS FROM INDIRAJI

Some of Mrs Gandhi's letters to me form part of the narrative in
Parts I to IV. However, there are quite a few other letters which are
interesting and bring out her personality, and thus have been included
in this section.

Mashobra
June 6, 1954

My dear Usha,

Aunty [refers to Mrs Vakil] has shown me your letter. I am so sorry things are not running smoothly. I am writing to Mathai but I suggest that whenever you have any such difficulty you might go and have a talk with him. Vimla has a tendency of throwing her weight about.

It is very lovely here & quite cold since we had a thunderstorm. I enclose two letters with instructions.

All good wishes
Indira

Miss Clark arrived on Friday. Jai also. Any news of Ira?
I have asked Vimla to send some things of mine. Ask her to also send a long sleeved pullover for James—his son Sambu has it.

Miss Clark was the teacher from Welham's School which the boys joined that year. Ira was the younger daughter of Mrs Vakil. James was the butler.

Mashobra
June 7, 1954

My dear Usha,

Do go off to Chamba. The Punjab Governor's car is coming back to Simla from Delhi on the 9th or 10th. We had thought that if you would like to spend a few days here, you could come up in it. It is now raining every day here and is quite cold.

Jai & her husband are in a rest house even further off than we are & they are a bit fed up. They are thinking of going on a bus ride to Kulu.

Please let the Handicraft board know that I cannot attend the Ranchi or the Srinagar meeting. I am sending in my resignation to Kamaladevi.

By the way, I heard from Moscow that our lady-friends who went there were constantly bickering and quarelling amongst themselves!

I thought I had a copy of Mridula's [refers to Mridula Sarabhai] working children scheme. But it is not here. If we have several copies, I should like you to give one to Mathai to show to my father & please send one to me. Otherwise ask Mridula to send it to the PM.

Indira

Mridula writes that she may come up on the 10th—let her know about the Gov's car. I have told the driver to get in touch with PM's house on the 9th morning. ING.

Jai is Mrs Vakil's daughter.

Mashobra
14.6.54

My dear Usha,

Can you find out if there was a Mr or Mrs Moses in our Embassy in Rangoon upto a year ago? And what post did he have? He is now in Trivandrum.

I haven't yet received the letter from the C. Social Welfare Board to which you refer.

Aunty wants the series of Spell-well (or is it Speedwell) books which are amongst the children's book in the small passage between my room and theirs. Also a book for forming the handwriting, I can't remember what it is called. (It is the one used in Elizabeth's school, I think.)

ING

P.S. Aunty Vakil wants to get 'Shabda Bodh' by Bhagat Singh M.A.B.T. and the three books following it in the same series. Please buy and send.

I find I have got the working children's scheme. But you must still get one for the PM.

ING

[On board Air-India International]
Flight between Cairo & Rome
3 a.m. (I.S.T.)

My dear Usha,

As everybody is going to be away from the house in Delhi I am rather worried about the security, especially as the house will be swarming with workmen. Is Mathai going to stay on there? I believe Bose will be on duty. Please ask him to be extra careful about the Ivory room & my bedroom. I have rather a flimsy lock on my cupboard & it is jammed with all kinds of things.

These long flights are terribly boring. I slept much of the time but my legs are aching & the rest of the time I was too tired to read. Seshan has been typing the whole time.

Shankar (of the Weekly) is also on the plane.

I hope every thing will be all right & you will have a good holiday.

Indira

Panditji and Mrs Gandhi used to travel by ordinary commercial flights. I think this is written in June 1955 on their way to the USSR at the invitation of Mr Bulganin and Mr Krushchev. The small drawing room had a number of carved ivory objects and was referred to as the Ivory Room.

Prime Minister's House,
New Delhi.
[Undated]

Usha

Here are 3 tickets for you & Mr & Mrs Gauba. Could you all come together? I don't want to send the tickets to Auntie Gauba in case she loses them!

ING

Prime Minister's House,
New Delhi.
[Undated]

Usha

I'm sorry I could not say goodbye—I suddenly realized I was late for my appointment with the V.P. & dashed off.

I hope you'll relax a bit while I'm away but do keep an eye on the boys. If there are any special children's films for Christmas—please arrange for them to go, if they want to. Ram Prasad can take them. I am leaving Rs 50/- with Auntie but you can always get money from Seshan.

ING

[Undated]

My dear Usha,

Thank you for your letter.

Please do whatever you consider best for Sanjay's picture. i think that wherever it is printed, it should say that it was taken by him—Sanjay Gandhi aged 10.

I have no objection to its being sent to the Weekly but will that not disqualify it for the competition? If however it cannot go for the competition because of the subject, it is better to send it to the Weekly instead. I hope this does not sound too involved.

I hope the dogs are well.

Shall be in Delhi on the 14th.

ING

The above is regarding a photograph Sanjay took of their dog.

May 28 [year not given]

Dear Usha,

It is so perfectly delightful here that one can't even imagine Delhi being 116° in the shade! This house is so tucked away between trees that one has the impression of its being the only house in the world. It is also considerably cooler than Simla.

Let me know if anything exciting happens.

Has any one taken down the pole with the fish streamers that we had put up in the garden? If not, please have it done.

Sincerely,
Indira

The above has obviously been written from The Retreat in Mashobra.

Raj Bhavan
June 1, 1956

Usha

Thank you for sending the letters . . .

Is the Darzi back? I told Vimla about getting some blouses dyed. Also left one pearl ear top with Mrs Atal for repairs.

1. Re gifts: We have to take a small gift for Lord Mountbatten,

b) small one for Eden

       "   " for Lady Eden

c) ditto for Sir Winston Churchill

(2) I hope the children are well . . .

(3) Please write to Mr or Mrs Frank Oberdorf (I do not have the address) giving them the dates of my stay in Germany. Tell them the boys are also coming.

Best wishes—Indu

Written before the trip in 1956 when Mrs Gandhi accompanied Panditji to London and other countries.

Raj Bhavan
June 3 1956

Usha

Your letter of the 2nd has just come.

Do write to the Oberdorfs. They have invited me to go on a motor trip with them & Kamalnayan Bajaj! If you let them know the dates, they will realise how impossible their proposition is.

What can have happened to the white silk? Have you asked Kali? It can only be in the cupboard in my bedroom or dressing room or in the godown. All keys are with Mrs Atal.

Indira

Raj Niwas
Simla-4
June 18, 1957

Dear Usha,

Thanks for your note.

Please tell Mr Sachdev not to go ahead with the house plans until PM has passed the estimates.

I am under such a tremendous mental strain these days that I doubt if I could find pleasure or rest in anything at all.

Pepi & Madhu are flourishing. Raja Sahib Bhadri is consulting every vet he can lay hands on about Madhu but the verdict is the same.

Love
ING

Raja Sahib Bhadri was Governor of Himachal Pradesh. Pepi and Madhu were the Golden Retrievers of the Nehru family.

Raj Niwas
Simla-4
21.6.57

My dear Usha,

Today is our last day of leisure for tomorrow afternoon we start on the tour which will be hot and dusty and fairly rushed. I wonder how the children will stand it—they have been having food trouble here.

You know how I never move without stacks of books. However this time everything seems to have gone wrong and I am stranded without anything to read. I have written to Amie but will you also send with her the book lent by Elisabeth Gauba. Tell Amie <u>not</u> to bring too many books on delinquents. I can't remember how many I have asked for. One is enough.

The conversation here centres almost entirely on the breeding of cattle and sheep. This is partly because of the Raja Sahib's great interest in the subject and partly because of various conferences on Animal Husbandry. I am so utterly ignorant on the subject that it gives me a proper feeling of humility.

There is a young man from Allahabad whom I would not normally have considered 'my sort' but he has a most remarkable memory and can recite poetry by the hour—it is <u>such</u> a relief after the talk of cows!

We shall probably be back in Delhi by the 14th July. Will you ask the boy's [sic] master to come every day from about the 16th until they go to school. They are both weak in History and Hindi. We will have to have the Hindi man too. Perhaps alternate days or whatever you think best. But do fix it up so as not to waste days on our return.

It is hot here so Delhi must be very bad. The monsoon is delayed by three weeks.

Indira

Mrs Gandhi was on the CSWB (Central Social Welfare Board). Hence the reference to the books on delinquents. The tour also probably was in connection with CSWB.

Jammu Tawi
June 29th '57

My dear Usha,

Thank you for sending the books and papers.

I read the 'Woman of Andros' when I was at school in England & again in jail. Thornton Wilder writes so very beautifully—it is almost poetry and I like reading him aloud for the sound of the sentences. I believe I have read all his books.

The journey from Kangra to Jammu was terribly terribly hot & we are all somewhat in a state of collapse. Kapur was really disappointed that his wife did not come but has decided to go with us.

This trip has been strenuous. We have swallowed quantities of dust. But on the whole it has been fun. The two 'holidays'—one day at Barot & one day at Manali were simply heaven. Manali is quite the most peaceful place on earth. Even Rajiv, who is such an ardent lover of Kashmir, had to concede that it was more beautiful! However they enjoyed Barot most of all because of the excitement of the funicular

This morning we added an item to the programme and visited the Jwalamukhi temple as well as the site of the drilling before leaving Kangra for Jammu. This means that the day began at 5 a.m. instead of the scheduled 7.30! However, it was worth it

For this bright idea we had to thank a young man who accompanied us from Jogindernagar. He is thin as a pin and was constantly making rude remarks about Kapoor's eating! His favourite topic of conversation is suicide! We managed to remain cheerful inspite [sic] of all.

In one of my letters I wrote of mental strain. All the circumstances remain the same and yet at Manali I slipped all burdens off, like a too-warm cloak.

Love
Indu

5.7.57

Usha

Thank you for sending the vests, pullover & ointment. Every thing was just right.

Kashmir is heartbreakingly beautiful. Every side you turn has its own loveliness —'Custom cannot stale its infinite variety.' We have discovered a gem of a place called 'Yus' [also spelled in Hindi]. We went there yesterday inspite [sic] of Sanjay's vigorous protests. 'Of what use is Yus?'

Every rose has its thorn and in Kashmir it's the politics which are [sic] poisoning the atmosphere.

There seem to be hordes of people wherever we go and social welfare institutions keep cropping up like rainy season mushrooms. In sheer desperation we have decided to go to Amarnath. We shall leave Srinagar on the 7th & Pahalgam the next day. Full moon is on the 11th.

The way we are always doing something—we shall be even more tired after the stay in Kashmir!

Love & good wishes,
Indira

Please thank Elisabeth for the books. Unfortunately since I last wrote there has been no time to read & even to write this I have had to get up at 5 a.m.

Guest House No. 1
Srinagar
7th July [1957?]

Dear Usha Aunty,

Thank-you for all that information about the I.G.Y.

Kashmir is very beautiful. Bakshi Sahab insists on us going to Pahalgam. We will be going there for two or three days.

Yours sincerely,
Rajiv

P.S. Everything seems to be going wrong—the Amarnath trip is off. Yesterday I had decided to return to Delhi immediately but as the boys simply would not agree to stay behind for a few days, we have now decided to go to Pahalgam (we are not allowed to go anywhere else). We return on the 13th & will fly to Delhi on the 14th July. Please inform the office & Mrs Atal.

                                                                    ING

The International Geophysical Year (IGY) was celebrated in 1957–58.

                                              [Postcard]
Usha

    This isn't any of us but it could well be. One of our most enjoyable days was the one spent on the lake, swimming, boating & surf-riding. We paid for this with sunburnt back and many oofs and ouchs!
    The Swami who impressed Teji Bachhan so much is here. We all had a session this morning with him. As a result we hope to be healthier, better looking & more intelligent!!

    Love from Rajiv, Sanjay & Indira
    12.7.57—Pahalgam

                                              [Undated]
Usha

    Thank you for your charming card.
    I am sorry this sari is so summery. But 'if winter comes, can spring be far behind?'

                                   ING

Mrs Gandhi is referring to a sari she gave for my birthday.

Raj Bhavan
Calcutta

My dear Usha,

I'm so glad you're going to Mussoorie. It should be lovely just now—especially the Happy Valley side.

I feel such a fool for falling ill just at this time. My temperature has been normal since the day before yesterday but the blood pressure & pulse is so low that the doctor is not allowing me to get up. I hope I can recover by the 3rd.

Give my love to the children. I am so bored all by myself.

Sincerely,
Indira

29.9.57

Raj Bhavan
Calcutta
3-10-57

Usha

Sanjay wants some sweets. Please send him a 2 lbs pkt of Kwality's toffees—he likes the white ones better than the brown.

I am still feeling very groggy & am going to Japan inspite [sic] of advice to the contrary from the doctor & others. If the colder climate does not help me to recuperate, I shall avoid the strenuous part of the programme & will come back with PM.

ING

Prime Minister's House,
New Delhi.
[Undated]

Usha

There is something I have been wanting to say to you for some days but there just hasn't been a leisurely enough moment.

Would you like to go to Madras with us? We are leaving by air on the 10th Jan. and returning on the 24th January. If it doesn't upset any of your plans, I should like you to come. There won't be much work but I want someone to keep an eye on the children if I accompany PM to Pondicherry for a couple of days. Think it over & let me know.

ING

Prime Minister's House,
New Delhi.
[Undated]

Usha

I tried to get Kamaladevi on the phone several times unsuccessfully. I thought I would write but in view of the excitement of the American Embassy I don't think it would be wise for me to put anything down on paper.

Will you please contact her—Kamaladevi. She has already agreed to be on the All India Committee. Would she be willing to help with the Delhi committee? If so, Mrs Asaf Ali would like to meet her. Tell Mrs Asaf Ali also.

ING

Prime Minister's House,
New Delhi.
17.3.58

Usha

This is just to say thank you for all the trouble you are taking over Paul Robeson. If you had ever met him and known what a truly grand person he is, you would realize that he is worth the trouble!

Compared with my Congress tours, this one is a picnic. One day we went to bed at 8.30 p.m. Of course we have to get up rather early.

Every day I discover anew what a strange place this world is and how little we know about it. Aizal is in the Mizo or Lushai Hills. The Lushais are all Christians. They are good looking and gay & have melodious voices. Unfortunately all their songs are based on hymns. They have much in common with the Burmese.

Good wishes & love
Indira

Love to Amie.

Raj Bhavan
Madras
10.12.58

Dear Usha,

I have received both your letters.

What <u>can</u> we do about the L.B.T.? Could Sangeet Natak give part of the money as a loan—that is, of course, if Gul & Marie Seton feel that they will be able to return it after the tour.

I have been feeling terrible—utter exhaustion, headache, occasional giddiness & to top it off, since the day before yesterday, I have unticaria & am looking rather like a boiled lobster, especially the face!

Madras city is one of the loveliest in India but I am afraid the Govt is going all out to ruin it in every possible way. I am depressed about some of the proposed 'improvements'.

ING

Raj Bhavan
Ooty
30.5.59

My dear Usha

This really is a delectable spot. Perfectly beautiful, the grass as green as in England.

There is no need for you to stay in the house but tell Mrs Mathias to keep a special eye on the boys' food. Tell her also that Hanna Reitsch [she was a German aviator] likes *dahi* for breakfast.

I hope Rajiv will spend some time with Hanna. I am sure he will find her interesting.

Please think of more people to invite to Hanna's lecture. It would be too awful if the hall were not full. Hanna might like to see the hall before hand.

What about arrangements for a mike? Kapoor can do this, if it has not already been done by the Max Mueller Bhavan people.

Who are to be ushers? I had suggested members of gliding or flying club. Has Kapoor done anything about this?

All good wishes

Indira

I had told Vimla I would telephone on 5th night. But am leaving Ooty in the afternoon so I do not know if I can phone in the forenoon.

Postcard sent from Afghanistan
Dwellings in Nooristan.
Nangarhar Province.

16.9.59

How nice of you to come to the Airport. This is a much more restful trip than most. Everything that sounds really interesting is too far off for us to visit. We meet the diplomats & the ministers twice a day, visit some beauty spots & eat quantities of heavenly fruit—melons & grapes.

ING

[1959?]

My dear Usha,

I went to Jagatsukh yesterday & met the Republic Day folk dancers team & danced with them again. They were so pleased, it was difficult to get away. By-the-way it is a really lovely place.

What with the dancing & two lots of strenuous exercises, besides riding, every bone in my body is aching today.

Best wishes,
Indira

Jagatsukh is a small village near Manali, Kulu. It used to be the capital of Kulu state at one time. The dance party for the Republic Day Folk Dance Festival in 1958 came from there. I stayed in the village later that year and to learn their folk songs and dances and told Mrs Gandhi about it.

Prime Minister's House,
New Delhi.
[1959]

Usha

So sorry to hear that you are down with 'flu—It leaves one feeling very weak and sorry for oneself. Don't try to get up before you are really well.

Indira

Prime Minister's House,
New Delhi-2.

My dear Usha,

This sari you have given me is really most attractive—I have it on, this morning and am sure to wear it a lot. Thank you so much for it, and for the sweet thought of getting it specially designed.

You were looking lovely last evening—the Kulu dress suits you well.

ING
20.11.59

With every good wish for a year of good health, good humour, good friends & good work!

Love,
ING, Rajiv, Sanjay
1959

A small card for my birthday from mother and sons.

New York
May 20 60

My dear Usha,

Your letter came yesterday—.

Today is the last day of my brief & whirlwind stay in this extraordinary city. I have had a wonderful time—interesting, stimulating, exciting. But now I am ready to come home. There is just so much one can stand. Anyhow I don't feel a vegetable any more, but am eager to be on the go—the question is how to achieve my end.

I started off wanting to write all kinds of things but my mind has wandered off & time is short too for I must bathe & get ready for the first appointment—it is 7:30 a.m.

Love,
Indu

[Postcard]

This is the coolest looking card I could find. I hope it will help your imagination, so that you can feel the breeze & the peace of the snow covered peaks which give birth to the roaring torrents. It's not too cool here, but cool or hot, it is the nearest place to heaven.

Love from us all.

ING
2.7.60

In June 1960, Mrs Gandhi, Feroze and the boys went together to Kashmir for the last time; in September 1960 Feroze died.

Prime Minister's House
New Delhi-11.

Usha dear,

You were kind enough to offer to gather material for my lecture tour—There are going to be four lectures but the most difficult one is 'Our ancient Heritage'. Could you jot down some points?—The subject is such a wide one & it is difficult to know what to say to an American audience.

Indira

Mrs Gandhi went on a lecture tour to the USA in 1962.

Prime Minister's House
New Delhi-11.

Usha

I hope you will excuse me on the 19th. I am so overwrought & depressed these days & hardly sleeping at night. Also the early part of the night is the only time which the boys & I have for a quiet time.

—Indira

The reference is to 19 November, Mrs Gandhi's birthday.

April 20th 1962

My dear Usha,

Letter from Col. Rao & Shastriji—also from Vimla & Aunty Vakil reached me in Birmingham, Alabama yesterday.

I am leaving New York finally on the 29th—staying a day in London & then returning home in first week in May. Could you find out if there is a possibility of PM's coming to London in May?

I see that there is a possibility of a Commonwealth Conference.

I have met some interesting people but I can imagine how dreadful such a tour would have been if one were absolutely alone. It has certainly given me the opportunity of meeting very different kinds of people & seeing out of the way places.

Love to all
Indira

Mrs Gandhi wrote this while on a lecture tour. Col. Rao was a doctor, I think, at the Safdarjang Hospital in Delhi.

Srinagar
12.6.63

Usha dear,

Srinagar is beautiful as always but becoming more & more of a town. We are surrounded by Delhi faces. It is warm (nothing compared to the plains, of course) in the day time.

I have so many dressing gowns & nightdresses but the ones which have come here are torn! However it doesn't matter. I have bought a rather nice dressing gown from Helen. It is a Sanganer print.

Talking of Helen—what about getting some of her things for the NYWF? Apart from the jackets & dressing gowns, she does wonderful things with quite ordinary cotton durries & namdah with just a touch of embroidery, or a fringe or a lining. Kitty [Shiva Rao] spoke to her but very vaguely & Helen does not know what is expected of her. She is understaffed & very busy in the summer season with tourist orders, so if we want her to give things for the Fair we must let her know at once a) What we want b) the quantity c) the sizes. Helen says she cannot choose, someone else has to do so. I have written to Pupul but could you speak to Prem [Bery] or whoever is handling the sales section at the Delhi end.

Helen showed me some coloured pictures of the Lake Palace Hotel at Udaipur. It's rather nice. Decoration by Mrs Contractor.

Thank you for the mail. Keep sending it.—Also the crossword puzzle.

With PM please send (i) Dental floss—it is in the glass over the wash basin (ii) 'jihvi' [tongue-cleaner]—same place.

As soon as you have any news of Rajiv's coming, please send telegram. If he does arrive on the 20th, he had better come up here as soon as possible on the <u>Viscount</u> plane. Not the Dakota. Sanjay & I will either return with PM or stay on until the end of the month.

Tomorrow we go to Gulmarg & stay on until the 17th or 18th, depending on PM's plans. If we decide to stay on longer in Kashmir we shall go to the Gurais (spelling?) Valley for a couple of days on the 29th.

PM was reading a book on Hinduism. If he has finished it, could he bring it for me?

Since you enjoy the heat, there is no point in commiserating with you!

Best wishes

Indira

P.S. In the second right-hand drawer of my writing table, there is a pile of note books. Amongst them, one is very thin, dark blue, stuck together with scotch tape. In it there are Kashmiri phrases written in Devnagari [in Hindi]. Please send. Mrs Atal will have Mrs Madan Rani Atal's address. Please post Pupul's letter.

Helen was Helen Stavrides, a Greek woman who had a boutique in Srinagar. Mrs Gandhi refers to Helen's items for the NYWF (New York World Fair).

New Stanley hotel
P.O. box 75
Delamere Avenue
Nairobi
Kenya Colony
Telephone 27456
15.12.63

Usha dear,

Just a very hurried line.

I shall have to send cards to the members of the Unesco Executive Board. Perhaps you had better have plain cards with greetings for New Year printed—or can you send off the cards received from Unesco with my name typed in? As soon as possible.

Am in terrific rush—just off to airport. Have rotten cold, cough, congested chest & so on. Rajiv & Dinesh Singh have been having a very gay & giddy time with all the balls.

It is quite cold here though Zanzibar was hot & very sticky. The celebrations have been very impressive & well done & also gay. The Africans have a great future before them.

I am very sorry Marie did not come. I think she got het up about nothing.

Love
Indira

Thank Vimla for her cable to Sanjay & give her my greetings.

I think this is when they went to Kenya for the country's independence celebrations.

26.6.63

Usha

Please find out what can be done about this adoption scheme.
We have had a wonderful trek to the Kolahoi glacier. Refreshing.
The magnificence and grandeur of the mountains gives quite a
different perspective to life.

The boys and I may go down to Srinagar today—It is Yunus's
birthday and there are big doings–dances and music on a *doonga*!

> Greetings to all
> Indira

Sent from Kashmir. A doonga is a poor man's house boat.

> Prime Minister's House,
> New Delhi

Usha

This little gift brings my very best wishes. Since you have plenty
of Channel No. 6, I thought some of No. 5 might be more welcome.

Last evening we were talking of opening books—Just now I
opened the birthday book (Shakespeare's) on your birth date, that
is, 30th July. It says:-

> 'Like a bold champion
> I answer the lists,
> Nor ask advice of any other thought
> But faithfulness & courage.'

Isn't it appropriate for you?
May the years bring fulfillment & ever increasing joy in living.

ING

*I had invited Mrs Gandhi and a couple of mutual friends for dinner
sometime in the early 1960s. I referred to the smell emanating from a
drain behind the home as Chanel No. 6. The next morning I received
the above letter.*

Prime Minister's House
New Delhi
March 19, 1980

Dear Usha,

Thank you for your card of greetings on the arrival of the youngest Mr Gandhi. I didn't reply earlier as I thought I would phone, but I have hardly a free moment in the daytime.

We are still stuck for a name.

With good wishes for your many activities.

Yours sincerely,
Indira Gandhi

When Sanjay and Maneka's son was born, I was not working for Mrs Gandhi. Thus I sent Mrs Gandhi a greeting card.

PART III

~

1970−79

~

TWENTY-NINE

THE BANGLADESH WAR

In 1969, after the death of President Zakir Hussain, the simmering differences between the Congress Party stalwarts—the Syndicate—and Mrs Gandhi began to surface, leading to a chain of events such as bank nationalization, the tussle over the election of the new President, and the split in the Congress Party. All these and other factors contributed to a change in the political climate in the country.

Mrs Gandhi was now much less dependent on the senior leaders of the party or the kitchen cabinet and others whom she had needed—and perhaps used—in the early stages of her political career. P.N. Dhar writes:

> The kitchen cabinet was described by her detractors as a shadowy group operating under the shelter of the prime minister. Its existence was looked upon as a symbol of Indira Gandhi's inadequacy rather than as an essential requirement for fulfilling the leadership role which, as prime minister, she was called upon to play.
>
> The struggle for power ended in 1969 when the party split, which brought Indira Gandhi into her own. By then she had disbanded the kitchen cabinet and organized a well-oiled secretariat staffed with an adequate number of aides.[1]

Mrs Gandhi was now in a confident mood and made two trips abroad in 1970.

In June 1970 Mrs Gandhi visited Mauritius where she was received with warmth and affection. During her visit, Sir Seewoosagar Ramgoolam, the Prime Minister, took her to the place where Indian indentured labour used to land in the nineteenth century. In the register, in the list of names, he showed her the name of his grandfather.

[1]P.N. Dhar, *Indira Gandhi, the 'Emergency' and Indian Democracy*, p. 134.

Mrs Gandhi also laid the foundation stone of the Mahatma Gandhi Institute. Because of the close cultural affinity between the two countries, a cultural troupe went with us to perform in Mauritius.

In October 1970 Mrs Gandhi went to New York to attend the twenty-fifth anniversary of the United Nations. The Indian delegation was large, consisting of ministers, high-ranking officials, and others. Mrs Gandhi also included Mrs Nandini Satpathy, a minister in her cabinet. She was concerned about the wardrobe and other details of Mrs Satpathy, and asked me to help her in this matter. I felt embarrassed and only spoke to her on the telephone, suggesting the woollens and other items she should take. Besides her usual engagements, Mrs Gandhi found time to meet intellectuals, journalists and artists and also to visit the theatre.

The overwhelming results of the elections in 1971 further boosted Mrs Gandhi's morale. P.N. Dhar writes:

> Her landslide victory in the general elections of 1971 brought her to the top of the political pyramid and gave her the confidence to assume the mien and manner of a confident leader.[2]

The above assessment seems true. After the Bangladesh war, when Mrs Gandhi was at the peak of her power, I think she gradually started depending less on people of calibre and more on lesser minds. Perhaps she found such people comfortable who were ready to comply with her wishes. Sycophancy started to surround her. I was reminded of a remark I had made to a friend when Mrs Gandhi became the Prime Minister. I had said that a lot would depend on not only the kind of people she encouraged, but also the kind she discouraged (as they are like hardy weeds which refuse to get uprooted easily).

Meanwhile, the situation in East Pakistan was becoming grim and in 1971 it started worsening, leading to a large influx of refugees into the country and increasing burdens and tensions. Besides the steps being taken to meet the challenge, Mrs Gandhi also felt it necessary to personally brief the leaders of the important Western nations

[2]P.N. Dhar, *Indira Gandhi, the 'Emergency' and Indian Democracy*, p. 134.

about the dangerous situation on the Indian border and its fallout on the country. She went to the USSR in September and on 4 October 1971 she left on a tour which took her to Belgium, Austria, the United Kingdom, the United States (where she had a frosty encounter with Mr Nixon), France, and Germany.

In addition to her official engagements, Mrs Gandhi was able to find time in London to see Igor Stravinksy's ballet *Rites of Spring* starring Rudolf Nureyev and the play *West of Suez* by John Osborne; in New York she attended a concert by the New York Philharmonic Orchestra; in Vienna she saw Beethoven's opera *Fidelio* and also visited the Spanish Riding School. In Paris Jean Riboud and his Bengali wife, Krishna, invited Mrs Gandhi to their artistic house for a get-together with interesting people, amongst whom were the artist Joan Miro, Langlois (head of la Cinémathèque Française), and Francois Mitterand whom Jean Riboud knew from the time when they were both in the French resistance during World War II and who later became the president of France.

According to Dom Moraes, in her talks with the political leaders of the countries she visited, Mrs Gandhi commented,

> It was genocide [in East Pakistan] and must be stopped. The implication was that though India wanted peace, she was prepared for war—she had furnished them with a background against which to interpret her subsequent actions. Now, she could turn her full attention to the matter immediately at hand.[3]

She returned to India about three weeks before the Bangladesh war began on 3 December.

On 3 December 1971 Mrs Gandhi went to Calcutta, where she was to speak at a public meeting at the Maidan and return in the evening. A meeting with some intellectuals (writers, theatre and film people) had also been arranged at the Raj Bhavan at 4.30 p.m. Around 3.00 p.m. Mrs Gandhi left for the public meeting. As she was delayed, I had to look after the people who had arrived for the 4.30 p.m.

[3]Dom Moraes, *Indira Gandhi*, p. 188.

199

meeting. Of those who attended I only remember Uttam Kumar, the Bengali matinee idol. Mrs Gandhi rushed back with S.S. Ray, the Chief Minister; Mr Dias, the Governor, also joined them. They sat down and an interesting conversation began between Mrs Gandhi and the writers and others. I took down a few points which were raised during the discussion, such as the cess of 5-10 paise on film tickets; processing facilities for colour films; employment and incentives for technicians; to form a cell to discuss and formulate ideas, to set up a cultural complex, and to utilize creative people.

In reply to a question Mrs Gandhi said that being the prime minister was not a burden if one acts and feels natural. With the Bangladesh war looming ahead, I remember her saying that what worried her was the glamour of war. She said that she found that those who had the glamour were not those who could take the war. She mentioned that the war in England (she had been there in the early years of World War II) had changed the spirit of the people as well as their health. People had also developed a taste for good music as at lunchtime the best musicians performed in public parks to ease the tension.

While she was speaking, Mr B.N. Tandon, Joint Secretary in the Prime Minister's Secretariat, who was sitting beside me, went out. In a few minutes he was back and passed me a small slip of paper which said: 'Pakistan bombs Srinagar, Pathankot and Amritsar airports.' I looked at him aghast. We hesitated to break the news at once. I remember at that time Mrs Gandhi was saying how on seeing anything beautiful, even a small leaf, she could immediately shed her tiredness. It all seemed very surrealistic. In a few minutes the meeting ended and she was shown the slip. There was no outward reaction.

In the meantime General Jagjit Singh Aurora arrived and was closetted with the Prime Minister. Thereafter we left for the airport. People in Calcutta, however, were unaware of what had happened and we saw the usual traffic and brightly lit roads and shops. When we entered the airport, there was a complete blackout. We sat in the plane for quite some time (perhaps escort planes were being arranged). I was not sure where or when we would land, but eventually it was New

Delhi, completely blacked out. There were only three or four people to receive Mrs Gandhi, and straight from the airport she rushed to attend a cabinet meeting. She made a midnight broadcast saying that the war had been forced on India and appealed to the nation to face the challenge valiantly. According to General Manekshaw, India was all poised to attack in the early hours of 4 December but by attacking on the evening of 3 December Pakistan took the onus of starting the war on itself.

The next day, that is, 4 December, while eating lunch Mrs Gandhi mentioned that while returning from Calcutta she had been reading Thor Heyerdahl's book on the 'Ra' expedition. I was quite amazed at the composure with which she was handling the crisis situation. Even when the war was raging, I saw her rearranging flowers in the vase before leaving for office. Perhaps it helped her to relax and rearrange her mind.

A noting I had made on 7 December 1971 is as follows:

> PM came back in the evening, took interest in presents for Sonia for her birthday on the 9th. We made a list of items of birthday presents as well as presents for X'mas. Also presents for Sanjay for his birthday on the 14th.
>
> Later in the evening, somebody came to see her, I presume Nandaji brought some astrologer. At 9 p.m. when we (Rajiv, Sonia and I) were listening to the news in the dining room, she walked in, had a peculiar expression, not worried in the usual sense, but I think she was. Then she said that 'all the Pandits seem to say that we are going to have hell till February'. May be this thought was disturbing her.

Mrs Gandhi was also concerned that not knowing the fate of the war, how the Republic Day celebrations would be held. I had noticed earlier also that when a crisis confronted her, her mind did not get bogged down and she looked ahead. A few people were invited, including E. Alkazi, Director, National School of Drama and Shanta Gandhi, Director, Bal Bhavan, to discuss the matter. It was decided that as the military parade down Rajpath would not be possible, celebrations should be held at the Vijay Chowk, and a special programme of spectacles with children and artists was devised. Although the war ended pretty soon, the planned form was adhered to for the 1972 Republic Day.

On 6 December Mrs Gandhi announced the recognition of an independent Bangladesh in Parliament. The decision of the United States to move its Seventh Fleet to the Bay of Bengal angered her. Rather than reacting diplomatically, she chose to express her ire publicly. She addressed a huge rally at noon at the Ramlila Grounds, accepting the challenge and expressing India's defiance of the US policy of intimidation. I remember how her speech aroused the people. Fortunately, the war ended soon thereafter and the Pakistan Army surrendered on 16 December. Though Mrs Gandhi must have been immensely relieved and no doubt felt satisfied with the outcome, outwardly she behaved normally, and birthdays and Christmas were celebrated as usual.

How her mind worked on 16 December is well illustrated in her own words:

> I was giving an interview to a Swedish T.V. team when the first news of the surrender came . . . As the interview proceeded, I was getting the information in bits and pieces. In the middle of it I had to go and meet the General [Manekshaw] who was in the next room to give me a report. I went back and answered two questions [to the T.V. team]. Then I made a statement in the Parliament. I came back and answered two more questions. Later I recorded a statement for the radio . . . While giving the interview, I was making up my mind—what to do and how. I think that being able to do several things at once without any tension is one of my main assets.[4]

Regarding the outcome of the war, it has been aptly stated:

> In delivering a decisive military victory, she had restored the national pride, so damaged by the 1962 Indo-Chinese debacle.[5]

Professor P. Lal, poet and the person behind the Writers Workshop in Calcutta, who has also transcreated the Mahabharata, in his letter dated 16 December 1971 to me wrote:

[4]Indira Gandhi, *My Truth*, p. 156.
[5]Jad Adams and Phillip Whitehead, *The Dynasty*, p. 239.

Pal

16 DECEMBER 1971

Usha-devi:

Please convey to Sm
Indira Gandhi my gratitude
& pride — gratitude for the
exemplary manner in which
she has led us during this
critical fortnight, & pride
because somehow, suddenly, I
feel more Indian. I have
always felt very Indian —
now I'm bursting, along
with the rest of my family!

162/92 Lake Gardens: Calcutta 45: Telephone 46-8325

He wrote further:

> I've just come to the 'sloka' in the Vana-Parva [of the Mahabharata] where Draupadi scolds Yudhishtra for unprotestingly accepting exile: [thus]
>
> > 'The Ksatriya who doesn't show courageous anger at the right time is scorned by everyone.'
>
> Please thank Sm. Gandhi for showing courageous anger at the right time.

She was no doubt the heroine of the saga of the Bangladesh war.

Mrs Gandhi and late M.S.
Subbulakshmi, the
well-known Carnatic singer
(Photo courtesy *The Hindu*
Photo Archives, © Kasturi
and Sons Ltd.)

Mrs Gandhi with the
author at an exhibition of
Madhubani paintings

Mrs Gandhi with her pet Golden Retrievers, Putli and
Pepita, at 1 Safdarjang Road, 1969

Mrs Gandhi with tribal dancers from Bihar in Teen Murti
House, Delhi, c. 1956

Mrs Gandhi against the Alps in Switzerland, 1981

Mrs Gandhi at the Presidential Palace in Rome, 1981

Mrs Gandhi in
Rabindranath
Tagore's room in
Shantiniketan

Mrs Gandhi with the autumn
colours she loved in Tallin,
Estonia, 1982

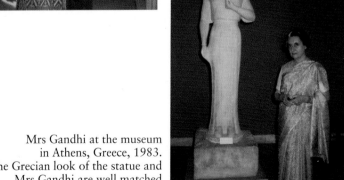

Mrs Gandhi at the museum
in Athens, Greece, 1983.
The Grecian look of the statue and
Mrs Gandhi are well matched

Mrs Gandhi looking for shells in the Andaman and Nicobar Islands, 1981 (Photo courtesy Photo Division)

Mrs Gandhi relaxing in the hotel in Tokyo, 1982

Mrs Gandhi with Varun and
Priyanka (wearing the mask) on
Christmas 1981

Mrs Gandhi, Sonia Gandhi,
Rahul and Priyanka in
Hawaii, 1982

Mrs Gandhi and family
with the King and
Queen of Spain in Delhi,
January 1982

Mrs Gandhi with Marie Seton, Pamela Cullen and Sonia
Gandhi in London, 1983

Mrs Gandhi with Dorothy Norman in New York, 1983

Mrs Gandhi with Melina
Mercouri, Greek minister
of culture and film actress,
at the amphitheatre in
Epidaurus in Greece, 1983

Mrs Gandhi and the author at the Parthenon in
Athens, Greece, 1983

~

THIRTY

SHEIKH MUJIB-UR-RAHMAN

After the Bangladesh war, when Sheikh Mujib-ur-Rahman was released from the Pakistan prison, he first went to London. On his flight to Dhaka, he stopped at the Delhi airport on 10 January 1972. He was a hero to many, including me. I found the following notes that I had made on the occasion of his visit to Delhi:

10.01.1972

This morning went to Palam Airport. Sheikh Mujib-ur-Rahman was arriving from London—after his release from Pakistan—passing through Delhi to Dhaka.

Miss Naidu and I followed Prime Minister's car. Rajiv and Sonia (expecting any day) went in Prime Minister's car. (Priyanka was born two days later).

At the airport, it was bitterly cold. The plane came at 8 a.m. Sheikh emerged looking lean in the face. He is tall.

The reception was formal which I thought constricted the atmosphere and the people's warmth (which there is in abundance), could not come through to the extent it should have.

He was a little nervous which only showed in the hands—put them in the pocket—took them out, etc. He peered over President Giri's address when he was reading it. He did not know all the formalities and had to be guided a little. He has a strong yet a gentle face.

From Airport, we went to the Parade ground for the meeting. He started to speak in English, but was asked to speak in Bengali. Then we followed the motorcade back to the airport. Crowds were not as much as one would have expected. May be it was too early and too cold.

On our return to the Prime Minister's House, Mrs Gandhi mentioned that Sheikh Mujib-ur-Rahman's imprisonment and its end reminded her of Fidelio (we had seen Beethoven's opera recently in Vienna, in 1971). She also said that Mujib-ur-Rahman had mentioned that Bhutto was popular in West Pakistan. Later she remarked that she hoped he would not be difficult with us. I asked, 'Bhutto?' She replied, 'No. Mujib.' I was surprised. She said that he still thought along old lines but that so much had happened since then. The question was of getting along with all sections and recognizing the need to bridge gaps. She mentioned [Maulana] Bhashani and others. She did not seem sure whether Mujib-ur-Rahman would be able to carry all of them with him.

In March 1972 Mrs Gandhi visited the newly formed Bangladesh at the invitation of Sheikh Mujib-ur-Rahman. It was an emotional visit, and what made the occasion even more celebratory was that we were there during the birthday of the Banga bandhu.

Mrs Gandhi also met some intellectuals; a few amongst them were those whose names had earlier been published as having been killed by the Pakistani *junta*, but who had evidently survived.

I had jotted down some points of the discussion:

Dhaka, 1972

Prime Minister said that 'in any struggle, it is the intellectuals who give a thrust.'

Question: How do you feel in Dhaka, victory of troops, elections and over minds of people of Bangladesh?

Answer: Mixed. It is not my victory.

Q. Calcutta is a doomed city. Reactions.
A. These are western phrases. Explained how Western nations spoke about India. Planning etc. Calcutta has many problems. Has not got over the problems of Partition.
Q. In May and June 1971, why didn't you give recognition?
A. World had to be prepared. Not ready for it.
Q. Some people feel here that we got liberation too early.
A. Liberation is never too early.
Q. Language problem. We lost a number of professors and some migrated to India early. What do you think of asking them to come here.
A. Your problem.

Q. Now artificial curtain is over, if a joint survey of art and architecture of this region (can lead to) an exchange of scholars.

A. Very good idea. Architects should pay attention to local material and needs of rural housing.

Q. I suggest cultural exchange should not be on official level.

A. Agreed. Govt. blamed—even (if) opposition not strong—it is the blame of Govt.

Q. What made you help our lost identity?

A. No doubt in my mind Bangladesh will be liberated.

Q. You said our suffering has enriched the world, how?

A. Any deep experience enriches the world. In west, such ideals materialistic—lack of values creating problems.

Q. What in your judgement have you inherited from your father?

A. One learns from so many people. Brought-up in atmosphere of ideas and ideals.

Q. What is the secret of your success?

A. Because I am not concerned about success. To do right is more important.

Q. What strength from Tagore?

A. Was very short time there (Shantiniketan). He reinforced ideals of . . . gave another dimension-cultural, (earlier) I had been in political atmosphere.

Q. Do you pray?

A. Many ways of prayers.

Prime Minister also said biggest mistakes made—not to change education and administration. Impressed by Illich de-schooling. Education should be continuing process. In west, intelligence equated with literacy.

Q. Bangladesh and India both profess in secularism. Are we doing enough to see that it is going down to the roots?

A. More important than religion is economics.

We were also taken down Meghana river for talks and lunch during the boat ride.

Towards the end of 1971, when the struggle and trouble in East Pakistan was looming large and casting dark shadows on India, I happened to see some films directed by Ritwik Ghatak. Ghatak came as a refugee from East Bengal. Being young and sensitive, he was traumatized by the Partition and its effects on the Bengali people, especially those who came as refugees. He made some films depicting their pathos. I saw two of them, part of a trilogy, *Meghe Dhaka Tara* (1960) and *Subarnarekha* (1965), as well as his classic *Ajantrik* (1958). I was very moved by his films. Unlike Ray's films which were beautiful and well crafted but had a certain detachment, the emotional intensity of Ghatak's films touched one's core.

Soon after I saw the films, when the Republic Day Awards were being considered, I suggested Ghatak's name and the Prime Minister included it. When the awards were announced, questions were raised in Parliament about Ghatak receiving the Padma Shri. The objections were due to the film maker's political leanings which were leftist and pro-Communist. I had neither known him nor his political background when I had recommended his name, and felt bad at having embarrassed the Prime Minister. I was sure I would be reprimanded, but Mrs Gandhi did not say a word. On the other hand, she defended the decision in Parliament. I was impressed and thought that the way she handled the matter conveyed the quality of self-assuredness necessary for a prime minister.

This was in early 1972, soon after the Bangladesh war, which must have stirred Ghatak since he was himself a refugee from East Bengal. Ghatak, I think, was so touched by the official recognition that he arrived in Delhi soon afterwards. He came to meet me. He was a tall and lean man, simple and almost childlike. One had heard of his eccentricities and drinking habit which may have helped in sparking his creativity but also led to the gradual disintegration of his health and work.

He also met Mr P.N. Haksar, Secretary to the Prime Minister, who was charmed by him. Ghatak expressed a desire to make a film on Mrs Gandhi without intruding on her. I think he even took one or two shots quietly in the driveway of the Prime Minister's House. As Mrs Gandhi was going to meet Sheikh Mujib-ur-Rahman in Calcutta, a ride with her in the plane was arranged in order to cover that event. But after getting out of the plane in Calcutta he disappeared and the idea remained where it was. He did make another film, *Titash Ekti Nadir Naam* (1973), in Bangladesh after this but drank himself to death in 1976 at the age of fifty.

THIRTY-ONE

THE SHIMLA ACCORD

In June 1972 Mrs Gandhi went to Sweden where she addressed the UN Conference on Human Environment. The awareness regarding the environment had begun to grow although it had always been close to her heart. She worked hard and carefully on the speech and it drew appreciation; the state visit followed. Mr Olaf Palme was then the Prime Minister. It was interesting to learn that he used to go to his office on a bicycle. The King hosted a lunch at his summer palace, Sofiano Palace, from where, across the sea, Denmark and the famous Elsinore Castle (of *Hamlet* fame) were visible. Due to my involvement with the film society movement in India and interest in the folk arts, I found time to visit the Swedish Film Institute and Skansen, the first open-air folk museum in the world, in Stockholm. From Stockholm, Mrs Gandhi went to the beautiful old city of Prague in Czechoslovakia. The love and care with which it has been preserved was impressive. Not one stone could be changed without permission. Mrs Gandhi attended a performance of *The Bartered Bride*, a comic opera by the great nineteenth-century Bohemian composer Smetana, and also visited the Magic Lantern theatre, an innovative audiovisual show, a mixture of cinema and theatre, created by Professor Jaroslav Fric. He later created the glass pathway at 1 Safdarjang Road which covers the path on which Mrs Gandhi was walking when she was shot.

The last stop was the beautiful city of Budapest in Hungary— Buda and Pest are situated on either side of the banks of the Danube. Mrs Gandhi also went to Lake Balaton where Tagore had stayed for a few days in 1924 and she planted a tree near the bust of the poet on the banks of the lake. She met some Hungarian intellectuals and saw a performance by a folk dance ensemble. I took the opportunity of visiting the Hungarian Academy of Sciences and the Ethnographic

Museum to see and learn more about the work of Zoltán Kodály and Béla Bartók regarding the documentation of Hungarian folk music. My interest in folk arts and crafts received an impetus while working with Mrs Gandhi.

On the flight back from Europe, Mrs Gandhi told me that I would have to accompany her to Shimla where the meeting with Zulfikar Ali Bhutto, Prime Minister of Pakistan, was to be held to settle the matters after the Bangladesh war. We reached Shimla on 30 June, a day before Bhutto's arrival, and were received by Dr Y.S. Parmar, the Chief Minister. An hour or so after our arrival at 'The Retreat' in Mashobra where we were staying, Mrs Gandhi told me to accompany her to see the place where Bhutto would be staying. We drove to the sprawling Himachal Bhavan.

Then followed a marathon session of rearrangement of furniture, etc. in the different rooms. Dr Parmar had thought that the Prime Minister would take a quick look around and come away, but Mrs Gandhi was very dissatisfied. The furniture had been kept in a slipshod manner, the colours of the upholstery did not match, and the curtains were often a foot higher than the floor. There was not much one could do at this late stage but Mrs Gandhi and I started to get the things shifted from here and there and to make the best use of what was available. Dr Parmar and the Chief of Protocol, Mehboob Ahmed, followed us around with consternation writ large on their faces. We went to the Chief Minister's house and got a few things from there, including his bed. We went to Raj Bhavan and picked up certain objects, including a deep-red raw silk bedspread. Mrs Gandhi asked me to speak to Rashtrapati Bhavan in New Delhi, asking them to send silver writing sets and stationery in the morning. We had started our work at around 5.00 p.m. and reached 'The Retreat' around 11.00 p.m. There had been no time to have tea or eat anything. Dr Parmar, I learnt, told someone later that his government had tried to do their best but the Prime Minister had international standards, which of course was true. The next day Mr Bhutto arrived accompanied by his daughter Benazir. I wonder if they realized the effort put in by Mrs Gandhi personally to make their place of stay somewhat better.

A similar exercise, though on a much smaller scale, took place in London in October 1983. We had stopped for a day on our way back from New York where Mrs Gandhi had gone to attend the UN General Assembly. The Commonwealth Prime Ministers Meeting was to be held in New Delhi in November. Queen Elizabeth II had been invited by the Indian High Commissioner for a meal before going on to New Delhi. When we visited the residence of the High Commissioner in Kensington, Mrs Gandhi spent an hour or two making the drawing room and the dining room more presentable and gave instructions about other changes to be made. In a way, Mrs Gandhi quite enjoyed these exercises and had once mentioned her desire to have been an interior designer.

While Mrs Gandhi and Mr Bhutto were busy with their talks, Veena Dutta (Sikri), a probationer in the Ministry of External Affairs who was attached to Benazir, and I took the young daughter of the Pakistani Prime Minister around sightseeing and to a craft bazaar arranged for her. I found Benazir not particularly exciting. She was lanky, rather gawky, and wore odd clothes. (It is said that she later improved her looks through plastic surgery.) She was then studying in the United States, at Harvard University, and later joined Oxford University. She must have had an academic and political bent of mind because after the Bhuttos left, I found a slip of paper in Benazir's room on which she had noted the names of the following books:

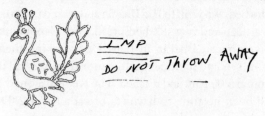

IMP
DO NOT THROW AWAY

Asia Book House:
Verghese: An End To Confrontation.
Subrahmanyam: The Liberation War.
Naik: India, Russia, China And Bangladesh.
Dalvi! Himalayan Blunder.

MULLIK: MY YEARS WITH NEHRU: THE
CHINESE BETRAYAL

MANKEKAR: PAKISTAN CUT TO SIZE.

MODEL BOOK SHOP:
DILIP MUKERJEE: Z.A.Bhutto— Quest for Power

Perhaps she took some of them from here for herself or her father.

The official talks between the two leaders and their delegations were going through rough weather and they almost parted on the afternoon of 2 July. Bhutto was returning on the morning of 3 July. He asked to see Mrs Gandhi personally and I remember him coming to 'The Retreat' in the evening. That night he was giving a return dinner at Himachal Bhavan where he was staying. I came across a note I had jotted down regarding the dinner, where the historic Shimla Accord was signed:

'The Retreat, Simla'   3.7.72
                                        1.15 a.m.

Have just returned from the historic meeting in the Himachal Bhavan.

Reached there at 8.30 p.m. for dinner. As soon as the dessert was finished, PM and Bhutto got up—everybody got up but realizing that they have gone for talks, then sat down. Soon after, Chavan, Jagjivan Ram and Fakhruddin Ahmed got up to join PM. After sometime, we went in the next room and gradually all the other guests were sent home, and only Pakistanis and Prime Minister's party remained. Soon the press started arriving. Mr Haksar came out of talks quite delighted and word started spreading—agreement has been reached. We started making frantic arrangements—two good chairs were brought out—a table was pulled out of a Pakistani guest's room. A sheet was arranged—was pink, damask— quickly got it ironed. Protocol arranged for the silver writing sets and small flags. We removed furniture from behind—put a vase of yellow foliage on a table behind—under President Giri's picture.

Big excitement—all press people, T.V. cameras, etc. huddled in front of the tables. Mr Haksar in great form. Everybody's nerves quite on edge.

Prime Minister and Bhutto entered room at about 12.30—there was clapping. Both looked quite serious. Signing took 5 minutes. We went straight to the car and back to The Retreat.

On way back PM talked a little—said they wanted to bring in U.N. in the withdrawal but they finally agreed to omit U.N., etc. She said Jan Sangh will hold rallies regarding withdrawal but that may strengthen our hands regarding Kashmir. She referred to Bhutto as basically a cold person and that is why he has to act theatrical.

A remark attributed to me by an author, 'Is it a boy or a girl?', when Mrs Gandhi and Bhutto came out after the meeting to indicate the success or otherwise of the talks, is absolutely false. I am not so brazen and gender-biased as to make such a silly remark.

In 1973, a meeting of the Non-Aligned nations was held in Algiers. Mrs Gandhi attended it and the participants were accommodated in villas in the suburbs of the city. Amongst the others, the colourful Libyan leader Colonel Muammar Gaddafi was present and so also was Idi Amin, who shortly before had thrown out the Indians from Uganda. In Algiers, he exerted a lot of pressure to meet Mrs Gandhi. Finally that hulk of a figure arrived, looking coy, as if butter would not melt in his mouth, accompanied by his retinue, which included a Sikh doctor and his wife, to impress Mrs Gandhi.

In April 1974 Mrs Gandhi visited Iran at the invitation of the Shah. One did not know then that he would be removed from the scene so soon. Tehran seemed to be a pretty modern city and the women were dressed in chic Western clothes. It was amazing how the smartly dressed women disappeared under the chador soon after!

Mrs Gandhi told me in Delhi that after the Shah's dinner the Iranians would be presenting a cultural programme and she suggested that perhaps we should also take a small cultural troupe. We quickly made arrangements to take with us Sonal Mansingh, Durga Lal, Madhavi Mudgal, and a Manipuri dance troupe. They performed after the Iranian programme at the banquet.

A visit to the beautiful city of Isfahan was also included in the itinerary.

In January 1975 Mrs Gandhi visited Iraq. Besides Baghdad, she also visited Mosul in the north. I was able to visit the Baghdad Museum and was impressed to see wonderful objects and artifacts of civilizations much older than India's. Unfortunately, much of this remarkable collection has been looted and destroyed in the recent war in Iraq.

In January Mrs Gandhi also went to the Maldives, which means—and indeed is—a 'garland of islands'.

In the seventies, Prince Charles came to India for the first time with Lord Mountbatten, who perhaps wanted to introduce the prince to India as he knew it. Mrs Gandhi hosted a lunch for the prince in the Mughal Garden of Rashtrapati Bhavan and invited young, interesting people to interact with him.

On his second visit in the early eighties, Prince Charles came alone. Mrs Gandhi invited him for a small family lunch at her house. Prince Charles had written as well as illustrated a couple of children's books, especially, I think, for his younger brother Prince Edward. He had brought copies of the book for Rahul and Priyanka. When all of them came out to the garden for coffee, the prince began to inscribe the copies for the children. Looking over his shoulder, when I commented, 'A very assured handwriting', the prince turned around with an incredulous look and said, 'Is it?' I was amused and somehow got the impression that he was not so sure of himself.

~

THIRTY-TWO

SANJAY AND MANEKA

After finishing his studies at the Doon School, Rajiv went to England for further studies and Sanjay was left alone at the school. However, due to a lack of adjustment and other problems he returned to Delhi without finishing his studies. Mrs Gandhi sent me to one or two schools in Delhi to make enquiries and Sanjay joined St. Columba's to complete his studies. After passing out, he was not keen on pursuing further academic studies, and as he had always been interested in cars, he went to study automobile engineering with the Rolls-Royce company at Crewe in England. He did not complete the five-year-long course as he felt that he had learnt the practical engineering part and the rest of the course was of no particular use to him. So he returned to India after three years.

On his return, I tried to interest him in other activities before he became involved in his car project. I thought rhythm might interest him and persuaded him to learn the *tabla* and arranged for a teacher. I think there were only a couple of lessons. Later the *tabla*s were being used as peg-tables in his room. I took him once to a private recital of Pandit Bhimsen Joshi's singing and another time to a screening of Canadian documentary films. But I do not think he was basically interested in all this.

Earlier Rajiv and Sanjay had been apolitical, or at least it seemed so. Politics were never discussed at meal times. However, a change began to take place when criticism regarding Sanjay's Maruti project started building up. One is not sure if he would have become active in politics if this had not happened. Perhaps Sanjay felt it necessary to counteract the criticism through political means. For his car project he needed help, financially and in other ways. He could not deal in such matters, nor could he approach officers directly. The person who came to his rescue was R.K. Dhawan. At that time he did not have much work, and perhaps it was a good opportunity for him to start cultivating Sanjay. He would ring up industrialists and others from the Prime Minister's House and they would come running as they were only too willing to oblige. They may have thought that the Prime Minister herself was taking an interest in these matters. However, I am sure she was quite unaware of all this. Along with the fortunes of Maruti, Dhawan's importance also started rising. Soon he started to be of use in other family matters and personal errands. He was efficient and would get things done. His name started to be mentioned at meal times and perhaps Mrs Gandhi gradually became aware of his existence and his efficiency. The process was very slow. Till then Kapoor had been handling political matters. He had political ambitions, and when he became an M.P., the void left by him gradually started to be filled by Dhawan. This process was accelerated only during the Emergency.

Sanjay used to be out the whole day from early morning till late evening. He was then working in his workshop, near Roshanara Gardens in Old Delhi. Sometimes he would bring a girl-friend. Before he started dating Maneka, I had jokingly told him one day that what he needed was a sardarni (Sikh woman). When Maneka came into the picture, I was not aware that she was from a Sikh family. When the matter became serious and I knew who she was, I teased Sanjay saying that I did not know he would take me so seriously. He retorted that after all I had been his 'guru'! (I wish he had considered me guru in other matters too!)

When the marriage date was to be fixed, Mrs Gandhi came to know that Maneka was not yet eighteen. She said she was not going to break the rules, so the wedding took place a month after Maneka turned eighteen. This time the wedding was held at Mohammad Yunus's home on 23 September 1974. Before Sanjay and Maneka got engaged, information regarding the ambitious and brash nature of Maneka and her family had reached Mrs Gandhi. She must have

217

felt awkward, so no notice was taken of it. Maneka herself has said: 'In my own home we are utterly informal and often brash in dealings with each other. The Gandhis observe decorum.'[1]

When Sanjay was courting Maneka, his spare time was fully devoted to her. After their marriage, he became more involved in political matters and especially after the Emergency he was occupied practically the whole day. Maneka started to feel neglected and restless and would often come to our office to ask Dhawan next door about Sanjay's programme. Sometimes she would sit down in our room to while away her time. Often she would talk about happiness. I knew this was no philosophical quest but revolved around her unhappiness at Sanjay's absence. Once or twice she also mentioned that Sanjay would one day be the prime minister. Maneka was spirited and intelligent, but at the same time she was ambitious and quite immature. Sometimes at meal times she would talk about the books she had read or was then reading, perhaps to impress Mrs Gandhi with her intellectual capacity. It must have been difficult for her to adjust to that household. Later during the Emergency she herself got involved actively in politics along with Sanjay.

[1] Jad Adams and Phillip Whitehead, *The Dynasty*, p. 246.

218

~

THIRTY-THREE

TURBULENT PASSAGES

By 1974, on the domestic front the situation was getting difficult due to economic problems, political turmoil, agitations, and strikes. 'It was altogether the most challenging period in the governance of the country', remarks P.N. Dhar.[1] Perhaps this and a combination of other factors depressed Mrs Gandhi. I came across a note I had written on 13 July 1974:

> Today while going to the electric crematorium to attend Yashodhara (Katju) Bhandari's funeral, prime minister mentioned for the first time that she is getting tired of life.
>
> On return, while eating her lunch, she mentioned that she is leaving instructions as to how to dispose off her body. Said she does not want any funeral, but wants the body to be put in a box and thrown or lowered from a small plane or a helicopter in eternal snows. She said she has had no peace in this life and this way at least will imagine that she will have it after; I said it is more important to have peace in this life. [She] Said that is not in her hands and is not possible. I disagreed.
>
> I said, nobody will agree to the disposal of body that way. Disposing the ashes that way seems possible. She said she doesn't want either to be cremated or buried. I said her way amounts to burial, but she didn't think so.

I wondered why she was in such a mood.

Mrs Gandhi again referred to this subject in the 1980s in her bedroom where Rajiv and Sonia were also present. When Mrs Gandhi saw our amused looks, she remarked with some annoyance that she was not joking.

In March 1975 I accompanied Mrs Gandhi to Madras where she

---

[1] P.N. Dhar, *Indira Gandhi, the 'Emergency' and Indian Democracy*, p. 237.

had gone for a one-day visit. On the return journey, soon after we had finished dinner, the plane was caught in a terrible turbulence and the pilot was trying his best to get the plane out of it. I am quite a coward where physical danger is concerned. I had already had a bad experience in 1966, and was thus very tense; I sat with my eyes closed remembering Him. The ten minutes of turbulence seemed like an hour. I later learnt that Mrs Gandhi had been quietly reading a book during this time. Before getting down I confessed my cowardice to Mrs Gandhi.

One night (in the morning I was to go to Shantivana for Panditji's death anniversary), while sleeping in my house, I suddenly woke up and felt a shadow standing next to my bed. Not sure if I was dreaming, I found myself asking, '*Kaun hai?*' (Who is there?). The next second the figure pounced upon me. I thought he was holding a string or wire in his hands and was going to strangle me. I struggled very hard and was thrown off the bed. The next moment I realized that I was under a rug, the point of a knife at my temple, and was being asked for the keys. There were apparently two men in the room and I believe a third outside. On realizing that the intruders were thieves, I started to tell them where the only key I had was likely to be. But they had gagged me and tied my hands and feet and perhaps could not hear me properly. Perhaps I passed out for a while because I do not know when they left. When I came around, I unwound myself and went to my mother's room across the veranda. My mother shrieked when she saw my dishevelled hair and swollen face. The next night I thought that I should sleep in my own room to get over the fear, but when I saw my mother pale at the idea, I agreed to sleep in her room for the next few days.

When Mrs Gandhi came to know of the incident, she along with Rajiv and Sonia came to see me. The next day she sent me the following letter:

28.5.75
11.30 p.m.

Usha

I am off to Gujarat again at the crack of dawn. My thoughts are with you. We all think that you are a brave girl & have given the lie to your own statement made not so long ago that you are a physical coward! It will take some time to get over the hurt & the shock. Take plenty of rest—not only physically but trying to calm thoughts & feelings.

Love

ING

The purpose of recounting the above incident is to link Mrs Gandhi's letter with the remark I had made in the plane on the return journey from Madras as well as to show her sensitivity and concern.

In early May Padmaja Naidu died. She was almost a part of the Nehru family. She along with her mother Sarojini Naidu were often guests at Anand Bhavan, in Allahabad. Padmasi, as the younger generation called her, had a certain grandeur (Raj Thapar describes her as 'looking like a grand African Queen').[2] She was big in size, and big-hearted too. She was always the centre of attraction due to her personality, humour, and *joie de vivre*. She was a generous person and gave her affection abundantly to everyone. That she had a soft corner for Panditji was well known.

Before giving Anand Bhavan in Allahabad to the nation, Mrs Gandhi sent me and Mr M.V. Rajan, who worked for the Nehru Memorial Fund, to have a look at the place and make an inventory of whatever there was. When I opened the steel cupboard in Panditji's dressing room it was almost empty, except for very few things. Amongst them was a small box with ashes (Kamalaji's or Motilalji's) and a notebook of poems. I could recognize the very flowery handwriting of Padmasi but thought it indiscreet to have a look. Very faithfully, I handed these things to Mrs Gandhi on our return to Delhi.

Padmasi lived alone, and though ailing she preferred a man servant and refused to have a woman helper. In early May she collapsed and was rushed to the hospital. On hearing the news I reached the hospital and was there till her end around 9.00 p.m. The doctor and I were alone in the room when I saw the line on the monitor flatten. Mrs Gandhi was away in Jamaica to attend the Commonwealth Prime

[2]Raj Thapar, *All These Years*, p. 400.

Ministers Conference. When I broke the news to Dr Karan Singh outside the hospital room, he went straight to telephone Mrs Gandhi. Mrs Pandit arrived in a taxi from Dehra Dun.

The body had to be kept for a day or two to await Mrs Gandhi's return. Lekha, Mrs Pandit's daughter, and I draped an orange saree on the body and tried to make Padmasi look as magnificent as she would have liked to. Luckily she died nearly a month and a half before the Emergency was declared. When I met her a few times earlier that year and conveyed my unhappiness about certain things (especially Sanjay), she would smile with sadness and pain in her eyes, but would not say anything.

Padmasi had made Mrs Pandit, Mrs Gandhi, and a relation of hers the executors of her Will. When they met after some time, the task of preparing an inventory of her apparel, jewellery, furniture, and other possessions was given to the lawyer, Mr Rajan, and me. The two men could hardly contribute to the task and used to sit around. I had to wade through her possessions. It was depressing work and the heat of June made it doubly so.

Padmasi used to appear before others immaculately dressed with matching flowers and jewellery. When I started to go through her belongings, I was saddened to see the disarray behind the façade. With no proper help, things were in a very disorganized state. What amazed me most was when I found pieces of jewellery tucked here and there in the drawers of the writing and dressing tables, mixed with papers and other things. It was a painful job and conveyed Padmasi's loneliness and helplessness in her ailing condition.

~

THIRTY-FOUR

THE EMERGENCY

The judgement of the Allahabad High Court in June 1975 which set aside Mrs Gandhi's election in 1971 on grounds of electoral malpractice created a grave crisis. It let to hectic activity in the Prime Minister's House. Many opinions and suggestions must have been discussed. Mrs Gandhi was most vulnerable at this point. There are different perceptions of what may have been going on in her mind. According to Mary Carras:

> She saw her self-respect, the esteem of others for her and all she stood for threatened. Because her sense of personal worth is tied up with her desire to achieve great things for India, the personal threat was perceived as a threat to the achievement of the beneficial national goals to which she was committed . . .[1]

While according to P.N. Dhar:

> At the moment of her supreme political crisis she distrusted everybody except her younger son, Sanjay. He disliked those of his mother's colleagues and aides who had opposed his Maruti car project, or had otherwise not taken him seriously. It so happened that these were the people who he rightly thought would advise his mother to quit office. He knew he would get into serious trouble if his mother were not around to protect him.
> She was blind to his shortcomings. Her concern for Sanjay's future well-being was not an inconsiderable factor in her fateful decision.[2]

He also writes:

> Whether she opted for the Emergency to save herself from loss of power or as shock treatment to bring the country back to sanity is also beside

[1] Mary Carras, *Indira Gandhi*, p. 100.
[2] P.N. Dhar, *Indira Gandhi, the 'Emergency' and Indian Democracy*, p. 261.

the point. The fact remains that both JP and Indira Gandhi, between whom the politics of India was then polarized, failed democracy and betrayed their lack of faith in the rule of law.[3]

There is no doubt regarding the validity of the above perceptions. There may have been other factors too. However, what is important is that at this crucial point, rather than following her own instincts and searching within herself, Mrs Gandhi's insecurity took over and she gave more credence to the opinions of those with lesser minds.

During this period Romesh Thapar rang me up and said that he was very disturbed and wished to meet Mrs Gandhi. I conveyed the message. I happened to be in the dining room when Mrs Gandhi mentioned Romesh's request and asked if she should meet him. 'Yes', said Rajiv mildly. 'Certainly not', Sanjay said categorically. This buttresses the point made above by Mr Dhar.

Earlier there had been a good rapport between Mrs Gandhi and Romesh Thapar, when she used to consult him and ask for suggestions. Over time her need for him reduced and distance also grew between them due to his critical appraisal of Sanjay and later of Mrs Gandhi. Those not happy about his influence, including some in the Prime Minister's Secretariat, also helped in this direction. The trouble with Romesh was that he was too blunt. He did not mince his words and had a low level of tolerance. Even his wife Raj admitted this: 'Romesh's strong language of censure, ... certainly no one would be able to stand for any length of time, however justified.'[4] His friends who were devoted to him, and there were many, knew that he did not take kindly to sham and underneath his explosions and harsh words, there was deep concern, no personal motivation or malice. The relationship between the Thapars and Mrs Gandhi degenerated, and Raj Thapar wrote:

We were wrong. We were wrong in supporting Mrs G as the catalyst— she was not capable of it. History does record catalysts but they were all people who knew what they wanted to do. She doesn't.[5]

[3]P.N. Dhar, *Indira Gandhi, the 'Emergency' and Indian Democracy*, p. 262.
[4]Raj Thapar, *All These Years*, p. 386.
[5]Ibid., p. 386.

Sanjay was very active during this time, and to drum up support for Mrs Gandhi, rallies were being organized near the Prime Minister's House. Our office was very small and also acted as a corridor. One day I.K. Gujral, who was Minister of Information & Broadcasting, walked into our office, summoned by Sanjay, and from the opposite door Sanjay entered. Sanjay was angry and shouted at Gujral about the poor coverage of the support rallies. This disgusting scene took place right in front of my table. The space was so small that it did not allow me to get out, so I had to sit through it as if nothing was happening. Gujral looked embarrassed but did not utter a word. After Sanjay left, we exchanged glances and then with folded hands I looked heavenwards.

Our room leading to the small sitting rooms where Mrs Gandhi or Sanjay met people was often used as a waiting room. One came across a number of people, some known and others unknown. Some years earlier when Mr Haksar was waiting in our room, I enquired how he was; his reply was that he felt like 'Neelkanth'. The reference to Shiva storing poison (in his throat) was, I think, because of Mr Haksar's need to store many things within himself and the burden he felt. A couple of times Mr Haksar told me that I was *bhavuk* (emotional). I replied, 'I am. So what?' His answer was that *bhavuk* people get hurt. I told him that I would rather be *bhavuk* and get hurt than not be *bhavuk* for fear of being hurt.

When the Emergency was declared on 25 June, somebody rang me at 8.30 a.m. at home that the news was on AIR. I could not understand and was bewildered. When I reached the office, I saw K.C. Pant sitting and looking depressed. Then a unit from AIR came to re-record the Hindi speech of the Prime Minister, which she had recorded in the middle of the night. It must have been quickly got ready and the language was obtuse. In the evening there was a telephone call from Pupul Jayakar, from Dorothy Norman's home in New York. As Mrs Gandhi went into her room, Sanjay and I followed her. To the anxious inquiries made, Mrs Gandhi tried to reassure Mrs Jayakar and Dorothy. When we came out of the room, the seriousness of the matter had not sunk into my head properly. I mentioned (as if they did not know) that I heard that some leaders have been arrested. Sanjay said, 'No, no.' Being the first day, perhaps he was a little nervous. In the beginning I reacted in my normal manner and even read out a few critical items and letters which appeared in the newspapers at the dining table. One day Sonia came into my room and told me that perhaps I should refrain from doing so. Perhaps she was concerned for my sake.

The atmosphere had begun to change. There was a lot of coming and going of certain kinds of people. I had my own way of gauging and measuring people, by noticing who entered from where. People like Jagjivan Ram, Swaran Singh, Chavan, and a few others would enter from the main entrance when they came to see the Prime Minister, but some others, the lesser ones, came from the side entrance through 'Dwarpal' Dhawan's office, perhaps after paying their salaams and checking on the mood of the house. We were spectators in our office-cum-corridor and those who entered from the side entrance had to pass through it if they had to meet the Prime Minister or Sanjay.

Seshan, Mrs Gandhi's personal secretary, was becoming gradually marginalized and feeling unhappy. Dhawan's importance was growing. I told Seshan that he should speak to Mrs Gandhi. He shook his head sadly and said it was no use. P.N. Dhar writes about Seshan:

Being a man of exceptional integrity, he was unhappy at what he saw was happening at the PMH [Prime Minister's House]. One day, after a heated argument that he had with Dhawan, he came to me with his letter of resignation. The only reason he stayed on was because I told him that by resigning he would please Dhawan.[6]

However, Dhawan's work was increasing and so also was his confidence, his grin, and his girth. He often used to boast that he was serving the king and not the *baingan* (brinjal). In a colloquial way *baingan* here refers to ordinary people. It reminded me of an operatic comic record we had as children in Lahore:

[6]P.N. Dhar, *Indira Gandhi, the 'Emergency' and Indian Democracy*, p. 320.

Khushamad hi mein amad hai.
Ek din raja ne kaha: baingan bahut achha hai,
Hamne kaha, tabhi to sar pe taj dhara hai.
Ek din raja ne kaha: baingan bahut bura hai.
Hamne kaha: tabhi to nam be-gun dhara hai.
Khushamad hi mein amad hai.

Only sycophancy pays.
One day the king said: The *baingan* is very good.
I said: That is why it has a crown on its head.
On another day the king said: The *baingan* is very bad.
I said: That is why it has the name *be-gun* (without merit).

It was an ode to sycophancy.

During the Emergency, a suggestion was made by someone that the signature tune of AIR should be changed, why I do not know. Pandit Ravi Shankar was assigned the job. When it was ready, he came with the recording to play it before Mrs Gandhi. She came and Sanjay followed her. When the music was played, Sanjay did all the talking, giving his opinion and comments. I was quite appalled, as he had no knowledge of music. What was disturbing was that Mrs Gandhi kept quiet and let Sanjay talk.

~

THIRTY-FIVE

SANJAY TASTES POWER

A lot has been written and said about Mrs Gandhi's relationship with Sanjay, especially during the Emergency. It was often said that Mrs Gandhi had a blind spot for Sanjay and was more attached to him. I had seen Rajiv and Sanjay grow up since their boyhood, at least till they went to study abroad. I cannot remember Mrs Gandhi showing any preference for one or the other. She was a concerned and devoted mother. She was very fond of children and said once or twice that she would have liked to have a large family, perhaps to compensate for her own lonely childhood. The criticism that she was not able to give much time to her children she countered by saying that it is the quality of time that the mother gives which is important rather than the quantity of time. In between her various tours and other engagements, she would always find time to interact with her sons and do things together and build a close bond with them. When Rajiv and Sanjay were in school in Dehra Dun, she wrote to them regularly from wherever she was, almost once a week. Her letters were neither impersonal nor literary and historical like those written by her father to her. They were personal and intimate, seeking to establish a firm emotional bond between them.

Sanjay had been headstrong and impetuous from his childhood. I think problems began to surface when he reached adolescence. Adolescence is difficult for all young people but more so for some. They then need a firmer hand to guide them and only a mother's emotional support and love is not sufficient. This could have affected the boys, especially Sanjay. They were fond of their father and must have missed him, which perhaps led unconsciously to some resentment too. Mrs Gandhi used to be quite worried about Sanjay and the company he kept, as is clear from her letter to me dated 17 October1961:

17.10.61

My dear Usha,

We were twelve hours late but the weather in Frankfurt is so bad that we cannot land, and are going to London direct. This means we shall arrive a little earlier. It was pouring in Geneva too.

Re gifts. We forgot to choose something for Mamie [Eisenhower]— but perhaps it isn't necessary. Ask Mrs P. [Pandit] I think we should include something suitable for Dorothy Norman & Mary Lord. We may or may not give it but it is best to have something. The usual stoles will not do.

I am terribly worried about Sanjay. I do hope he is all right. He has made some friends now but they seem to be rather a blood thirsty lot, mainly interested in pigeon shooting! Sanjay must be encouraged to read in Hindi & English.

In the packet of notes I left with Amie for you, there were one or two notes which were rather torn. I do not know if Amie remembered to check whether they were usable or not before handing them over.

Until Beirut there were only 3 first class passengers. But at Beirut, 28 Saudi Arabians, including women, have got on. They are terribly noisy.

Indira

It was the start of the Maruti project. With its affairs becoming embroiled in controversy, Sanjay started getting worked up and he began to move towards active politics. In an interview given to Mary C. Carras in 1978, Mrs Gandhi had this to say about Sanjay:

He's not basically interested in politics . . . In fact, he wouldn't have been in politics at all but for the criticism and tremendous attack on him. He wanted to stand for Parliament because he felt that only he could reply to the false allegations.[1]

Whether the allegations were false or not is another matter, but it is true that earlier Sanjay had not shown any interest or inclination in politics and neither had Rajiv.

The Emergency and what transpired during that period I still find difficult to comprehend. Sanjay's role is understandable. But Mrs Gandhi was a shrewd, perceptive, and intuitive person. How

[1]Mary Carras, *Indira Gandhi*, p. 250.

229

and why she allowed these qualities to be clouded is an enigma. It seems that the long-term view was sacrificed for the short-term view. There is some substance in what P.N. Dhar writes:

> With all her known strengths, there were points of vulnerability: Sanjay seemed to know them better than anyone else and exploited them most cynically. . . Mrs Gandhi was, in some ways, afraid of her son, at least to the extent of fearing his displeasure.[2]

Having tasted power without any political or historical understanding or experience, Sanjay—with his mix of ideas, idealism, and arrogance—must have thought that it was easy to put things right and in a hurry. It is in this context that Sanjay 'thought his mother a ditherer who would act only when pushed by a person with stronger convictions, or when the circumstances left no alternative'.[3] I think perhaps to a lesser degree Rajiv also later shared this perception.

Mrs Gandhi could be a 'ditherer' and procrastinate in some cases, but she was also an astute and experienced person. So these delays must have been due to the complexity of the problems and her concern regarding the fallout that her decisions might have. Perhaps sometimes it is better to dither than to take quick and cut-and-dry decisions. Her muddling through often had a method.

Mrs Gandhi's style of decision making was her own. She did not take decisions in a hurry and weighed the pros and cons in her mind without disclosing them to others till she had made up her mind. Mary Carras echoes this; she spoke to many of Mrs Gandhi's colleagues and others, who told her that Mrs Gandhi liked to have a series of options and no one would know what she was likely to do. As events developed, one or the other option closed. She would then work up the situation and take the most desirable decision.

Perhaps in the two most tragic decisions of her political career—the Emergency and Operation Blue Star—either Mrs Gandhi was not allowed to take the decisions in her own style or perhaps things moved too fast and left her no alternative.

[2]P.N. Dhar, *Indira Gandhi, the 'Emergency' and Indian Democracy*, pp. 325-30.
[3]Ibid., p. 329.

~

THIRTY-SIX

AN UNHAPPY INTERLUDE

The nature of work was changing and there was hardly any work for people like me. I was also trying to get over the frightening event which occurred at my home in May 1975. I therefore thought that a change of scene would be helpful and asked for leave. That was the first long leave I took and I was out of the country for over two months. Thus I was able to avoid being in the office for that period during the Emergency. When I returned, I found Mrs Gandhi sullen and cold with me for some time. She must have guessed the reason for my long leave. As time went by my feeling of unhappiness due to the lack of work and the atmosphere in the house was I think evident.

In early 1976 I decided to write a short note to Mrs Gandhi. Rather than being critical I took the onus upon myself. My note conveyed something like the following: 'I find myself growing stale and feel that the PM needs a person with a fresher mind and attitude. I would also like to devote some time to music, which I have neglected. Any feeling which persists should be taken note of. Thus I am sharing my feelings with the PM.' Our relationship was never based much on words, for we used to understand each other even without them. I knew that Mrs Gandhi was aware of my unhappiness and would understand the feelings which had prompted me to write the note. Earlier whenever I left a note on her table, she had always responded with a comment, or otherwise with her initials, conveying that she had seen it. This time the note never came back. After a month or so, I met Mr Haksar at the farewell party Satish Gujral gave for his brother, I.K. Gujral, on his being appointed ambassador to the USSR. I mentioned my note to Mr Haksar, observing that I had not received any response. His cryptic reply was: 'You are a good address.' I was not sure what he meant. In my position, one could talk to very few people. When I used to talk to Pupul Jayakar, she used to give a weak smile and hardly say anything.

In the meantime, plans were being drawn up for India's participation in the cultural programme being organized by the Smithsonian Institution in Washington D.C. to observe the United States bicentennial celebrations. I was also on the organizing committee, and the committee decided to send me as the leader of the Indian group of folk artists for the Folk Life Festival to be held in the US capital. I was happy because this provided me an opportunity to do something close to my heart, and also I could be away from an unhappy situation.

After a fortnight in the United States, we went to Canada from where I was due to return to Delhi while the troupe was supposed to go for an extended tour to some European countries. Our high commissioner in Ottawa, Mr U.S. Bajpai, without asking me, sent a message on his own to India requesting that as I was doing a good job as the leader of the troupe, I should be allowed to continue to travel to Europe as well. I am sure this could not have pleased Mrs Gandhi, but nevertheless the permission was given. Thus I was out of the country for over two months. The performances were much appreciated everywhere. It was a wonderful breather for me.

We had not stopped in New York, but while changing our flight to Europe from there, I rang up Dorothy Norman from the airport to say hello. The first remark she made in her deep voice was: 'What about Sanjay?' I tried to reply as best as I could on the telephone.

On my return to Delhi I again faced coldness from Mrs Gandhi and her aloof manner towards me continued. I did not know what to do. But when in January 1977 she announced the elections, I decided to wait till the elections were over before taking any decision. The results of the elections decided my fate as my job, which was co-terminus with that of the Prime Minister, was terminated automatically along with hers.

~

THIRTY-SEVEN

DOROTHY NORMAN

Mrs Gandhi had met Dorothy Norman for the first time in 1949, when she accompanied Panditji on his visit to the United States. Dorothy was a humanist, a champion of civil liberties, and a very warm and generous person. She also had an interest in the arts and literature and thus she knew a large number of people in these fields. Because of their mutual interests and Dorothy's emotional warmth, a very good relationship developed between Mrs Gandhi and Dorothy. She was like a mother, a friend, and an agony aunt to whom Mrs Gandhi could express her feelings and thoughts which she could not to others. Mrs Gandhi herself wrote to Dorothy: 'I can tell you things which I wouldn't dream of telling anyone.' Dorothy Norman visited India in 1950 and 1952. Mrs Gandhi met her whenever she was in the United States. They exchanged warm and affectionate letters for three decades, except between 1976 and 1980.

Given their friendship, Dorothy was very pained at the declaration of the Emergency. Below are excerpts from some of her remarks:

> On June 25, 1975, she [Mrs Gandhi] declared an unprecedented state of internal emergency. The nature of her act shocked defenders of democracy and startled proponents of civil rights. Friends of India and many Indians who had long worked to help in the struggle for freedom could not at first believe the news ... After waiting for ... a reasonable time, we realized with a pang, that the alarming actions were correctly reported. I called a meeting of those perturbed by the Emergency measures. We issued a statement that expressed our concern.[1]

[1]Dorothy Norman, *Indira Gandhi*, p. 148-49.

Some excerpts from the statement:

> We deplore these events, especially in India, because there democracy
> was established after a long struggle for freedom led by some of the
> greatest contemporary exponents of human rights, and also because
> the respect of democratic India for human rights was for so many years
> a beacon light for all newly independent and developing countries ...
> We therefore, call for the restoration of these rights in India.[2]

I am sure that the 'democrat' in Mrs Gandhi, which I believe she
was at her deepest core, must have also been affected. In a letter to
Dorothy dated 19 September 1975 Mrs Gandhi wrote: 'If you can
bear to accept a gift from the "Great Dictator", here is something
which I had kept for you some years ago.'[3]

There was almost no communication between them for five years
and it was resumed only after the tragic death of Sanjay in 1980,
when Dorothy says she wrote to Mrs Gandhi 'as woman to woman
about her loss'. An excerpt from Dorothy's letter dated 6 August 1980:

> It is so long since we have corresponded, at one level I do not quite
> know to whom I am writing; at another level, I am writing to the person
> I did know ...[4]

On 14 September 1980 Mrs Gandhi replied. An excerpt:

> ... you know how fond I have been and have remained of you. And that
> is why the last years I have felt sad. I do not want to enter into controversy.
> The past is over, let it lie, but some things have to be said. The falsehood,
> the persistent malicious campaign of calumny must be refuted. You know
> me well enough to appreciate that I am neither authoritarian nor cold.
> But I am not effusive and perhaps this is misunderstood.[5]

Mrs Gandhi met Dorothy in 1982 during her state visit to the
United States and for the last time in October 1983 when she went
to New York for the General Assembly of the United Nations. On

[2]Dorothy Norman, *Indira Gandhi*, pp. 148–49.
[3]Ibid., p. 149.
[4]Ibid., p. 153.
[5]Ibid., p. 154.

both these occasions Mrs Gandhi found time to have long talks with Dorothy over dinner and lunch. Dorothy accompanied Mrs Gandhi to Puccini's opera *La Boheme*. For lunch Dorothy brought along with her Luise Rainer, the heroine of the film *Good Earth* based on Pearl Buck's story. The last time I met Dorothy was in 1991 in New York, when she was ailing after a stroke. She died three or four years later.

~

THIRTY-EIGHT

A KIND OF FAREWELL

In March 1977 when the election results started coming out, one knew there would be a big setback but it was difficult to believe its actual extent. It seemed unbelievable that the Prime Minister would lose. I had the radio on the entire night of 20 March and could not sleep a wink. On 21 March my duty was in the afternoon. I reached 1 Safdarjang Road around lunch time. Our office was next to the dining room. I did not know how to face the situation and what to say. I decided just to walk in. As I entered, Mrs Gandhi was sitting at the table facing me. Realizing my predicament and to cover the embarrassment, she smiled and said, 'Usha, you must return the fat lady.' I was taken aback and asked, 'Fat lady?' She replied, 'Yes. The fat lady which was taken on loan from the National Museum.' A couple of years earlier she had been keen to have a sculpture in the drawing room. We made inquiries at the National Museum and were told that they might be able to loan a not particularly valuable piece from their collection. I went to the Museum and from their storage in the basement I selected a headless and footless torso of a voluptuous lady of the Pala period, which was loaned with a proper receipt, etc. Mrs Gandhi was referring to that sculpture. I knew that these remarks were made to lighten the grim situation. This was just like her.

In the days to come all of us began sorting out things and getting ready for the move to 12 Willingdon Crescent. One day when a chest was lifted from her bedroom, Mrs Gandhi noticed that dust had collected behind it. She remarked about the inadequacy of the way cleaning was done and asked for a broom and herself started sweeping. It took some days to sort and pack everything and move to the new house and then to rearrange things. There was a shortage of staff, and very often Sonia herself used to cook. I continued to go regularly, but after the major work was over, there was not much left for me to do. Job or no job, I would have continued to go, but when I found that Sanjay and Dhawan were still going strong I thought that continuing would be meaningless and not very pleasant. Loyalty for me has a different meaning. It is not just sticking to people. Marie Seton once wrote to me: 'To my mind there is only one kind of loyalty, either to work or in relation to people. It is that you are loyal to the best in them and in yourself.' I thought that would not be possible and continuing in the present context would be unproductive. My sister Urmila was going to Bombay and I decided to accompany her. When I told this to Mrs Gandhi, I noticed a sad smile on her face. She had guessed that it was a kind of farewell.

After spending a few days in Bombay, we went to Poona. We were keen to go to Acharya (as he was then called) Rajneesh's ashram and to listen to his lecture. Things were not so difficult then and no AIDS check ups were required. Only hair was sniffed at by his tall foreign disciples at the entrance as the Acharya was allergic to perfume. The Acharya's lectures used to be based on a few questions which his disciples would send him the previous day. I found his lecture impressive and engrossing and his style original. One of the questions asked was: the Acharya has always commended the quality of courage; but even Napoleon and Hitler had courage and what did the Acharya have to say about that? I remember Acharya Rajneesh saying that the quality of courage is the same; there is no bad or good courage. In an ambitious and aggressive person, courage takes an evil and destructive form, while in an evolved person courage becomes the power to do good for other people. Acharya then added that the trouble was that many of the so-called good people lacked the quality of courage and were thus ineffective.

In 1981 an important disciple of the Acharya, Ma Yoga Laxmi, came to Delhi to meet the Prime Minister and try to persuade the Government to allow their ashram to move out of Poona due to its location in a congested area. The places they suggested for moving to were sensitive from the security point of view. Mrs Gandhi asked me to interact with them. While all this was going on, those who controlled the inner politics within the ashram were able to persuade the Acharya to move to the United States. All this happened very suddenly. I am not very sure if Ma Yoga Laxmi knew about this decision, but she left Delhi suddenly.

~

THIRTY-NINE

THE END OF ANOTHER PHASE

On my return from the Bombay-Poona trip, I would drop in at 12 Willingdon Crescent from time to time but not regularly. Mrs Gandhi kept up her pattern of meeting people and a number of them—not the rich or powerful, but workers and others—used to come. However, the atmosphere used to be strange. Although Rajiv's and Sanjay's rooms were across the corridor, I do not think there was much communication between the two families, although outwardly the family pattern of eating together continued. Rajiv told P.N. Dhar that 'he had been a helpless observer of his brother's doings'. Mr Dhar writes of Rajiv: 'He told his mother in my presence, 'you have been brought to this pass by Sanjay and Dhawan.' She said nothing in reply but looked forlorn.'[1]

However, it is interesting that although Rajiv barred Dhawan from the Prime Minister's House after becoming the Prime Minister, two or three years later, he not only brought Dhawan back, but also made him an M.P.

One day in early October 1977, just when I was planning to make my evening tea, Vimla Sindhi, who lived a couple of houses away from Mrs Gandhi, rang up and said that there was police outside Mrs Gandhi's house and they had come to arrest her. I left the tea making, got into my car, and rushed to Mrs Gandhi's house. When I reached 12 Willingdon Crescent, the scene I saw saddened me. Earlier the police cordon outside the Prime Minister's House used to be for protecting the Prime Minister from unruly demonstrations and protestors. This time the cordon was to detain Mrs Gandhi and to prevent people from coming out or going in. I saw Nirmala

---

[1] P.N. Dhar, *Indira Gandhi, the 'Emergency' and Indian Democray*, p. 355.

Deshpande, who had been close to Vinobha Bhave, walking towards the gate and also being stopped. I urged the policemen to let us go in but met with no response. Suddenly I heard a voice: 'Let Ushaji go in.' It was Kiran Bedi, who was in charge of the situation. I had not recognized her in her uniform. Mrs Gandhi had felt proud when Kiran Bedi became the first woman IPS officer and had encouraged her. Realizing the delicate situation, I did not wish to give an inkling of recognition. After saying 'Thank you' in an impersonal manner, I walked in along with Nirmalaji. When I entered the house, I found Mrs Gandhi walking in and out of her bedroom. She was pleased to see me and asked me to help Sonia pack her bag. We did not know where she would be taken and for how long. I remember saying that perhaps it might be to a hill-station and suggested that a shawl should also be kept.

In another room, a Sikh police officer was waiting for Mrs Gandhi. The look on his face was uneasy and sheepish and I am sure he did not like his assignment. He was trying to be friendly with Rahul and Priyanka.

When finally Mrs Gandhi left with the police, Rajiv and Sanjay, together with their wives, decided to follow her. Rajiv asked me if I could stay with the children. I readily agreed. They returned around midnight.

I think the Janata Party made a very big mistake in arresting Mrs Gandhi. Till then Mrs Gandhi had been feeling low and had even talked about retiring to the hills. If they had left her alone, she may or may not have come back to active politics. But by treating her as they did, they put her back up. 'Now, as throughout her life, objections and obstacles merely strengthened her resolve', as Katherine Frank writes.[2] From then onwards she was ready for the battle.

After a long time, I found plenty of time on my hands and started thinking of ways to occupy it. Music had always been my first love but I had been out of touch for a decade or so. My music teacher in the meantime had died. I started going to the Dhrupad singers, the

[2]Katherine Frank, *Indira*, p. 169.

Dagar Brothers, who lived very near my house. I had always been attracted to the Sanskrit language also, but had never learnt it. It was too late to learn a language like Sanskrit at this late stage, but I started to go to Bharatiya Vidya Bhavan to get some idea of the language and was fascinated by whatever I came across. I realized that Sanskrit was not merely a language but also an unfathomable ocean from which arose our cultural traditions and concepts. I will have to be reborn to learn the language.

Other activities which occupied me during this period were accompanying a Japanese film team to record and film music in some places and helping the ICCR (Indian Council for Cultural Relations) organize a South Asian Festival of Performing Arts; this was perhaps the first festival in which our neighbouring countries participated.

Himachal had always fascinated me. I was familiar with the Kulu valley. In 1958 I stayed in a village, Jagatsukh, to learn about the life as well as the folk music and dance of the people. However, I had never been to Chamba on the Ravi river, earlier a feudal hill state. Thus I took the opportunity to visit it in 1978. It was interesting to see an old hill town built in the usual Indian style, with houses around narrow lanes, compared to the later sprawling hill stations with bungalows developed by the British to suit their way of life. Amongst the arts and crafts of Chamba, I was particularly keen to see the rare art form of the Chamba *rumal* (miniature paintings translated in embroidery). It was disheartening to see its complete decline, as it had once prospered under the patronage of the rajas. Later, after I joined the Delhi Crafts Council, we made efforts to resuscitate this art form and were successful in doing so.

In April 1979 the Dagar Brothers were going to sing in my house. While inviting other people, I suddenly thought of asking Mrs Gandhi too. She agreed and came with Rajiv and Sonia. The latter stayed on but Mrs Gandhi decided to leave after the singing of the first raga. When I went to see her off to the car, she told me that Mr Haksar's mother had died. The next day I got a message asking if I would accompany Mrs Gandhi to Mr Haksar's house at 4.30 p.m. I reached 12 Willingdon Crescent at 4.00 p.m. It was quite hot, and on reaching

Mr Haksar's home we did not find anyone waiting for us. I was surprised. We rang the bell, but no one appeared. The security person and I went around the house. After some time the front door opened and an elderly lady peeped out sleepily, no doubt wondering who was disturbing them during their afternoon siesta. She was Mrs Mushran, Haksar Sahib's sister, and she took us to Haksar Sahib's study. Haksar Sahib must have been resting as well because he took some time to come. By then I realized that no prior information about our visit had been given. There had been some strained relations between Mrs Gandhi and Haksar Sahib. When Sanjay's Maruti car project had become controversial, he had spoken and advised Mrs Gandhi frankly, as only he could, and had been sidelined. However, Mrs Gandhi being a very correct person wished to pay her condolences. Perhaps she felt embarrassed to call on him alone and to inform him of her intention to visit beforehand. Mrs Gandhi did not speak a word. Mrs Mushran sat staring coldly at Mrs Gandhi. During the early period of the Emergency, Pandit Brothers, a firm owned by Mr Haksar's uncle and his brother-in-law, Mr Mushran, had been raided, allegedly at the behest of Sanjay and both the gentlemen had been taken to the police station in handcuffs. Mrs Mushran had obviously not forgotten the humiliation suffered by her husband. To cover the embarrassment, I talked incessantly with Mr Haksar. I was quite amused by the entire episode.

I had known Swami Ranganathananda of the Ramakrishna Mission for a long time, and whenever he used to come to Delhi I would go to meet him. Besides being very spiritual with a deep knowledge of the Vedanta, he is very widely read on different modern subjects as well and was a wonderful orator. I always enjoyed meeting him, because while being respectful one could also talk to him as a friend. I think he was also interested in what was going on in the country. Once when he was in Delhi, after Mrs Gandhi had lost power, I went to see him. I asked: 'Swamiji, you knew Mrs Gandhi well. Why did you not speak to her regarding the Emergency?' I remember his wise words; he said that advice is sought. I realized then that it was for Mrs Gandhi to have consulted him if she so desired and spiritual people such as Swami Ranganathananda do not waste their words and advice. They give it only to those seekers who are keen and ready to receive it. Swamiji is now the President of the Ramakrishna Math and Mission.

When Swami Ranganathananda visited Delhi again, I told Mrs Gandhi that he was going to speak at the ashram in the evening. She expressed a desire to go and we both went along with a security person and sat quietly in the audience. Swamiji of course saw us, but we did not meet him.

After 1977 one started noticing a change in people's attitudes, even of those people one thought one knew well. Their smiles of recognition became weaker and some leading journalists passed snide remarks at social gatherings. Of course, there were very civilized people too. When I met Mr Badruddin Tyabji at a function, he asked me how I was. When I replied, 'We are untouchables these days', he touched my arm and said smilingly with a twinkle in his eyes, 'Very touchable for me'.

PART IV

~

1980–84

~

FORTY

RETURN TO POWER

After defeating Mrs Gandhi in 1977, the Janata coalition government could not hold itself together for long. In early January 1980, after the elections, when it became clear that Mrs Gandhi would be the prime minister, I was in a dilemma. Should I go to greet her or not? If I went to congratulate her, it may seem that I had come looking for a job again, but if I did not go, it could be misunderstood too. So I decided to go. Mrs Gandhi was in her room working at her table. When I peeped in, and before I could say anything, she started talking as if there had been no interregnum in our relationship. She said that Republic Day was approaching and that the Parade and the Awards had to be looked into, that the French President Mr Giscard d'Estaing was coming, and that I should talk to the Foreign Secretary about some arrangements. I was very amused, as I knew that all this talk was to cover embarrassment. I approached her and said, 'Please let me put my arms around you and congratulate you first.' I had no particular desire to rejoin her, but nevertheless decided to do the couple of errands she asked me to do. When I next visited her after a few days to inform her about what she had asked me to do, she did not pay much attention and I felt she was avoiding me. I tried once again and got the same impression. I knew her and realized there was something more to it. I had done my duty and decided not to go again. Someone told me later that she was considering taking me back, but when she mentioned this before her family, Sanjay did not approve. This suited me fine, as I had not gone to the house with this idea at all.

In April, Urmila, my sister, and I went to Banaras to celebrate the sixtieth birthday of Pandit Ravi Shankar. The ride in a 'bajra' (a special big boat), accompanied by music from a 'shehnai', and topped by 'thandai' and 'mithai' was memorable. There was a musical evening at his house, too.

In June I went to Manali with my family. It was there that I heard of Sanjay's accident in an air crash on 23 June 1980. I could not believe it at first, and left for Delhi by bus the next day. When I reached the Prime Minister's House, Mrs Gandhi was in the adjoining house on Akbar Road, standing on the same pathway on which she would be assassinated four years later. Rajiv was bringing in the urn containing Sanjay's ashes. Mrs Gandhi was in charge, giving various instructions. In her private moments of sorrow, she always took charge of difficult situations, having been used to them since her childhood.

I wanted to be of help and soon found myself involved in looking after the deluge of condolence letters, which had started to pour in. One day while sorting out the letters, I heard a PA taking a message from Mr Sadasivam. As I knew Mr Sadasivam and M.S. Subbulakshmi well, I took the telephone to speak with them. They were in Delhi and wanted to meet Mrs Gandhi to convey their condolences. On the spur of the moment I asked Mr Sadasivam if Subbulakshmiji would sing a couple of bhajans for Mrs Gandhi. They readily agreed. When they arrived, they sat on the carpet and M.S. started singing. On completion of the bhajan she looked towards me, and I coaxed her into singing three or four more. I am sure Mrs Gandhi must have been touched by Subbulakshmiji's soulful voice which had a healing touch.

It took me two months to go through all the condolence messsages. In the meantime, Mrs Gandhi was thinking of having me back and asked Pupul Jayakar to speak to me, which she did a couple of times. I did not find myself prepared to rejoin and evaded giving any proper reply. One day I was in Mrs Gandhi's room with some condolence letters when she handed me a thin file; this was the proposal from the Prime Minister's Secretariat regarding my job. Knowing me, she perhaps felt that I should be confronted directly in this matter. I felt embarrassed, but as I was not ready for it, I mumbled something about personal problems, which was also true. Later I was ashamed and felt that if Mrs Gandhi thought that I could be of even a little help to her in the most difficult job she was holding, I must assist her. Thus I

248

joined her in September, nine months after she became the prime minister. When I met her after formally taking over, I told her that it was the fourth time that I had rejoined her and that there must have been some 'sambandh' (connection) between us in our past lives. She merely smiled and went on with her work.

In October Mrs Gandhi went to Bombay for the inauguration of the NCPA (National Centre for the Performing Arts) as well as to attend some other functions. During that time, a memorandum was circulated regarding the Indira Gandhi Pratibha Prathishthan, a brainchild of A.R. Antulay, at that time the chief minister of Maharashtra. It was a very ambitious project, involving large funds, for the promotion of art, artists, writers, etc. However, the link between the project and Antulay, a political person, was perplexing. The use of Mrs Gandhi's name was also disturbing. On her return to Delhi, I prepared a note for Mrs Gandhi, and after she had seen it I wrote to Mr Antulay asking for certain clarifications. No reply was received from him. It was later learnt that the project was:

> named after the Prime Minister and thus enabled him [Antulay] to pretend that his entire venture had her support . . . [It] was nothing more than a convenient cover for the use of funds for political and partisan purposes.[1]

As far as I know the project did not take off.

In February 1981 Mrs Gandhi visited the Andaman and Nicobar Islands. She visited the Cellular Jail, known as the Kala Pani, where many of our freedom fighters had been incarcerated and quite a few died. One was shaken to see the torture chamber and the hanging room. One forgets the heavy price paid by the many valiants in the attainment of our freedom.

In the Little Andaman, she was upset to see the administration's efforts to 'civilize' the Onge tribals by dressing the usually half-naked women in thick khadi sarees and blouses, which were cumbersome and restricted their movements. Mrs Gandhi felt that if considered necessary, the tribals should be given something simple and functional

[1]Inder Malhotra, *Indira Gandhi*, p. 248.

to wear. The concerned authorities later sent her some sketches for her approval.

While driving along the sea, she asked the car to be stopped. Although it was dusk, she wanted to wade in the sea water and pick up sea shells and even borrowed a torch from the security person for the purpose.

~

FORTY-ONE

CIRCLING THE GLOBE

FOREIGN VISITS

1981

From 1981 onwards Mrs Gandhi travelled abroad extensively. The first trip was in May 1981, when she went to Geneva to address a WHO meeting and then visited some UAE countries. It was suspected that the Air India Boeing which was to have taken Mrs Gandhi had been tampered with. Therefore, within two or three days, an Indian Airlines plane was got ready. However, being a smaller plane, it had to hop for refuelling via Oman and Cyprus. Mrs Gandhi had expressed a desire to spend a day in a quiet place after addressing the WHO meeting. After lunch with the President of Switzerland in Bern, most members of the Prime Minister's party left for Zurich. Mrs Gandhi, accompanied by Ambassador Gurbachan Singh and his wife, the doctor, the security person, and I went to a delightfully beautiful place called Vitznau, on Lake Lucerne. When I entered Mrs Gandhi's room in the quaint hotel, she was looking wistfully towards the lake and said that she had not experienced that kind of quiet and silence for a long time. In a letter to Dorothy Norman from Zurich dated 9 May 1981, she wrote: 'I managed an evening (and) . . . morning at a heavenly lakeside Chateau Hotel. It will be a memory like Wordsworth's host of daffodils!'[1] She told the ambassador that she remembers coming to this place many years earlier with Feroze when both were studying in Europe.

The next day we went to Zurich. Mrs Gandhi showed interest in going to a department store, so she, the ambassador's wife, and I went to a store. Mrs Gandhi's interest was in visiting the toy section

---

[1]Dorothy Norman, *Indira Gandhi*, p. 156.

to look for some things for Rahul and Priyanka. One could see that she would appraise them imagining what would give joy to the children and enjoying the exercise. She picked up a really big stuffed monkey, a mechanical car, and other objects.

The woman in her enjoyed such visits which became almost impossible later on. Earlier in London and New York, if time permitted she would go to a book shop and loved browsing through them. Amongst personal things, she was not interested in cosmetics, as she hardly used them, but sometimes a pretty housecoat would catch her fancy.

From Switzerland Mrs Gandhi went to Kuwait and the UAE. In these countries, with the exception of Mrs Gandhi, no women were invited to the official meals. In Kuwait I insisted that I be included in their official dinner as I wanted to make a point that there is no segregation in our country. As there were no other women besides the Prime Minister, I had to be accommodated at the main table. This was quite impossible in conservative Abu Dhabi. However, a special party was arranged for the Prime Minister to meet the wife of the Sheikh and other important ladies. The ladies all sat in long rows in the big hall and food was served by maids who were all Pakistanis. They were happy to talk to me in Punjabi. Although a women's gathering, it was surprising to see the sheikh's wife in a beak-like contraption to cover the face.

In August 1981 Mrs Gandhi went to Kenya to address the United Nations Conference on New and Renewable Sources of Energy as well as for a state visit. She also went for a half-day safari to Keekorok Game Lodge, approximately 280 km from Nairobi. Maneka accompanied Mrs Gandhi on this visit and I think she used to feel a little left out, more so when both she and Sonia accompanied Mrs Gandhi to Europe in November of the same year.

A meeting of CHOGM (Commonwealth Heads of Governments Meeting) was to be held in September 1981 in Australia, so Mrs Gandhi went on an extended tour. In addition to Australia, this visit included Jakarta, Fiji, Tonga, and the Philippines. In Fiji, besides Suva, the capital, she also went to Lautoka on the western coast, where Indian indentured labour had landed in the nineteenth century. The University of the South Pacific conferred an honorary degree on Mrs Gandhi.

The next stop was Tonga Island, a very small island. It was a fascinating place inhabited by Polynesians and so different from other places and people one had seen. The royal family though corpulent were gentle and cultured. Recently I read somewhere that many Polynesians possess the 'thrifty gene', allowing them to retain calories; thus they suffer from obesity. Due to lack of proper accommodation, Mrs Gandhi and a few of us were put up in a house belonging to the royal princess who was away. What was especially interesting was the feast the King hosted which was held in an open ground. For the VIPs there was a little raised platform. A large number of the islanders also attended the feast and they and the rest of our party sat on the ground in long rows. We learnt that the food had been brought by the people and thus there was community participation; it had a tribal flavour. There were long trough-like low tables which were piled with whole chickens, chunks of meat and marine products, interspersed with watermelons, coconuts, and other fruit. One had to use one's fingers to pick and eat with relish! I could see the vegetarians amongst our party standing at some distance with their faces turned away; they went hungry. After the feast, the people performed their folk dances. The whole affair was quite charming.

From Tonga, Mrs Gandhi travelled to Melbourne, Australia to attend the Commonwealth conference. One night she knocked at our connecting door in the hotel. She had just heard the news on television of the assassination of Anwar Sadat, President of UAE, and felt she had to share it with someone. In the early morning the assassination at the parade was being shown on television, and this time I knocked at her door to apprise her of it. For the Retreat we went to Canberra, and Mrs Gandhi found time to visit a kangaroo park.

The last stop was Manila. President Ferdinand Marcos and his wife Imelda had been keen for some time for a visit by Mrs Gandhi. President Marcos and his high-powered wife, Imelda Marcos, were at the airport to receive Mrs Gandhi. She left accompanied by President Marcos in the car, and Mrs Marcos asked me to come in her car although this was not according to protocol. One could see that she was smart in appearance as well as otherwise and did not believe in rigidly sticking to protocol. She was also the governor/mayor of Manila and in that capacity she gave a luncheon that was even more impressive than the state banquet given by the President the previous evening. Afterwards she took Mrs Gandhi and her party in a small van on a guided tour of the city, and with a microphone in her hand she pointed out some buildings and other improvements made under her.

In the second half of October 1981 the Prime Minister went to attend a conference of the International Cooperation for Global Progress in Cancun, Mexico, a town on the Atlantic coast. On the way to Mexico, there was a two-day state visit to Romania, when Nikolai Ceausescu was very much there. In Cancun, over twenty important heads of state and governments participated, including Chancellor Bruno Kreisky of Austria, Prime Minister Pierre Trudeau of Canada, Prime Minister Zhao Ziyang of China, President Francois Mitterrand of France, Prime Minister Zenko Suzuki of Japan, President Jose L. Portillo of Mexico, President Ferdinand Marcos of the Philippines, Prime Minister Margaret Thatcher of the United Kingdom, President Ronald Reagan of the United States, and others. The purpose of the North-South Summit was to work out a new and just international economic order. In addition to the conference session and other formal functions, Mrs Gandhi hosted small lunches everyday for more informal interaction with the participants. I found time to visit Tulum, a Mayan site some distance away. After the conference Mrs Gandhi went to Oaxaca to see the old ruins of the ancient Mesoamerican Zapotec and Mixtec civilizations. In Oaxaca town, the indigenous people reminded us of our tribal peoples from north-east India.

This was the most hectic period of the tour. On her return from Cancun on 27 October Mrs Gandhi left for Bulgaria, Rome, and Paris on 6 November. On this trip both Sonia and Maneka accompanied the Prime Minister. From 1975 to 1980, Maneka along with Sanjay was in an over-confident mood and drew more attention to themselves. With Sanjay's death, Maneka lost this sheen and became vulnerable. Sonia who was in the background in the Emergency period became more confident now.

After 1967, this was Mrs Gandhi's second trip to Bulgaria, where she was conferred an honorary degree by the University of Sofia. Sonia, Maneka, and myself, accompanied by the daughter-in-law of President Zhivkov, visited the old town of Plovdiv to see the Roman amphitheatre and other old sites and buildings. Soon after reaching Rome, Mrs Gandhi went to the Vatican to call on the Pope. While she was with him for more than half an hour, the rest of the party was in the anteroom. I was itching to take a photograph of the Pope with my newly acquired camera, and when the official crew entered with the party I joined them to fulfil my desire. Mrs Gandhi also addressed the FAO Conference. The President of Italy, Mr Alexander Pertini, gave a lunch in Quirinale Palace, in the topmost room, which had earlier been the attic; the glass panels all around gave a beautiful view of old Rome.

The next stop was Paris, as beautiful as ever. Mrs Gandhi was to receive an honorary doctorate from the Sorbonne University. She wished to give her speech in French. She had been out of touch with the language, so she had worked hard at it from Delhi onwards. The French were impressed and appreciative of her gesture. She also visited the Pompidou Centre for a chat with some intellectuals. I remember Peter Brook amongst them, who later directed the play *Mahabharata* with an international cast. She also went to see a ballet at the Opera Comiqué. Mrs Gandhi stayed at the Hotel de Marigny, an old palace with beautiful furniture and tapestries, where generally only heads of states stayed. The same honour was accorded to her in Moscow, in 1982, when arrangements for her stay were made at the Kremlin.

1982

United Kingdom, March 1982

The Festival of India in the United Kingdom was being planned for a couple of years. It was to be inaugurated in London jointly by Mrs Gandhi and Mrs Thatcher in March, and consisted of interesting functions and programmes. The formal inauguration was the concert at the Royal Festival Hall. After the beautiful rendering of her musical composition by M.S. Subbalakshmi, Ravi Shankar's composition, *Ragmala*, was performed by him and the London Philharmonic Orchestra, conducted by Zubin Mehta. Other programmes included an Indian exhibition of science and technology and an exhibition of classical Indian art at the Hayward Gallery.

Saudi Arabia, April 1982

In April Mrs Gandhi visited Saudi Arabia. Rajiv also accompanied her. Being a conservative country, the experience was different. Regarding the dress code, sarees were all right but blouses had to be long-sleeved. Mrs Gandhi had some made but I refused to invest in something which would be of no use later, so I quietly picked up a few khadi blouses from Mrs Gandhi which she used to wear on her tours in India to prevent the sun and dust from affecting her skin. The first stop was Jeddah. Najma Heptullah had also reached the city. She had cordial relations with the Saudis and her grand uncle, Maulana Abul Kalam Azad, was originally from Saudi Arabia. Mrs Gandhi included her tailor master in the party to give him an opportunity to do *umrah*. It was her idea and spoke of her consideration and thoughtfulness. The tailor's father, Muhammad Hasan, had worked for Panditji since the Anand Bhavan days in Allahabad. Later he was a part of their household in Teen Murti and Safdarjang Road. After his death his son took his position.

The reception given by Prince Majed, Governor of Makkah, was not too formal, and surprisingly both Najma and I were also invited. This was not so in Riyadh. The banquet hosted by King Khaled and the lunch by Crown Prince Fahd were meant exclusively for the men, except of course Mrs Gandhi! The Queen also hosted a dinner for Mrs Gandhi. It was interesting to see these otherwise veiled ladies in French haute couture dresses and loaded with diamonds. I was not sure if justice was being done to the dresses! In Arab countries seating was in long rows of chairs kept against the walls, so you could only talk to the ladies on either side of you if they understood the language.

On the day we were to leave, Crown Prince Fahd came for talks as well as to accompany the Prime Minister to the airport. The talks were taking time and Rajiv, Najma, myself, and one or two Saudi officials were waiting in the hall. I suddenly got into a little mischievous mood and persuaded one of the Saudi officials to take off his cloak and headgear to drape them over Rajiv to take a photograph. The official felt quite nervous as he did not want to get caught if the VVIPs entered the hall.

USA, July–August 1982

In end July, Mrs Gandhi went for a state visit to the USA and was accompanied by Rajiv, Sonia, and their children. In New York she was invited for lunch at the Metropolitan Museum to which some important cultural personalities had been invited. Before leaving for Washington D.C., Mrs Gandhi called on the Secretary General of the United Nations, Javier Perez de Cuellar, and presented a sculpture to the UN. In Washington D.C., in addition to the official reception at the While House, other engagements included meeting with the Editorial Board of the *Washington Post*, delivering an address to the National Press Club, meeting with scientists, and a television interview.

The state banquet hosted by President and Mrs Reagan at the White House, though formal, had an informal and cheerful atmosphere. Mrs Reagan's dress was inspired by a sari. Guests sat at round tables with one important host at the table. At our table, Vice-President George Bush (Sr) found himself sitting between Usha Narayanan (wife of our Ambassador K.R. Narayanan) and myself. I told him that he was sitting between two dawns (Ushas) and he was quite amused. After the banquet there was a concert by the New York Philharmonic Orchestra conducted by Zubin Mehta on the White House lawns.

Mrs Gandhi stayed two more days in New York. Here she met the mayor, businessmen, and other people, as well as some interesting American women. Among them I remember Martha Graham, a pioneer of contemporary American dance, and Gloria Steinem, a feminist. Mrs Gandhi was also able to meet her old friend Dorothy Norman after their long estrangement during the Emergency. They had long talks and we all went to see the play *Amadeus*.

Mrs Gandhi returned to India via Los Angeles, Honolulu, and Tokyo, stopping a day each at these places.

Mauritius and Mozambique, August 1982

Almost a fortnight after returning from the United States trip, Mrs Gandhi left for Mauritius and Mozambique towards the end of August. This was the Prime Minister's second visit to Mauritius, the first being in 1970.

From Mauritius, Mrs Gandhi went to Mozambique, where she was received by President Samora Machel himself. Besides the banquet given by him, he also had a small informal dinner the next evening, where along with a few ministers, the President's wife Graca Machel was also present. (President Machel later died in an air accident. His wife is now married to Nelson Mandela.) Mrs Gandhi visited the Revolution Museum where she was received by the then Foreign Minister, Mr Chissano. The Museum traced the history of the country's struggle against Portuguese rule. One could see that, compared to the British, Portuguese colonialism had been very harsh. Due to the lack of educational facilities during the period of colonial rule, when Mozambique gained independence there was hardly any infrastructure for the governance and other needs of the country and people from other countries were being invited to help in this direction.

Along with the Ambassador's wife, I visited two important artists, a muralist who was also a poet (the walls of his room were covered with large murals) and a sculptor (of wood). I was able to persuade Mrs Gandhi to visit the sculptor whose name was also Chissano, whose house was a veritable museum of his works. Both the artists visited India in early 1984 at the invitation of Mrs Gandhi.

USSR, September 1982

Mrs Gandhi left for the USSR in the third week of September 1982.

While driving from the airport with Ambassador Vishnu Ahuja

and his talented wife Amina, Amina referred to the beautiful sarees that Mrs Gandhi wore during her visit to the United States a couple of months earlier. I told Amina that it was not only the sarees, but the way Mrs Gandhi carried them that made the difference; the same sarees on Amina or on me would hardly be noticed. Amina then remarked: 'Yes, she has *jama-zebi* (gives grace to clothes).' On reaching the Kremlin, when Amina and I entered Mrs Gandhi's room, I told her that I have learnt a new word—*jama-zebi*—and described the context in which the remark had been made. She smiled. I am sure she must have been pleased.

Besides the usual official engagements, Mrs Gandhi was taken to Star City to view the Soyuz spaceship model, and she also met the Indian trainees, Rakesh Sharma and Ravish Malhotra. Rakesh Sharma later accompanied the Russian cosmonauts into space. One evening was free and when the Prime Miniter showed interest in seeing a ballet, the authorities put up a special programme for her at the Bolshoi Theatre. It included excerpts from *Spartacus* and the well-known ballerina, Maya Plisetskaya, though advanced in years, also put in an appearance as a special gesture.

After Moscow, the next stop was Tallin, capital of Estonia, which had some Nordic flavour. A special programme of Estonian music and folk dances had been arranged for us. Estonia is well known for its special annual community singing festival in which approximately 80,000 people participate. The next stop was Kiev, capital of Ukraine, on the banks of the Dnieper river. Having been greatly affected by World War II, the war memorial in the city consisted of a mammoth figure of a woman on the banks of the river. Mrs Gandhi was conferred a degree by the Kiev University; she attended a special performance of a classical ballet group and visited some beautiful old churches.

1983

In June 1983 Mrs Gandhi left for a visit to Yugoslavia, Finland, Denmark, Norway, and Austria.

She had visited Yugoslavia many times, first with her father, and then by herself when President Tito was still alive. This was the first time she was visiting the country after his death. She visited the Tito Memorial Centre. She also gave the Raoul Prebisch lecture at UNCTAD VI on Peace and Development in Belgrade. In his last years President Tito had separated from his wife, Madame Jovanka Broz. Mrs Gandhi especially asked to meet her. We went to her small modest place. One could see that she was very touched by Mrs Gandhi's gesture of visiting her even when she was living in obscurity. Perhaps she had no help, and when she herself brought in the tea trolley, I jumped to help her.

The next stop was Finland for a day, where Mrs Gandhi visited the Parliament and also opened an exhibition of Indian handicrafts at the National Museum. Before the banquet hosted in her honour, she attended a programme of the youth choir at Temppeliankio Church. The next day she was taken for a cruise on board the icebreaker *URHO*.

From Finland, Mrs Gandhi went to Denmark. On the first evening the dinner was at the famous Tivoli Gardens in Copenhagen. The next day she visited the island of Odense to see the house and museum of Hans Christian Andersen. She attended the lunch hosted by the Queen and the banquet given by the Prime Minister. She also gave a lecture organized by the Council for International Development Cooperation.

Norway was the next stop. Mrs Gandhi visited the Parliament and also opened the Nehru Photo Exhibition at the Munch Museum. We were then taken to Bergen by plane and stopped at Ullenvang for the night. The next morning we went sightseeing down the beautiful Hardenger Fjord in the frigate *Trondheim*. The scenic beauty of the Fjord was a memorable and enchanting experience.

After Norway, the last stop was Austria. In Vienna Mrs Gandhi visited the Houses of Parliament. The lunch given by the Federal President was hosted in the beautiful old Hofburg Palace; its ambience and antique furniture had been well maintained, and imposing portraits of Queen Marie Therese looked down from the walls. The next day Mrs Gandhi left for Innsbruck on her way to Alpbach for the 'Dialogue Congress', where she delivered the keynote address.

In September 1983 Mrs Gandhi left for a visit to Cyprus, Greece, Paris, France, and the United Nations in New York City. The first stop was Cyprus, where President Spyros Kyprianou himself received Mrs Gandhi. She visited the Cyprus Museum, the Museum of National Struggle, the Tomb of Archbishop Makarios, and the Kykko Monastery. She also inaugurated the Jawaharlal Nehru Avenue, opposite the House of Representatives.

From Cyprus, she went to Greece, where she visited the imposing ruins of the Parthenon on the Acropolis in Athens. In addition to the banquet, the Greek Prime Minister had also arranged for a small and informal gathering of eminent personalities from literary and artistic circles. The next day she left for the famous Apollo Temple at Delphi by helicopter, and on the way stopped at the impressive ancient amphitheatre at Epidaurus. Melina Mercouri, the well-known actress who was then the Minister of Culture, accompanied Mrs Gandhi. Basically Mrs Gandhi's interests and inclination were more towards the arts, literature, nature, etc. as she herself often mentioned in her letters to Dorothy Norman. However, having chosen a different course in her life, I think such visits and encounters fulfilled her genuine interest, even though for a short while, and gave her joy and relaxation,.

On her return, in the evening she saw the performance of the Greek tragedy *Oedipus Rex*. Before her departure the next day, she visited the Goulandris Museum of Natural History and the Archaeological Museum. Mrs Gandhi herself looked quite Grecian and I took some photographs with Greek sculptures. In Paris her stay was more in the nature of a stopover; she attended a dinner hosted by the President of France.

The main purpose of the visit to New York City was to attend the General Assembly session of the United Nations. However, she also managed to pack a lot of other activities into the programme in addition to attending the United Nations. She met the Editorial Board of the *New York Times*, a group of writers and intellectuals, and received the UN Population Award. She was also able to meet and have long talks with her friend Dorothy Norman, and attended a performance of Puccini's opera *La Boheme*. While looking for information on the current cultural events in the newspaper, I noticed that *Edmund Kean*, a one-man play by Raymund FitzSimons, was being performed, in which Ben Kingsley (who had played the role of Gandhi in Richard Attenborough's eponymous film) was starring. When I mentioned this to Mrs Gandhi, she asked me to send flowers to the actor and we also went to see the play. After the performance—I do not know whose bright idea it was—rather than going out by the exit door we found ourselves being taken onto the stage and then into Ben Kingsley's green room. He had gone in for a wash as he had a wig on in the play. We had to wait for a few minutes till he came out in his dressing gown. Both he and we were quite embarrassed.

On the way back to India, Mrs Gandhi stayed for a day in London. There I read a notice in the paper about a concert at the Barbican in which Yehudi Menuhin was playing in the first half. We went to the concert and Mr Menuhin, pleased to learn of Mrs Gandhi's presence, joined her after the interval. As mentioned earlier, Mrs Gandhi also spent a few hours trying to spruce up the drawing and dining rooms by rearranging furniture, paintings, and other objects in the Indian High Commissioner's residence, because the Queen was invited for dinner there before she came to India for the CHOGM.

1984

Libya and Tunisia, April 1984

Mrs Gandhi's last visit abroad was to Libya and Tunisia, in April 1984. When our plane reached Tunis, it began to circle rather than land. Being a nervous flier, I began to worry, but after almost ten minutes, the plane began to descend. When it finally landed I saw a car racing the plane on the tarmac. It was Colonel Gaddafi, driving himself, with his wife beside him. One learnt that as he was getting late and wanted to receive Mrs Gandhi personally, he sent a message that the plane should land only after he had reached the airport. The scene had to be dramatic, like him!

A visit to the Military Academy for girls was also arranged. It was impressive to find a venture like this in an Arab country. What was amusing, however, was to see the young girls in uniforms bearing rifles but also sporting pigtails and earrings under their berets.

Mrs Gaddaffi hosted a ladies' tea party for Mrs Gandhi and the atmosphere was not as conservative as that of other Arab countries.

Tunisia had quite a different flavour, in its language, food and culture due to the French influence. We were there hardly for a day.

~

FORTY-TWO

MANEKA

Sanjay's tragic death on 23 June 1980 was a terrible shock for everyone, especially Mrs Gandhi and Maneka. Maneka with her three-month-old baby was very low. Both she and Mrs Gandhi must have made efforts to adjust to the changed situation and Mrs Gandhi would have tried to help her in her own way. However, there were people who tried to fan Maneka's ambition and political importance by comparing her to 'Durga' and in other ways. They, I am afraid, muddied the situation more than they helped Maneka. Mrs Gandhi doted on Sanjay and Maneka's son Feroze Varun. Sometimes, she would have all the three grandchildren sleep in her room and fussing over them gave her great joy.

Since I was working from the Secretariat, I was not aware of the situation in the Prime Minister's House, but over time I could sense the power equation changing. Gradually perhaps Maneka began to feel sidelined, especially with Rajiv's rise to power. She may have thought of building her own power base by starting the Sanjay Vichar Manch along with some of Sanjay's friends. A meeting in this connection was planned in Lucknow in March 1982. Mrs Gandhi had asked Maneka not to attend it. I think Maneka was getting ready for a confrontation. While Mrs Gandhi was in London for the UK Festival, information did start reaching there that Maneka was removing some of her things from the Prime Minister's House.

A day or two after our return from the UK, while leaving the office I looked into Sharada Prasad's office. In his usual tongue-in-cheek style, he said that there was trouble in the Prime Minister's House. I was upset and, not knowing the seriousness of the situation, thought that perhaps I could be of some help. Rather than going home, I decided to go to the Prime Minister's House first. The gates, which were generally kept open, were closed. The security officer on duty, who should have been inside, was pacing outside on the pavement. I stopped the car and asked to go in. He replied with a sheepish smile that there were strict instructions not to allow anybody in. I felt unhappy and left after ten minutes. It was only through the media later that one knew what had happened.

I think, knowingly or unknowingly, Maneka crossed swords with Mrs Gandhi in the power game. The saddest fallout of this incident was that both Mrs Gandhi and Varun were deprived of sharing their love and affection. Mrs Gandhi must have been deeply affected, but being proud she kept her pain to herself. At her funeral, when four-and-a-half-year-old Varun was taken near the pyre to pay his last respects, the ritual seemed meaningless, as Mrs Gandhi's intense desire to see him during her lifetime remained unfulfilled.

~

FORTY-THREE

THE LOYALTY FACTOR

Mrs Gandhi was affected by the difficult situations that she had to face after 1977 as well as the wavering loyalties of certain persons. In the 1980s things began to change and she gradually started to trust fewer people. The loyalty factor, i.e. personal loyalty, began to play an increasingly important role. When Mrs Gandhi was out of power, Pupul Jayakar gave moral and emotional support to her. In 1980, after coming to power, Mrs Gandhi offered the Ministry of Culture to Pupulji. Pupulji was a person of ideas and did not like getting embroiled in the nitty-gritty of administration and official responsibilities. Hence, she did not accept the offer. Nevertheless, her role and power became more important than that of a minister. She now wielded special influence with Mrs Gandhi and wished to be involved in all aspects of art and culture, not only handlooms and handicrafts.

The idea of a Festival of India in the United Kingdom had been mooted on a very modest scale before 1980. Under Mrs Jayakar, it was transformed into a mega festival. Festivals in other countries also followed. They no doubt created an impact but almost became an industry.

When a new Secretary to the Prime Minister was to be appointed, Mrs Jayakar suggested the name of Dr P.C. Alexander, a capable bureaucrat, who after retirement was working for the GATT in Geneva. Pupulji had had a good rapport with Dr Alexander when he was Secretary, Ministry of Commerce and she was the chairperson, Handicrafts and Handloom Export Corporation. Dr Alexander writes: 'Pupul Jayakar, who had been strongly urging me to come back to India (from Geneva) telephoned me . . . That I should straightaway inform the Prime Minister of my willingness to accept the job . . .'[1]

---

[1] P.C. Alexander, *My Years with Indira Gandhi*, p. 30.

With Dr Alexander's appointment, Pupulji's power grew further.

Mrs Gandhi had known Pupulji over a period of time. She appreciated her aesthetics, her excellent work in the handlooms industry, and her sensitivity towards the arts. However, one could see that Pupulji's need for Mrs Gandhi was more than Mrs Gandhi's need for her. Her eyes used to light up when she was with Mrs Gandhi. Raj Thapar comments that 'what I have not forgotten was Pupul's beatific expression whenever her eyes looked up at Indira, in almost adoration of the goddess, as if transported into cloud number nine . . .'[2] Perhaps two persons mattered the most to Pupulji: J. Krishnamurti and Mrs Gandhi. They were very different people but Pupulji's effort was always to bring them together.

In 1983 Pupulji persuaded Mrs Gandhi about the need to set up an Arts Council to oversee and direct the cultural scene, much like the Council of Scientific and Industrial Research in the field of science. The Arts Council was to consist of some eminent personalities. According to Pupulji, culture was vitally important and without the establishment of a central cultural presence the atmosphere would be vitiated; she believed that a central cultural perception was more important than the functioning of any institution.

I was a little concerned about the proposal and did not think that the science scene and the art scene could be equated. Hence, I sent my comments to the Prime Minister, noting that no doubt the cultural scene had been stagnant and needed to be reviewed, but that the setting up of another super-body could lead to the imposition of more power controls and levers at a high central level, which could stifle creativity rather than stimulate it. Also, I was not sure if it was a good idea for a few people, no matter howsoever eminent, to direct the vast multilayered and complex cultural scene in the country. However, the Arts Council was set up, but after a couple of meetings it disappeared, like a bubble.

Mrs Gandhi enjoyed the arts and found pleasure and relaxation in them. In 1956 she wrote to Dorothy Norman: 'My main interest

[2]Raj Thapar, *All These Years*, p. 316.

still remains as it was much more in Art and Literature, but I feel that certain essential things have to be dealt with first.'[3] The 'essential things' she referred to was her intense sense of duty which was always uppermost for her and which she pursued from the beginning till the end. Marie Seton wrote to me in 1966 about this:

> The inside of her [Mrs Gandhi] will never enjoy the situation. The whole conflict always has been between natural inclination and duty. This is a terrible conflict for any human being because there is another form of duty (the most difficult to adhere to) and that is to what one is at the deepest level of one's being. The problem is to know what is the deepest level.

Mrs Gandhi and I shared many similar interests and tastes, and in a quiet way I tried to keep her informed about various happenings in the cultural sphere and arranged meetings between her and various artists, writers, and others. Whenever possible, she visited exhibitions and theatre performances both in the country and abroad. Given her heavy work schedule, these activities nurtured her spirit and provided relaxation to her. The communication between us was never much based on words but more in the nature of osmosis. Somehow I think we knew and understood each other. I respected her privacy and learnt to distance myself whenever necessary. When I had reservations about certain matters I did not have to say anything and quietly distanced myself inwardly, and she knew it.

[3]Dorothy Norman, *Indira Gandhi*, p. 30.

~

FORTY-FOUR

A GROWING DISTANCE

Earlier, I had always worked from the Prime Minister's House, be it Teen Murti or later 1 Safdarjang Road. When Mrs Gandhi was alone, my role used to be work cum being a kind of companion. After Rajiv and Sanjay got married, the house with the sons, daughters-in-law, and later the grandchildren became more like a home and she greatly enjoyed the togetherness, having missed it in her childhood. When I rejoined work in 1980 I made two requests. The first was that I should be permitted to work from the Secretariat rather than from the Prime Minister's House. There were two reasons. I was happy that Mrs Gandhi was surrounded by her family. A good relationship had developed between Sonia and Mrs Gandhi, and Sonia understood and fulfilled many of her personal and emotional needs. I did not wish to be entangled in the affairs of the Prime Minister's House and the family. The other reason for my asking to work from the Secretariat was that I needed more space and independence as well as an area earmarked for my work.

The second request was regarding the designation. When she became prime minister in 1966, I had been designated social secretary, which has a specific connotation. My work could hardly be categorized; it was to assist her in whatever area—personal, social, cultural—she needed my help. In 1980, therefore, I was designated Officer on Special Duty (OSD).

Mrs Gandhi had agreed to my requests. Thus, besides some personal work I also started looking after cultural matters. It worked well for some time, and I would go to the Prime Minister's House from time to time. However, over a period the physical distancing began to gradually affect our relationship, as she was used to having me around the house. I knew that she was not reconciled to my not working from the house, an arrangement which she was used to and which suited her better.

Gradually, my work in the Secretariat began to be affected. I mustered enough courage one day and spoke about this to Mrs Gandhi. She commented that I was sensitive. But the conversation did not particularly help in resolving matters. I felt sad because earlier it was the sensitivity of our relationship that had been a bond between us. I came across a note I had written to Mrs Gandhi when she became prime minister in 1966, in which I had said: 'Perhaps you will say that I am sensitive, which I am and ask why not? Under a sensitive person like you, one expects sensitivity to thrive.'

Over a period of time the distance grew, as reflected in a rather harsh comment she made in a note in 1983, 'The work that was previously handled by you . . . I now have to do all by myself, often having to stay up until the early hours.' It made me unhappy, but it was not possible to go back to the earlier pattern.

The fallout of all this was that the space between us was now occupied by others. Amongst them was Dhawan who was in the PM's House from the morning when Mrs Gandhi started the day till she retired at night, day in and day out. There was no doubt about his loyalty but gradually there was hardly any work he was not handling—personal, official, or political. This influence gave him a further high as well as access to almost all channels of communication to the Prime Minister.

Mrs Gandhi was now surrounded by persons in the house, including the family and a few other outsiders, whose influence mattered. But perhaps this led to her sources of information and perceptions getting restricted.

Towards the latter part of 1983, the earlier syndrome of my being a square peg in a round hole had reappeared, and I seriously began to wonder if there was any purpose in my continuing to work. However, I thought I would be grossly misunderstood if I asked to be relieved and decided to continue for some more time. I did not know then that Mrs Gandhi had so little time left and I would not have forgiven myself if I had raised the question of leaving.

In April 1984 I sent Mrs Gandhi a slip asking for a few days' leave for personal reasons. Marie Seton was in Delhi from London to receive the Padma Bhushan award and she came to my house which I had by then renovated. Marie liked it and the next day when she visited Mrs Gandhi, perhaps she mentioned something about my flat. When my slip asking for leave came back to me, I was surprised to see Mrs Gandhi's comment on it which was unconnected to what I had written. It said, 'Marie Seton told me that UB has vastly improved her house.' She also told Marie that she had no place of her own. This comment perhaps conveyed her sense of insecurity about her own future. Nobody knew then that her future existed only for six more months.

~

FORTY-FIVE

OPERATION BLUE STAR

Two important international gatherings took place in Delhi in 1983: NAM (Non-Aligned Meeting) in March and CHOGM (Commonwealth Heads of Government Meeting) in November. A large number of heads of state and governments attended both the sessions. The functions—conferences, banquets, and informal lunches hosted by Mrs Gandhi for small groups—were well organized and handled by her with her usual charm and grace. These conferences were good from the public relations point of view. The banquet seating for the large number of NAM delegates posed a protocol problem. An interesting way out was devised; round tables were arranged and given numbers. Mrs Gandhi sat at No. 7 (as it was the 7th NAM) instead of No.1. She also went from table to table to interact with the guests.

The cultural programme began with nearly twenty Rajasthani folk musicians entering the hall in their traditional costumes and carrying their instruments. Playing and singing, they wove their way around the tables before getting onto the stage. Other items were of classical dances. President Fidel Castro had brought with him his friend, the Nobel Laureate Gabriel García Márquez. He was so thrilled with the programme that he told Mrs Gandhi the next day that on returning to his hotel room after the dinner, he rang his wife back home to say that he had never seen a programme like the one he saw that evening.

At the same time, in 1983, trouble was brewing in different areas—Assam, Kashmir, as well as Sri Lanka. The most serious, however, was the Punjab imbroglio, which had been continuing for some years and had become a festering sore. It was a very complex and vexing issue, and Mrs Gandhi was discussing and listening to the advice of many people. But 'she no longer had skilled advisers and negotiators' to assist her.[1]

When Operation Blue Star took place on 6 June 1984 it was a terrible shock to everyone. It was difficult to believe that Mrs Gandhi could have taken such a decision herself.

According to Arun Nehru, 'she was scared of attacking a house of God.'[2] It is learnt that she had pujas performed in the hope that some sort of miracle might resolve the crisis in the Golden Temple, and that she told those who were persuading her to take such drastic action that in the grey areas in history—that is, in unsolvable situations—the only thing to do was to play for time, wait and hope. What triggered her decision.

It is difficult to say what would have happened if Mrs Gandhi had gone according to her own inner voice, and not given in to plans that were not in tune with her instincts. But perhaps things had reached a point of no return and there is no purpose in asking the question.

The tragedy of Operation Blue Star was traumatic for everyone, but more so for the Punjabis. I never used to send notes on political and serious matters, but this time I did send a note, excerpts from which are:

July 18, 1984

The Punjab issue has been exercising everyone's mind. Being a Punjabi and having passed through the traumatic experience of the Partition, people like us are more affected.

The situation as it exists today is very complex and one thing has led to or is leading to another.

It is important to understand the psyche of a Punjabi. The Punjabis, especially the Sikhs are a fearless and proud people. This is what makes them what they are, self-reliant, enterprising, hard working and full of vitality and vigour. This is the reason that after the trauma of Partition the Punjabis were able to rehabilitate themselves so well. If these qualities are not understood or misunderstood it can create problems for those who administer the Punjabis

[1]Katherine Frank, *Indira*, p. 479.
[2]Ibid., p. 478.

in the same way as people in some other areas where the people may be more submissive. Punjabis are doers and understand deeds better than words. Too much of arguments, strategies and procrastination frustrates them and not being used to inaction or frustration, their energy then can go in negative and wrong directions.

I think ways have to be found to release the anger and resentment (justified or not) from the people's hearts and minds. A kind of cleansing is necessary for loosening the knots of the mind and making it more receptive.

Things were not the same after Operation Blue Star. Being an intuitive person, I think Mrs Gandhi had an inkling of what might come. On her last visit to Kashmir, on 28 October, she went to meet the Shaivite savant, Lachchmanjoo, in his ashram near Nishat Bagh. He told Mrs Jayakar later: 'She [Mrs Gandhi] spoke of death. She felt that her time was over and death was near.'[3] In December 1984, when I visited the Ramakrishna Math in Belur, I was told by a swamiji that in October Mrs Gandhi had written a letter expressing similar sentiments to another swamiji.

[3]Pupul Jayakar, *Indira Gandhi.*

~

FORTY-SIX

OUR LAST MEETING

On Saturday, 27 October, while leaving the office, I looked into Sharada
Prasad's room. He mentioned that the Prime Minister had gone to
Kashmir for a day. I was surprised as usually a circular used to be
issued regarding the Prime Minister's tours.

On Sunday, 28 October, I went to the UK High Commissioner's
residence to attend a reception in honour of Princess Anne. While
driving back and passing 1 Safdarjang Road, I suddenly decided to
go in as I had not met Mrs Gandhi for a few days. When I walked
into her study, I found her standing near the table and Priyanka was
watching television. When I began to speak, Mrs Gandhi raised her
hand to restrain me, and I realized she was also watching television.
The film was Jane Austen's *Pride and Prejudice*. As both grandmother
and granddaughter were busy watching the film, I went into the dining
room where Sonia was beginning her dinner.

When the film ended, Mrs Gandhi and Priyanka walked in. Mrs
Gandhi, considerate as she was, remembering that she had stopped
me, asked, 'Usha, you were going to say something?' When I asked
her about her Kashmir visit, she said she had gone to see the chinar
trees in their autumn splendour, but she was disappointed as the leaves
had not yet turned fully to the autumn colours. She also talked about
the shrinking Dal Lake and how the Convention Centre had further
encroached upon the lake and spoilt its beauty. Mrs Gandhi had been
unhappy about the environmental pollution of the Dal Lake and often
conveyed her concern to the state government. After saying goodbye,
when I went to my car I realized that the children had played a prank
and had changed my car key. I had to come back and found Rahul
and Priyanka giggling at having fooled me. That was the last time I

met and talked with Mrs Gandhi. The next morning, 29 October, she left for Orissa.

On 29 and 30 October I went to the office and completed some notes on which I had been working. As my work in the Secretariat had been affected, I had begun to work out my own agenda keeping Mrs Gandhi's interests in view. I visited Jaisalmer, in Rajasthan, and saw the state of affairs regarding its conservation. In Kinnaur, in Himachal Pradesh, I was disturbed to see the effects of video parlours (also showing blue films) in the remote and peaceful valley, where a young boy, when restrained by his father, had committed suicide. Due to Mrs Gandhi's deep interest in the tribals and their welfare, I had started a dialogue with the concerned officer in the Planning Commission for holding a seminar for the reappraisal of the tribal policies then in force. I also made a suggestion for hosting a Southeast Asian Cultural Festival every two years. I completed the notes and sent them to be placed before the Prime Minister on her return. An invitation from the National School of Drama about a play, *Mattavilas*, to be held from 1 to 5 November had been received. I sent it along with a short note.

> The play MATTAVILAS is going to be presented
> by the National School of Drama from 1st to the
> 5th November in their Open-air Theatre. It is a
> Hindi translation of a seventh century Sanskrit play.
> It has been directed by the Guest Director,
> Shri Kaavalam Panikar, a well-known theatre person from
> Kerala.
>
> Perhaps PM may be interested to see it.
>
> (Usha Bhagat)
> 29.10.84

P.M.

Mrs Gandhi returned from Orissa on the night of 30 October, tired after a hectic tour. As was her wont, she presumably must have looked through some important papers before retiring around midnight. My notes were returned to me unseen after 31 October, except the one regarding the play; she had seen it and had underlined the date, indicating that perhaps she may have liked to attend its performance on that day.

~

FORTY-SEVEN

EKLA CHOLO RE

On the morning of 31 October, I received a phone call from a PA in the Prime Minister's House around 9.15 a.m. saying that there was a message from the Prime Minister that she had a television interview at her South Block office (Peter Ustinov was going to the Office from Akbar Road), and I should see if everything in her room was in order. (After some days, the same PA told me that as he was putting down the receiver, he heard the sound of shooting.)

Meanwhile, not being aware of what had happened at Safdarjang Road, I reached South Block around 10.00 a.m. As I was parking my car, an office driver told me, rather casually, that there had been some shooting at the Prime Minister's House. I was alarmed and thought that perhaps there had only been an attempt. I jumped into an office car and rushed to 1 Safdarjang Road. I found Mr Sharada Prasad on the telephone trying to reach Rajiv, who was on tour in West Bengal. Mrs Jayakar and Mr Natwar Singh were also there, standing in stony silence. A little later Dhawan returned from the hospital, shaken and in tears. Mrs Gandhi's personal servant, Nathu Ram, was leaving for the All India Institute of Medical Sciences, and I quickly got into the car in which he was travelling.

News of Mrs Gandhi's death had not yet spread and there was no crowd at the hospital. We quickly went to the eighth floor where the operation theatre was located. Sonia was sitting in the anteroom in a daze with a cousin of Mrs Gandhi, Sheila Shungloo, who happened to be in the hospital for her husband's treatment. Soon other people began to arrive. I hung around in the veranda. After some time Dr K.P. Mathur, Mrs Gandhi's personal physician, came out of the operation theatre looking dejected. He said, 'Her body is like a *chhalni* [sieve]', meaning that it was riddled with bullets. One was sure it was all over, but the announcement was not being made as the President was out of the country and Rajiv and the Principal Secretary to the Prime Minister were also out of town. Around 1.00 p.m. when Dr Karan Singh was leaving, I took a lift with him as I could foresee a lot of work ahead.

As soon as the announcement of Mrs Gandhi's death was made, we started clearing up the dining room and had the legs of a divan cut to make a low platform for keeping the body. After embalming and other formalities, the body arrived in the evening. Having seen Mrs Gandhi for years in the house in different moods—active, happy, low, angry—this homecoming, her last, was very sad. Her face had become puffy and a little discoloured. It was better that she could not see herself as she would not have approved, being always so well groomed and careful about her appearance. Her relatives and friends sat there the whole night.

The next morning the body was moved to Teen Murti House. Crowds poured in to pay their respects during the days the body lay in state, grief writ large on their faces. Arrangements were somewhat haphazard. Begum Ali Yavar Jung mentioned to me later that one missed Mrs Gandhi's dignified handling as in earlier situations. I brought a group to sing Mrs Gandhi's favourite bhajans, especially Rabindranath Tagore's *Ekla cholo re* (Walk alone), which seemed appropriate for the occasion.

~

EPILOGUE

When I thought about Mrs Gandhi's desire to visit Kashmir two or three days before she died, I realized that her love for Kashmir and the chinar was a constant refrain that occured throughout her life, from her youth right till the end. In a letter to her father from Srinagar dated 11 June 1934, when she was sixteen, she wrote: 'Ever since I first saw the chinar, I have been lost in admiration. It is a magnificent tree.'[1] In 1957 she wrote to me, again from Kashmir: 'Kashmir is breathtakingly beautiful. Every side you turn has its own loveliness. Custom cannot stale its infinite variety.'

Katherine Frank has summed it up well:

Again and again in the coming years, Indira would return to Kashmir at times of great joy, stress, danger, defeat and grief . . . Whatever religious faith she possessed was permeated by the landscape of Kashmir—her idea of paradise—one of the rare constants in her life.[2]

Her sudden wish to visit Kashmir a day or two before she left for Orissa perhaps conveyed her intense desire to have her fill of the beauty of Kashmir, especially the chinar, for the last time. Maybe she realized her end was near, as conveyed in her last words in Orissa on 30 October.

I am here today. I may not be here tomorrow. I do not care whether I live or die. I have lived a long life in the service of my people. I am only proud of this and of nothing else. I shall continue to serve until my last breath and when I die I can say that every drop of my blood will invigorate India and strengthen it.

[1]Sonia Gandhi, *Freedom's Daughter*, p. 118.
[2]Katherine Frank, *Indira*, p. 85.

In an interview to Fatma R. Zakaria for the *Times of India* on 11 September 1984 Mrs Gandhi had told her:

… There is hardly any time left. One has come to the last stage… What is left now. My time is almost over now.

Later, after Mrs Gandhi's death, Fatma Zakaria wrote in the *Times of India*, 18 November 1984:

There was a special kind of tranquility about her throughout the two hours and more of the interview… She was not the Indira Gandhi I had known for almost two decades… She appeared to be more at peace with herself than I had ever seen her before.

Girilal Jain wrote in the *Times of India*, 4 November 1984:

Indira Gandhi once said to me: I have a lot of work to do and I shall do it whatever it takes. Finally it took her life… Indira Gandhi's commitment to India's unity and security was unqualified.

After Mrs Gandhi's death I received two letters from Marie Seton, in November and December 1984 respectively. She came to Delhi in March to receive the Padma Bhushan and left on 6 June. The following excerpts are revealing:

Usha, . . . all the months I was there, I realized the risks that Indu was existing under. I was acutely sad about her and extremely worried as to the deplorable effects of Maneka's playing of cat and mouse with her over Varun . . . . I have now a certain feeling of relief that she is out of the misery she was suffering. The blessing is that she went as nearly as humanly possible in the spirit of Joan of Arc, whom she told me, had inspired her, in childhood and youth. Later, I'd jokingly say, 'Joan is showing!'
. . . It appears that beneath the conscious surface, I was prepared, not that I anticipated either the day nor the circumstances . . . I'm perfectly certain she guided herself in expectation to face whatever was going to happen. And I think that had she been able to choose this particular Karma, she would not have attempted to avoid it. I must tell you, Usha, that I believe you contributed to Indu and no less to me, the day you brought the two of us together (in 1955)!

No doubt Marie was emotional and a little dramatic, but she felt deeply for Mrs Gandhi and understood her various moods and states of mind. She herself died in February 1985, three and a half months after Mrs Gandhi. Aunty Gauba died in early November 1985. All three women who knew each other and had also played an important role in my life died just within a year of each other.

My job was coterminus with Mrs Gandhi's, and so it ended with her demise. Within a week of her passing away, therefore, I wrote to Rajiv:

> It has been a privilege and a great experience to work for Mrs Gandhi for a span of about thirty years. I feel that my duty has ended now. I am always there if any help is required. I am sure that with your calm, poise and sincerity you will be able to surmount the difficulties. Wishing you all the best for the future.

I realized it was the end of an era. Someone had mentioned, perhaps B.K. Nehru, that Mrs Gandhi was the last of the old generation and Rajiv the first of the new generation.

When I look back, a whole panorama stretches before me, of glorious moments, major upheavals, happy and fulfilling times, and great tragedies. I saw five deaths—those of Feroze, Panditji, Sanjay, Indiraji, and then Rajiv. The last three were almost like Greek tragedies.

I am not sure if I believe in destiny, but I do not know how else to describe it. If there had been no Partition, I would not have come to Delhi and joined Aunty Gauba's School, where Rajiv and Sanjay came to study, which in turn led me to work for Mrs Gandhi at a time when she was hardly involved in political work. One could not have imagined then that she would be the prime minister one day. There were interruptions in our work and relationship, and yet we came together again and again. Was it destiny or was it mere coincidence?

Although I was associated with Mrs Gandhi for thirty-one years, I think, as I have mentioned earlier, that I remained a square peg in a round hole. This created problems, but I think the friction and sometimes the lack of adjustment to the situations also provided me with a perception to see people and things in a different light and from a different perspective.

During this period I came across a large number of people of all hues—great and dynamic, simple and ordinary—as well as social climbers and ambitious characters. They all reflected the shades of 'sat', 'rajas', and 'tamas' as described in the Gita. It has been a great experience and lesson for me. The realization was that what really matters is being simple, sincere, unpretentious, and genuine.

While assessing Mrs Gandhi, there is a tendency to either put her on a pedestal or to denigrate her. She would have disapproved of both. She knew her weaknesses and strengths. She was, above all, a human being, a dedicated and hard-working person who thrived on challenges.

~

BIBLIOGRAPHY

Adams, Jad and Phillip Whitehead, *The Dynasty: The Nehru-Gandhi Story*, London: BBC Books.

Alexander, P.C., *My Years with Indira Gandhi*, New Delhi: Vision Books, 1991.

Ali, Tariq, *The Nehrus and the Gandhis: An Indian Dynasty*, with an Introduction by Salman Rushdie, London: Picador, 1985.

Carras, Mary C., *Indira Gandhi: In the Crucible of Leadership: A Political Biography*, Bombay: Jaico Publishing House, 1980.

————, 'Indira Gandhi: Gender and Foreign Policy', in Francine D'Amico with Peter R. Beckman, eds., *Women and World Politics: An Introduction*, Westport, CT: Bergin & Garvey, 1995.

Dhar, P.N., *Indira Gandhi, the 'Emergency', and Indian Democracy*, New Delhi: Oxford University Press, 2000.

Frank, Katherine, *India: The Life of Indira Nehru Gandhi*, London: HarperCollins Publishers, 2001.

Gandhi, Indira, 'Manali: A Place for Contemplation', *Sunday Statesman*, Delhi, 13 July 1958.

————, *My Truth*, New Delhi: Vision Books, 1982.

Gandhi, Sonia (ed.), *Freedom's Daughter: Letters between Indira Gandhi and Jawaharlal Nehru, 1922–39*, London: Hodder & Stoughton, 1989.

———— (ed.), *Two Alone, Two Together: Letters between Indira Gandhi and Jawaharlal Nehru, 1940–1964*, London: Hodder & Stoughton, 1992.

Hutheesing, Krishna, *We Nehrus*, Holt, Rinehart and Winston, 1967.

Jayakar, Pupul, *Indira Gandhi: A Biography*, New Delhi: Penguin Books, 1995.

Kalhan, Promilla, *Kamala Nehru: An Intimate Biography*, Delhi: Vikas Publishing House, 1973.

Malhotra, Inder, *Indira Gandhi: A Personal and Political Biogarphy*, London: Hodder & Stoughton, 1989.

Masani, Zareer, *Indira Gandhi: A Biography*, New Delhi: Oxford University Press, 1975.

Mehta, Krishna, *This Happened in Kashmir*, Calcutta: Signet Press, 1954.

Mohan, Anand, *Indira Gandhi: Personal and Political Biography*, New York: Meredith Press, 1967.

Moraes, Dom, *Indira Gandhi*, Boston: Little, Brown, 1980.

Norman, Dorothy, *Indira Gandhi: Letters to an American Friend, 1950–1984*, Orlando: Harcourt Brace Jovanovich, 1985.

Pande, Mrinal, ed., *Indira Gandhi: Smriti-Sandarbh* [in Hindi], New Delhi: Hind Pocket Books Private Ltd., 1990.

Sehgal, Nayantara (ed.), *Before Freedom: Nehru's Letters to his Sister 1909–47*, New Delhi: HarperCollins Publishers, 2000.

Seton, Marie, *Panditji: A Portrait of Jawaharlal Nehru*, London: Dennis Dobson, 1967.

Thapar, Raj, *All These Years: A Memoir*, New Delhi: Seminar Publications, 1991.

~

ACKNOWLEDGEMENTS

Grateful acknowledgement is made to the following for permission to reprint copyright material:

Rahul Gandhi and Priyanka Gandhi Vadra for the extracts from *Freeedom's Daughter* and *Two Alone, Two Together*, edited by Sonia Gandhi

P.N. Dhar for the extracts from *Indira Gandhi, the 'Emergency' and Indian Democracy*, published by Oxford University Press, © P.N. Dhar

Suresh Mehta for the extracts from *This Happened in Kashmir* by Krishna Mehta

Orient Paperbacks for the extracts from *My Truth* by Indira Gandhi, published by Vision Books

HarperCollins India Ltd for the extracts from *Before Freedom* by Nayantara Sahgal, published by HarperCollins Publishers

HarperCollins Publishers Ltd for the extracts from *Indira: The Life of Indira Nehru Gandhi* by Katherine Frank, published by HarperCollins Publishers © 2001 Katherine Frank

Pamela Cullen for the extracts from *Panditji* by Marie Seton

Jaico Publishing House for the extracts from *Indira Gandhi: In the Crucible of Leadership* by Mary C. Carras, published by Jaico Publishing House

While every effort has been made to trace copyright holders and obtain permission, this has not been possible in all cases; any omissions brought to our attention will be remedied in future editions.

~

INDEX